Chester Elul 1st 2005
Nicolaitau Aug 1st 2005

THE HOME WATER SUPPLY

How to Find, Filter, Store, and Conserve It

Stu Campbell

A Garden Way Publishing Book

Storey Communications, Inc.
Pownal, Vermont 05261

To C. W.,
who weathers my cranky bouts with writer's block
like a willow.

ACKNOWLEDGMENTS

Authors and illustrators of the following books did much to educate me in specific areas: *Planning for an Individual Water System, Water Systems Handbook, Do-It-Yourself Plumbing Handbook, Manual of Individual Water Supply Systems,* and *Domestic Water Treatment.* I'm particularly indebted to Fred Powledge for exhaustive research done in preparation for his book, *Water.*

Much of the information herein is borrowed from publications of the Federal Cooperative Extension Services, as well as from state and municipal agencies, including the Washington Suburban Sanitary Commission (WSSC) in Maryland, the East Bay Municipal Utility District (EBMUD) in the San Francisco Bay Area, and the Denver Water Department (DWD). These data and the know-how are in the "public domain," but their assistance must be acknowledged.

Special thanks to the H.A. Manosh Corporation (Manosh B'Gosh) of Morrisville, Vermont, particularly Emmett Morton, Stuart Roe, Bill Gabaree, Jay Hull, and Stuart Manosh.

The friendship and expertise of Kerr Sparks Jr. has been invaluable, as has help from Phil Wagner and U.S. Soil Conservationists Gene Fellows and Carlton Piper of Lamoille County, Vermont.

Illustrations by Bob Vogel

The name Garden Way Publishing is licensed to Storey Communications, Inc. by Garden Way, Inc.

Copyright 1983 by Storey Communications, Inc.

Printed in the United States by The Alpine Press
Fifth Printing, June 1990

Library of Congress Cataloging in Publication Data
Campbell, Stu.
   The home water supply.

   Bibliography: p.
   Includes index.
   1. Water-supply—Handbooks, manuals, etc.   I. Title.
TD345.C35   1983   628'.72   83-1635
ISBN 0-88266-324-0

CONTENTS

iv

AUTHOR'S NOTE

It's time we all understood more about the common substance we call water. I haven't until recently, so I'm as guilty as anyone else. I grew up, and still live half each year, in northern New England, a part of the country where forty-five inches of annual rainfall is the norm. That's well above the national average, and *far* more than the rest of the world gets.

Around here it's almost never a question of whether we'll find water, it's a matter of where. Lakes and ponds and rivers and streams crowd the landscape. Ninety-five to 97 percent of the wells we dig yield an adequate supply of water for any family—as long as they go deep enough. There's underground water almost everywhere, though its quality isn't always perfect. Most of my life I've taken water for granted, and have wasted it shamelessly.

Contrast in Forecasts

Turn on the evening news from WCAX-TV in Burlington, Vermont—forty miles from where we live—and you'll hear weatherman Stuart Hall announce, "It looks like showers again through the weekend, with lingering cloudiness on Monday." Nasty weather brings us *our* water.

That same night, meteorologist Joel Barlett of KPIX San Francisco, three and a half hours from my wintertime job, is probably saying, "Our weather satellite picture shows continued high pressure over California. The storms we can see out here in the Pacific are expected to pass north of us tomorrow, into Oregon and Washington. The forecast: continued sunny with no outlook for precipitation over the next four days. Earliest chance of rain: Friday. At least we've got our fingers crossed for Friday. . . ." And San Francisco is in the north—the wet part of California.

In places like Vermont or Seattle much of our day-to-day conversation centers around water—about getting what we need into our homes for sure, but more about keeping the rest of it *out.* Just down the road in California, our most heavily populated state, and throughout the Southwest, drought and fear of water shortage are a constant specter. This geographical contrast is just one of thousands of examples. Figures may *claim* there's more than enough fresh water for everyone on the planet, but it's been doled out with horrible inequity.

A few nights ago I realized I've lived in at least ten different rural homes—long enough in each to learn some of the ins and outs of their water systems. I've been supplied by springs and wells, a pond, a brook, and two lakes. Except for one bout of dysentery in Spain, I've never been made sick by water. And I've never been seriously in want of it.

I've only worried about water when something went wrong. As Ben

1

Franklin said, "When the well's dry, we know the worth of water." I've learned enough to fix things—sometimes. But I'm not a mechanic. Nor am I a chemist, and my understanding of water's physical properties extends maybe three paragraphs beyond eighth-grade general science. I've been led to believe my genes retain a speck of that ancient Druid ability to dowse—or locate unseen water below ground. I've witnessed and felt some astonishing things with a dowser's instrument, but I'm not completely sure I'm a believer.

Do It Right

My experience and skeptical nature *do* make me a believer in trying to do things right. I'm in favor of hiring competent (or better) professional tradespeople to do any job as important as installing a water system, because I want it done properly the first time. Unless you're exceptionally handy, I recommend you do the same. The more I learn about it, the less I trust waterworks designed, built, or even modified by amateurs like me.

I favor maximum communication and cooperation between customers and the experts who handle water—and all its myriad problems—for a living. You should understand all you can about what to expect from a well-driller, pond-maker, or plumber. You should not try to go it alone. Consulting with the best people you can find will save you money in the long run. I've learned that lesson the hard way.

We're all afraid of what we don't understand. In these days when there's so much else to be afraid of, we can at least understand something as fundamental as our own water supplies. The more we know about where water comes from, how it behaves, how it comes to us, and what can happen along the way, the more comfortable we can be with it.

Organization of Book

This book will take you through a straightforward progression. First, it explains what water is, what it can and can *not* do. It will focus briefly, through a wide-angle lens, at man's long-term relationship with water. As we'll see, we've made the same mistakes with it over and over again.

We'll talk about where water can be found, and about ways men have devised to find it when its presence is disguised. We'll discuss how to reach, redirect, and capture water. We'll trace the various ways it can be moved from where it is to where we live. Once we've got it, we'll learn how to keep it. More often than not, we need to treat it in some way before we can use it. This book tells how. We'll look at the plumber's art of quietly distributing water to the most convenient locations in our homes. We'll investigate some of the ways water can be controlled, and we'll learn how to protect and conserve what water we have.

In 30 B.C., the Roman poet and satirist Horace expressed a longing many of us still share today. In the twilight of his life he wrote, "This used to be among my prayers—a piece of land, not so very large, which would contain a garden, and near the house a spring of ever-flowing water, and beyond these a bit of wood."

Independence like this is the goal for rural people everywhere. Country folk, especially people who grow things, are more attuned to water, maybe, than city dwellers who see water as something that comes from a tap. But complete independence, even with water, is simply impossible—no matter how far out of town we choose to live. The biggest lesson to be learned about water is that what's yours is mine and everybody else's—as we'll also see.

Still, we can go a long way down the road toward self-sufficiency, and there's plenty of help along the way. Federal agencies, Cooperative Extension Services, local water districts, associations of water-servicing professionals, and water-equipment manufacturers have contributed a wealth of experience and expertise to this book. I acknowledge that much of what I've learned since the immensity of the rural water question hit me has come from their literature.

As already outlined, this book follows a general sequence of events, from locating water until it arrives safely at your kitchen sink. Many of the topics discussed won't fit your particular circumstances and can be safely skipped. Numbers in brackets at the ends of paragraphs are cross-references, suggesting pertinent sections you might turn to for further information.

1 YOU, ME, AND WATER

1. WATER

We *are* water.

The fact is, we have more water molecules in our bodies, by far, than any other. A human being who weighs 150 pounds carries at least 100 pounds of water around with him all the time. To lose just 10 of those water pounds would be fatal. What's more, we all need a minimum of about two quarts of water a day. Without it, even the healthiest man will be dead in twenty-four to ninety-six hours. It's that simple.

We're borne for nine months in a womb filled with fluid that, for all practical purposes, is an imitation of sea water. After birth we trade carbon dioxide for oxygen in our lungs, organs that have developed considerably since some snout-nosed ancestor of ours waddled ashore with stumpy finfeet and gasping gills, long before the first light of recorded time. Still, after billions of years, the critical point of gas exchange in our lungs takes place in a film of—that's right—water.

Uncomfortable as the idea might seem, conditions here on earth which allow us water may be unique in all the universe. Life, as we know it, began here about 4½ billion years ago with the advent of water, and for billions of years thereafter all life was contained in it. It all began for us when two gases combined to form a liquid, and, fortunately for us, that bond between one oxygen atom and two hydrogen atoms has proven to be a stable relationship ever since.

Goethe, the German philosopher-poet, reminds us quite accurately, "Everything originated in water. Everything will be sustained by water." For one thing, without the hydrogen that water supplies, photosynthesis in plants could not occur. And that's just one of an almost endless list of examples of the sustenance water gives us. It's second only to air in importance to life.

We came from the sea, we're told, and in our present evolutionary state, we've never really left it. We just found a way to carry the sea with us, always, as we ventured farther inland. It was this sobering thought that prompted Lorus and Margery Milne, authors of *Water and Life,* to coin the phrase "our portable ocean." It exists in each of our body cells.

Prehistoric man saw water as fire-quencher, meat-softener, food-cooker. Also as indispensable drink. "The ways of man are fresh water ways," the Milnes continue. An early tribesman had no choice but to live near his water source. If he needed to leave it, he took it with him in coconut shells, mammal-skin bags, ostrich eggs, through recorded time in clay pots and wooden casks, now in steel drums, canteens, Thermos bottles, and plastic containers. Man's first highways were on water, and that substance still transports the better part of all our moving goods.

The prehistoric water system.

4

Replaced in Body

Our "portable ocean" is far from permanent. Water in the human body is completely replaced seventeen times a year. That's approximately once every three weeks. Each of our individual cells is filled with water that's just passing through. The liquid leaves our bodies by several routes: through the skin, through the kidneys, through the intestines, and out of the nose and the mouth—the same way it came in.

For all our present concern about water cleanliness, we *can't* drink perfectly pure water. Pure water only steals essential salts from us as it passes out of our system. Our very health depends to a large extent on some of the dissolved minerals found in natural water everywhere.

With its 200 or so parts per million of minerals in solution, water varies greatly in different parts of the world. The human body has a broad range of tolerance for all sorts of substances, and usually adjusts to these changes whenever we travel. But it's the toxic substances like mercury, lead, cadmium, and zinc that, once absorbed, cause deadly problems. In small amounts these poisons are harmless, but they accumulate in our bodies over time, and can eventually kill us.

Because our relationship with water is so intimate, there are scholars who insist that man has evolved according to both the quantity and *quality* of his water supply. And there's not the slightest evidence the work of evolution is complete. We'd all be smart to keep that in mind.

2. WATER PROPERTIES

Water is a unique material. We all know a lot about it because we're in constant contact with it. Much about water is common sense. On its own, it's subject to gravity, just like everything else. It flows downhill—never up—and it's always trying to level itself. Yet it's easily influenced by outside forces. And when it is, it performs in strange ways and seems to go in impossible directions.

Water takes on various disguises. We're most familiar with its liquid state, but it's often found as solid ice, or as water vapor—a gas. It's startling to realize that only 0.32 percent of the world's water is where man can use it: in the atmosphere, in fresh water lakes and streams, and in the top half-mile of the earth's skin.

Water is nature's stingiest substance when it comes to giving and receiving heat. Only a few rare eutectic salts can store more heat energy longer than water can. Whole systems of thermal studies are based on the Btu (British Thermal Unit)—the amount of heat needed to raise the temperature of one pound of *water* one degree Fahrenheit. It's this innate thermal sluggishness that makes the oceans, and all other water, earth's most massive temperature stabilizer. Without it, we'd immediately experience deadly hot-and-cold fluctuations.

Before we can even think about working with water we must understand that, unlike another common fluid, air (and most other things), water cannot be compressed. A cubic foot of water fills one cubic foot of space. That's *it*. When it gets colder—below the point of 32° F. or 0° C.—it doesn't contract. It gets bigger. This fact alone causes massive containment problems wherever there are large temperature variations.

Evaporation

Water molecules have an affinity for one another. When heated they become hyperactive and will begin an excited dance. If the heat is enough,

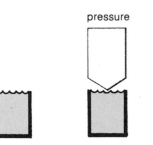

pressure

x amount of h20   same amount of h20

pressure

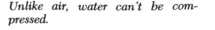

x amount of air   smaller volume air

Unlike air, water can't be compressed.

they'll jig off into the atmosphere, sticking together so well they pull one another away in a molecular daisy chain. You and I know this process as evaporation. And evaporation is another way to spell water loss.

Further, water has the reputed ability to purify itself—a reputation that's not entirely warranted. Known as the "universal solvent," it does its best to assimilate whatever it contacts, does so indiscriminantly and with a high degree of success. There *are* materials, of course, both natural and synthetic, that water can neither dissolve nor pass through. But it almost always carries with it things animal, vegetable, and mineral. That's not necessarily bad.

Among water's healthiest inhabitants are aerobic bacteria which, given enough of the oxygen they need to survive, will devour much waste matter that larger creatures—including humans—find distasteful, or sickening, or harmful. In this sense, water *is* self-purifying. But sometimes it needs help.

These unchanging phenomena, along with others, make the existence of modern water systems possible. We can't understand waterworks until we understand about water itself.

3. WATER AND MAN

Earliest man went to the water. Later, "civilized" man did his best to bring water to himself. The more man's culture developed, the more involved his water problems became. We learned early on, for instance, that water combined with soil results in silt. In practically the same moment we discovered irrigation, we found that irrigation canals filled with just that—silt. So we spent an inordinate amount of time digging it out. And still do.

The ancients quickly became skilled at collecting, storing, and distributing surface water. The Garden of Eden, if such a place really existed, was probably somewhere in Asia Minor, between the Tigris and Euphrates Rivers. The Babylonians, Mesopotamians, Persians, and Phoenicians dug reservoirs to contain "Adam's ale," still a common nickname for water, as well as canals for watering the desert.

Twenty-one hundred years before the birth of Christ, Hammurabi, king of Babylonia, patted himself on the back and wrote, "I brought the waters and made the desert bloom." Piles of silt dug from *his* canals can still be seen today. Later, and in other parts of the world, the Chinese, the Incas, the Greeks, and the Romans did the same.

Part of Egypt's successful experiment with civilization had to do with the *shadoof*, or water sweep—a bag, a long lever, and a counterweight—which allowed men to lift water into canals *above* the level of the Nile. After the shadoof came a more sophisticated lifting device called the *sakia*, a primitive waterwheel with buckets, powered by oxen. Our need to lift water still persists. In the present chapter of man's story, we try to pull or push water uphill with machines we call *pumps*. We're somewhat better at it than our Egyptian predecessors, but elevating water is still a major headache.

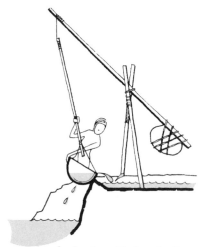

The shadoof enabled early Egyptians to lift water from the Nile.

One of Elements

The Greeks, you'll remember, saw water—along with fire, earth, and air—as one of the four primary elements. They accepted much of their water from springs, and directed it through extensive waterworks. Philosophical leaders in Greece, like Plato, tore their hair out worrying about erosion on land denuded by man, because the resulting runoff fouled drinking water and made people sick. Plato may have anticipated that history would not be kind to those nations who used their water unwisely. . . .

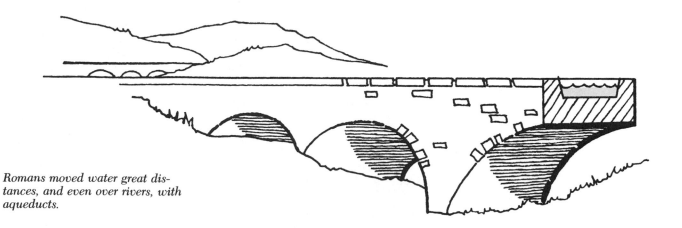

Romans moved water great distances, and even over rivers, with aqueducts.

The first public water system was probably in Rome, where bathing—also public—became a way of life. The Romans constructed over 200 aqueducts. These elaborate tiers of arches were marvelous architecturally. Equally impressive was their ability to move great quantities of water to the capital from elsewhere in the Empire. All by gravity. But that's not all. In addition to their aqueducts, the Romans built water tunnels, cisterns, fancy baths, and sewer systems. They also used lead pipes and drank from lead goblets, and poisoned themselves in the process.

In Greece, Rome, and cultures everywhere the essential nature of water makes it a highly symbolic part of many religious ceremonies. In the Bible, backbone of the Judeo-Christian ethic, shallow wells like those dug by Abraham are mentioned early in the Old Testament. Deep wells—the kind we know today—came relatively late in history, as did geologists and hydrologists.

It's been said that all wars have been fought over water, either directly or indirectly. And there's reason to believe *that* explosive potential for conflict will intensify. The Goths and Vandals who eventually conquered Rome, almost by default, weren't educated enough to appreciate the complex water system that fell into their hands, and disuse led to ruin. The Middle Ages saw great setbacks in water technology, as in almost everything else. That's when the dowser, who'd been waiting in the wings, came on the scene....

Human records show that many centuries later, in 1791, a British scientist by the name of Henry Cavendish was able to combine a bit of hydrogen with exactly half a bit of oxygen for the first time in a laboratory and come up with man-made water. The experiment involved a loud explosion, but the result was something man had known plenty about for some time. So Cavendish's experiment is only a faint whimper in the pages of science:

$$2H_2 + O_2 \rightarrow 2H_2O.$$

What's most ironic about man's long history with water is that as soon as he tried to match the natural world to himself, by coaxing water out of its traditional realm, problems of shortage were alleviated in some places, but erosion and subsequent pollution problems immediately took over. And they're only getting worse. The Aztecs all but committed cultural suicide when they cut all the trees around what is now Mexico City to make charcoal for their fires.

There are lessons to be learned from all of this, particularly for those who wish to manage land, and food, and water, and their own lives.

4. WATER POLITICS

Today it's no news to anyone that fresh water does not exist in equal amounts everywhere. The contrast between Seattle and Tucson is an absurdly obvious example. What's far less obvious to most of us—including many land speculators—is how settlement patterns often develop around inadequate water sources. Too few thorough studies are done on the water supply for an area, and rarely are accurate projections done on the demands to be made on that supply. As it stands now, there are few restrictions on the number of people, farms, or industries that can draw from a given water source. Laws will surely get tougher.

It's imperative that we each see ourselves within the framework of the bigger water picture. In this country, for instance, migration to the Sun Belt continues, despite the fundamental fact that our Southwest, for all its good weather, is an arid region at its wettest. In West Texas, New Mexico, and Arizona, wells have been drilled, dams, reservoirs, aqueducts, and canals have been constructed, accessible bodies of surface water have been tapped, and vague judgments have been made about how many people can be served by the apparent supply.

Flow May Reverse

Some demographers—people watchers—now project that within the next two decades the population flow will reverse itself, and people will head back to the Snow Belt where at least there's enough water to go around. On a personal level this means: If you're considering trading your land in Ohio, with its well or spring, for the dry warmth of Arizona, you could be making a long-range error in judgment.

In this final quarter of the twentieth century, many of us still believe there's an endless supply of fresh water. We expect it to be delivered automatically—at the turn of a tap. Only when our automatic systems fail are we surprised, and when the water doesn't run, we're helpless to know what to do.

As the population of the United States disperses more and more, community water systems will reach farther and farther into the hinterlands. But for those of us who live beyond town water and sewage lines, and cling, out of necessity in many cases, to private water supply and delivery systems, water supplied automatically will remain as much a necessity as the automobile—another machine few of us understand completely.

Water technology is improving by leaps and bounds—every day. It's also getting more complex. It's impossible, as an average consumer, to stay abreast of it all. A modern water system may have as many as eight components:

1. The water source itself.
2. A pump.
3. A storage tank.
4. Distribution pipe.
5. Water treatment equipment.
6. Disinfection equipment.
7. Electrical controls.
8. Housing for all of this.

Each of these ingredients needs to be understood separately, and their combination correctly sequenced as the system is being designed. Without knowledge of water itself, and a sound overall blueprint, an owner-built water system can be a Rube-Goldberg nightmare, constantly in need of maintenance, change, upgrading, and money.

5. WATER'S IMPERFECTIONS

How far afield do we have to go to find "safe" water? To the suburbs? To the mountains? To the backwoods of Vermont? In 1969 Vermont's health commissioner, Dr. Robert Aiken, asked the U.S. Public Health Service—now the Environmental Protection Agency (EPA)—to survey the state's water supplies. Dr. Aiken suspected that water quality in Vermont, of all places, was degrading to near the crisis level. And he was right.

Of the 214 village, town, city, and individual water supplies tested for bacteriological, chemical, and radiological contamination, *none* was described as "excellent," only 9 were rated "good," 69 were rated "fair," 69 "poor," and 67 were tagged "undesirable—unfit to drink." Samples taken from 13 supplies showed toxic levels of lead, 34 exceeded the mandatory limits for iron, and 45 exceeded the mandatory limits for manganese.

The surveyors also found an all-but-universal apathy on the part of Vermonters toward the whole fresh water problem. They found, "In only twenty-seven cases did customers express dissatisfaction with the quality of their water supply. Fifteen of these complaints were for chlorine taste. The people of Vermont, almost to a man, believe that their water, obtained from mountain streams and brooks, is the best in the world. Even when confronted with bad sample results (both physical and bacteriological), this belief still persists. Over and over again the statement, 'No one has ever died (or gotten sick) from drinking our water,' was made to members of the survey crew. This attitude, coupled with tight finances, makes it very difficult to obtain improvements."

The situation in Vermont only illustrates the larger fact that pollution has become an almost impossibly intricate problem. Contamination, according to the EPA, means "the presence in water of any foreign substances (organic, inorganic, radiological, or biological) which tend to lower its quality to the point that it constitutes a health hazard or impairs the usefulness of the water."

"Safe" water, as the EPA defines it, is "free from harmful bacteria, viruses, and parasites." As a commodity, truly safe water is becoming a rarity.

Linked with Population

The seriousness of rural population problems correlates directly with human population density and its accompanying livestock—both of which produce undesirable waste. Pesticides and insecticides, obviously toxic, enter the water supply readily, as do other synthetically produced chemicals, sewage, waste water, and detergents. As you'd expect, as rural population increases, unspoiled water decreases.

But another recent EPA study found that "59 percent of rural individual water supplies examined failed to meet the bacterial standards, and fecal contamination was confirmed in approximately ¾ of these cases." Further investigation showed that "nearly every system had one or more facility deficiencies," and that "very few systems were constructed to prevent the entrance of contamination." So no place is totally safe.

General pollution of our streams, lakes, and rivers is only part of the problem. Industry, which for years vomited waste materials into our waterways, became a convenient scapegoat for our frustration about unclean water. Manufacturing waste is partially to blame, of course, but it's also a case of the public pot calling the industrial kettle black. Too often the fault lies within city and small-town water systems, or worse, in the plumbing of our own homes.

Too Critical?

Still, certain questions inevitably arise when it comes to water contamination. As we learn more and more about water chemistry and water hygiene, aren't we also learning more and more about what can be wrong with it? Are we getting paranoid about water, judging it too harshly? Haven't some of the impurities now found in an Alaskan stream always been there?

Some probably always have been. Once upon a time the earth may have abounded with pristine water. But it's not likely. It's water's nature to harbor microorganisms, harmful and otherwise, as well as to dissolve solids and pick up some poisonous minerals. Simply by drinking water, man has been killing himself ever since the beginning.

The more he tampered with it, collected and directed it, the more hazardous the water became. Water running in the Roman aqueducts was probably highly contaminated, by modern standards. Anthropologists now suspect that many diseases, organ malfunctions, and untimely deaths among the ancients were a direct result of water imperfections—exactly the case with modern man. That such things couldn't be explained at the time didn't make *their* impure water any less a problem.

There's no question water was cleaner then than it is today. Centuries ago the Chinese had fewer people to pollute Yangtse River water with coliform bacteria from human sewage, and the Egyptians, when they still had pharaohs *didn't* have detergents strong enough in phosphate to pollute the Nile. The Thames may have been an open sewer back then, but England in Shakespeare's time knew nothing of pesticides, herbicides, and insecticides that could dissolve and run off as toxic effluents into drinking water. And there was no way the American Indian could have foreseen asbestos plants that would one day dump thousands of tons of cancer-causing particles into Lake Superior. These types of problems can be, and have been, dealt with on a collective political basis.

The message so far can be reduced to one sentence. If you see a private, individual water system as a way to escape the difficulties men have always had with water, you're probably throwing quarters down the wrong wishing well.

2 FINDING WATER

6. HYDROLOGICAL CYCLE

The total volume of water on this planet is finite and constant. What's always been here will probably always be here. It may move around in various ways, but the sum of all Earth's water *never* varies. Thomas Canby, in the *National Geographic*, says the same water used by John the Baptist is still around somewhere, though its molecules are by now widely dispersed. And as Joseph Cragwell, former chief hydrologist for the United States Geological Survey, puts it, "Water: they're not making any more of it."

Hydrology, as the word itself suggests, is the study of water, its properties, how it's distributed and circulated throughout the world. Hydrological maps describe where large portions of water exist at any given time, where they go, and what state they're in. Geohydrologists also try to map water that's underground, where it can't be seen. They admit tracing groundwater is an imprecise science at this time, and they're quick to remind us that water, like air, is a substance we all own in common, together with all other water-using creatures and plants. It's in a constant state of flux, moving its wealth to and fro with more or less general consistency. Most of us are able to borrow from the World Water Bank easily, but there are more than a billion people in the world—also stockholders in the bank—who don't have access to an adequate fresh water supply. Getting it costs them dearly.

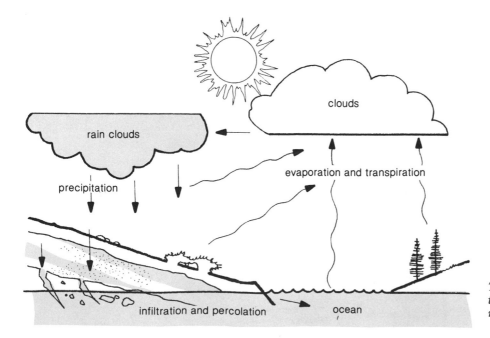

The hydrologic cycle of water lifted to the clouds, released to fall, then returning to the seas.

Man is forever trying to predict and control the hydrological cycle to his own advantage. But without much success. It's too immense and powerful to be fully understood now. We *do* know that each and every water molecule on earth belongs to the ocean at least part of the time. All start out there; all end up there eventually.

Ever since land usurped the ocean's complete dominance of the earth's surface, the two have been in conflict. Where sea meets shore there's a continual effort to wash the land away. Rain and surface water also join forces to peel off topsoil and pull it back to the sea from far inland. As though in retaliation, land sends back its sourest, saltiest minerals to make the ocean ever more bitter. As both spectators and participants in this colossal drama, it's easy to see that our perpetual enemy is erosion. Its ally, water, steals billions of tons of topsoil from us every year.

The average rainfall throughout the world: about twenty-eight inches a year. In the United States we're fortunate to exceed the world average by about two inches, with thirty inches a year. About 92 percent of all rain that falls either evaporates or runs, unused, to the sea. As we already know, less than 1 percent of the world's water is fresh and available to us. The oceans contain 97 percent of all water at any time, leaving 3 percent that's fresh. A third of this fresh supply is frozen in the polar ice caps, and in glaciers, while another third is locked in "aquacludes," geologic formations that do not release their water.

Continual Cycle

Water is continually circulated from oceans, to air, overland, underground, and back to the sea. There salt water is reincarnated as fresh through evaporation. When water vapor in the atmosphere moves over land mass, it may cool and condense to form clouds, which may in turn give up their moisture in the form of precipitation: rain, snow, sleet, or hail. Any water that reaches the earth and escapes immediate evaporation is a potential water source for man.

Water that penetrates the soil moistens the earth and may be snatched by plant roots, which take it in and give it right back to the atmosphere through a process called *transpiration.* Water that drains past plant roots may reach a lower level where all spaces between soil particles are filled with moisture. This area is called the *zone of saturation,* and the liquid here is known as *groundwater.* The uppermost surface of groundwater is called the *water table.*

Rain or melted snow that doesn't sink into the ground, and isn't returned to the air, but collects in streams and lakes, is called *surface water.* Because its movements are so easy to see, a great deal more is understood about sur-

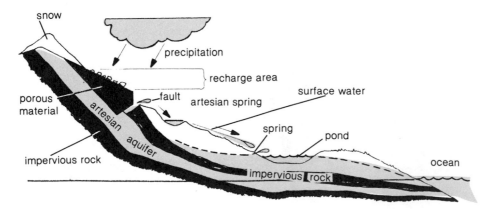

Some common hydrological terms are illustrated here.

face water than about groundwater patterns. Even so, both are part of the larger hydrological cycle, which, in its simplest form is this: what evaporates, precipitates, and eventually evaporates again.

Any homeowner in a rural setting is wise to understand many alternative types of water systems and supplies. There may be several options. One supply may be strong enough to serve several homes, while another will always need help from one or more back-up supplies. In the end, you may find water, or lack of it, a big enough concern to decide it's best to choose a homesite within a community system, where water of acceptable quality is piped to your house, under pressure.

7. SURFACE WATER

Surface water, our most obvious and traditional water source, has fallen victim to civilization. Most of it is polluted. A lot of what becomes surface run-off has come from the sky, as *meteoric water*. Even before this precipitation hits the ground, it may contain some minerals, gases, and as you've no doubt heard, acids picked up from industrial smoke. Secluded lakes in the Adirondack wilderness of upper New York State have been poisoned by acid rain. Fish there are killed by industrial wastes coming from hundreds of miles away. As we pollute the atmosphere we pollute water—long before it ever reaches us. (104)

Yet rainwater remains relatively free of bacteria. Only when it reaches the ground does it become contaminated with microorganisms. Stream levels and bodies of surface water may go up and down according to the weather. A benign brook, in the Sterling Valley four miles from my house, becomes a violent torrent during and after a thunderstorm, sometimes rising as much as eight feet. Other streams may be influenced more gradually by weather that's happened counties away.

Not all surface water, of course, comes from the sky. Much of it comes from the ground, at springs and in spots where a body of water intersects the water table. This explains why certain streams continue to run full, even through long periods of dry weather. Some surface water finds unsaturated soil and filters into the ground. When it reaches an impermeable surface and can no longer move downward, it might stay put or be deflected sideways. This can happen at, or below, the earth surface.

In a sense, snow is surface water held in suspension. It stores water until the temperature rises above freezing. Snow pack in the mountains of the western United States is a vital water resource, and people who live there watch it with intense interest. The snowfields and surface water in the Lake Tahoe Basin of California are guarded with Doberman-like ferocity by the U.S. Forest Service. The almost pure water in the jewel of a catchment basin is always being eyed by parched neighbors who surround it.

Much of our country is dotted with surface water, as any airplane ride over the eastern, southern, midwestern and northwestern states will show. We love to play in it and near it. Surface water is America's number one recreation medium.

Unlimited Supply

It's said that our neighbor to the north, Canada, is one of the few countries in the world with an unlimited supply of fresh water on its surface. (106) Lake Superior, which separates us from Canada near the middle of our northern border, is the largest body of fresh water on earth. In fact, the Great Lakes all together contain a quarter of all the fresh water in all the lakes and rivers of the world.

The quality of surface water changes all the time. It contaminates itself, and the reverse, purifies itself, though to a much lesser extent. We can't rely on natural treatment processes to keep our surface water healthy, as some believe.

Dissolving minerals, sedimentation, natural filtration, the growth and decay of plant materials, aeration, and sunlight are all factors that influence water, for better or worse. If we take drinking water from streams, lakes, and ponds, we're putting our health on the line, even though there may be times when the water is perfectly safe. The treatments we perform in rural homes, to eliminate pathogenic organisms, impurities, and chemicals, are only attempts to supplement, enhance, or recreate natural processes. And sometimes it's more expensive to treat surface water than it's worth. . . .

8. GROUNDWATER

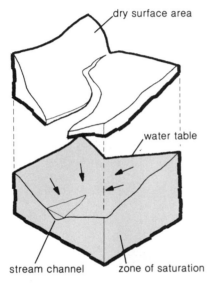

Lift the dry surface area, as we've done in this drawing, and you expose the water table. Note that this isn't a flat table, but slants towards the stream channel.

Some say it's a science. Others insist it's an art. Either way it's agreed that locating groundwater is not always an easy task. Getting it out of the ground once you've found it may be far simpler. And there's an abundance of knowledge about *that*. . . .

A vast majority of the 10 million or so families in the United States who have private water systems use groundwater as their primary source. Our Water Resources Council estimates that about 97 percent of all the fresh water in the nation is underground. In the mid-60s somebody calculated that all the underground water on earth equals about three years of rainfall on the entire planet. So there's plenty down there.

The Water Systems Council, an organization of pump manufacturers with an obvious interest in promoting its machinery, goes on quite correctly, "A major advantage to private wells and water systems using the groundwater supply is low cost. Except in heavily populated areas, it is less expensive to install and maintain a private system than it is to pay the significant piping and operating costs of a central system—such as a rural water district."

The earth stores its moisture in water-bearing formations, in loose soil, and in rock crevices, fissures, and cracks. Some soils are waterproof and hold almost no significant wetness. Underground water, like a glacier, often moves slowly, sometimes as little as a few feet a year. Sometimes it moves rapidly upward. Its motion is encouraged by gravity, capillary action, temperature, and pressure.

Porous strata that accept water easily are sand and gravel, of course, but also loam, sandstone, limestone, and sandy limestone. Clay, shale, marl, marble, and granite do not.

Be reminded that the top surface of ground saturated with water is called the *water table*, a favorite term among geologists. The name is a little misleading, however. Unlike most "tables," the water table is frequently *not* flat, but may slope and follow the contour of land above. (It's a mistake,

Use a dishpan, sand, and water to understand the term water table. Left, the top of the saturated zone is the water table. Middle, a "lake" is created when sand is removed to below water table level. Right, water table slants from source of water supply.

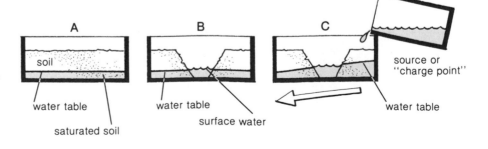

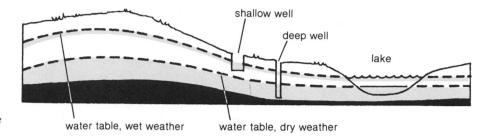

Here's why some wells go dry during droughts. Note well at left doesn't reach water table in dry weather, while well at right has water year-round, and level of lake changes with seasons.

shallow well

deep well

lake

water table, wet weather

water table, dry weather

however, to assume the water table *does* conform to land surface. It often runs contrary to it.) A water table also moves up or down depending on its supply.

Useless Water

Immediately above the water table there may be porous material containing water particles that are "stuck." They can't move because there are not enough of them to collect and flow with gravity. This thin area, known as the *capillary fringe*, is just one of many places where water exists, but in a form that's useless to us. It's always been one of man's frustrations to know that water is just beyond his grasp. This fact probably inspired the too-often quotation of the line, "Water, water everywhere, nor any drop to drink."

Moving groundwater, reachable or otherwise, may find its way to land surface or to a place beneath other water—in a stream, a lake, or even the ocean floor. The formation in which it runs may not be, *probably* won't be, level. Water always takes the path of least resistance. In other words, it may be *impossible* for water to seek its own level, as is its wont. Seasonal changes, as well as weather, cause differences in elevation and the extent of groundwater slopes.

An *aquifer*—another indispensable part of the geological vocabulary—is any formation that holds and transfers groundwater. Water within an aquifer, by definition, is free to move and can be recovered. An *aquastat*, on the other hand, is a geologic structure that contains no water and is impervious to it. To have an aquifer, there must be an aquastat to provide a bottom.

The best aquifers are in coarse sand and gravel, or openings in limestone, sandstone, or broken lava. At the same time, because there's so little chance of water penetrating silt, clay, and solid metamorphic rock like marble, groundwater is usually found in layers and at greatly varying depths. There

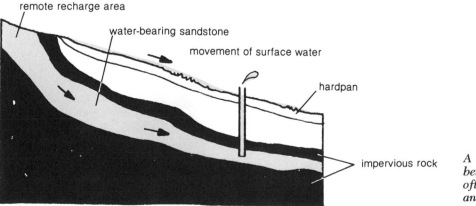

remote recharge area

water-bearing sandstone

movement of surface water

hardpan

impervious rock

A layer of sandstone sandwiched between layers on impervious rock often provides an ideal setting for an artesian aquifer.

may be water far above one water table in an entirely different rock formation. These high pockets are sometimes called *perched aquifers*.

Recharging takes place when water enters an underground water basin at a rate equal to or greater than the discharge flow. Charging normally happens at high ground, and discharge at lower outcroppings of rock. It's easy to see how an aquifer's slope creates hydrostatic pressure, particularly toward the lower end where the water pushes up against impermeable rock.

The earth has experienced some major changes during its lifespan. The northern United States was once buried under ice, and the Southwest, though it's hard to imagine it, was not always desert. A great aquifer stretches from the Carolinas to Florida, and at its southern end the water table is as shallow as five feet. One of the biggest aquifers in the world, a remnant of an ancient fresh water sea perhaps, runs from Nebraska to western Texas. Here water that fell as rain or snow during the Ice Age—10,000 years ago—is now being pumped out of the ground. The problem is that it's not being replenished.

Artesian Wells

At one time the conquering Romans were astonished to discover tons of water flowing from an open well near Artesium, in what is now Artois, a province of France. Today, any similar well that stands higher than the aquifer from which it originates—even if the water height does not reach the surface—bears the name "artesian well."

The term artesian, contrary to what many believe, has nothing to do with depth. But it has everything to do with pressure. An artesian well may be deep, but many are shallow. A *non*artesian well simply pokes into the water table somewhere. As water is pumped from it, the water table can be lowered if it's not replenished.

An artesian situation develops when water is confined beneath an impermeable layer of rock or hardpan, and the pressure that builds from the weight of the overburden and the weight of water at higher elevation ex-

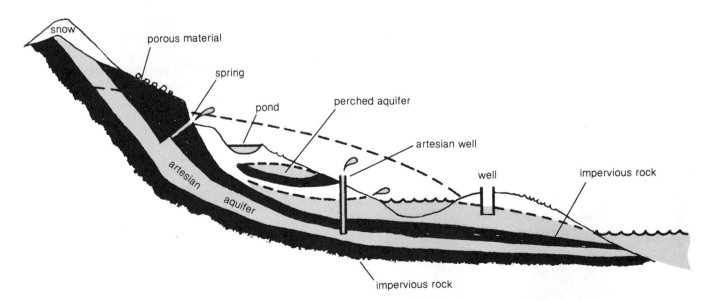

Water under pressure in artesian aquifer will rise to surface in spring or in artesian well, but will not in well that doesn't reach the artesian aquifer.

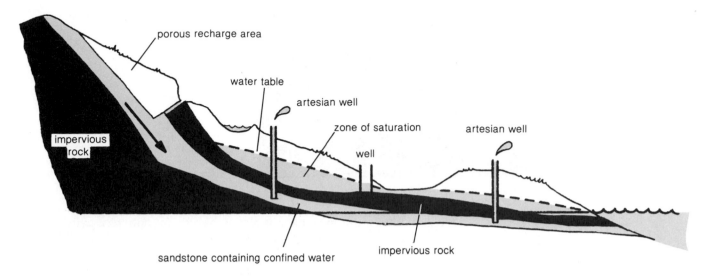

porous recharge area

water table

artesian well

zone of saturation

artesian well

impervious rock

well

sandstone containing confined water

impervious rock

The depth of a well often determines whether it is an artesian well. Note that wells on left and right are deep enough to reach the artesian aquifer, while center well only reaches the zone of saturation under the water table.

ceeds normal atmospheric pressure. If a well bit punctures rock layers that press down on this kind of subterranean pool, water can rise in, even gush *out* the top of the well pipe. Hence an artesian well.

The frustration is that there seem to be few hard and fast rules governing the behavior of groundwater. And this fact inspires great debate and conflict among water "experts." Most textbook diagrams tend to be theoretical and oversimplified.

Movement of groundwater is sometimes likened to blood circulating in our bodies. *Primary* water, as it's called by some, may rise from deep within the earth as a result of artesian pressure. This central point of uplift is what dowsers call a water *dome.* Once it reaches its full height, water spreads out in different directions, into secondary streams called *veins.*

These underground arteries can be deep or shallow, potable or not, few and far between, or right next to each other and nearly parallel. They may even move. You can see veins of water flowing or seeping from ledge where roads have been blasted through it. They're particularly apparent in winter when frozen.

Always Changing

There's very little you, or I, or anyone else can do about the geologic structure below the surface of the ground, except penetrate it with a digging machine or drill and hope for the best. That's *not* to say what's down there isn't changing. All kinds of pushing and squeezing are going on. After billions of years the earth is amazingly plastic, still. Stresses change with movement and weight shifts. Cracks open and close. New ones are split. Water is the weakest player in this game of underground power struggle. It goes where everything else does not.

There are those who believe earthquakes, dynamiting, lightning, strong vibrations, even bulldozing or felling a heavy tree can alter the course of groundwater. Indeed, there are countless stories about wells that have drawn good water one day, only to go inexplicably dry the next.

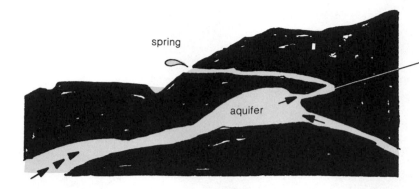

spring

crack in rock

aquifer

Water will move uphill if, as arrows indicate, it is under pressure, and if it finds a crack in a rock, and emerges as a spring.

We'll see that water movement is closely linked, not only to gravity, pressure, and nudging from surfaces next to it, but also to that heavy blanket of air that surrounds us all—the atmosphere. We know that atmospheric pressure changes regularly, enough to be measured by even the simplest barometer. These air changes can also affect groundwater, particularly as it relates to height within a well.

Most groundwater has a temperature somewhere between 40° and 60° F. Unlike air temperature, its warmth fluctuates only a few degrees over an entire year. Some water, rising from great depths, can be hot, some salty or brackish. The chemical character of groundwater depends almost entirely on where it's been and what it's passed through.

There is no foolproof or scientific way to find groundwater. Every search for it is a fascinating gamble.

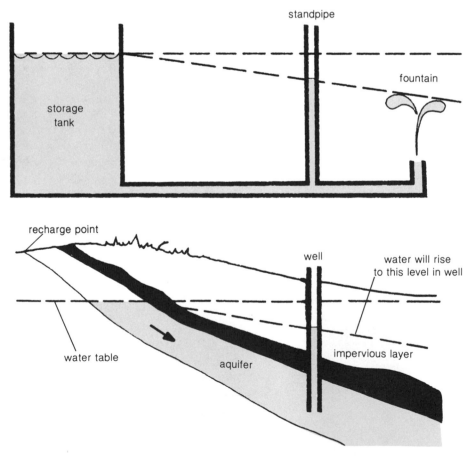

standpipe

fountain

storage tank

recharge point

well

water will rise to this level in well

water table

aquifer

impervious layer

Friction influences any fluid under pressure. The farther water must travel from its storage tank (top), the greater the pressure loss due to friction, and the less it will rise. The walls of an aquifer (bottom) will also generate friction. The farther a well is located from the aquifer's recharge point, the lower the level of water in the wall.

9. DOWSERS

Get help from experts before trying to find—or develop—a groundwater source. Contact a groundwater geologist, an Extension Service hydrologist, the Soil Conservationist at your nearest U.S. Department of Agriculture office, or an engineer who specializes in water.

The EPA recommends against dowsers—"water witches," as they're sometimes called. A few scientists who study water scoff at people who say they can find groundwater with a forked stick. Some academic water experts and professional well-drilling associations are fond of articles like "How the Water Witch Drowned in the Well," stories that ridicule the mystical water-seekers.

While most scientists say no, one USDA forester, whose hobby was dowsing, is quoted in the Agriculture Department's 1955 yearbook, entitled *Water*. "I grasp the ends of the twig with palms upward. As I start I have the butt of the stick pointing up. As I near moving water I can feel the pull as the butt end begins to dip downward. When I am over the water it's straight down, having turned through an arc of 180 degrees. A stick of brittle wood will break under my grip as the butt dips downward. Pliable sticks will twist despite efforts to hold them straight."

Those who like to make order out of nature will never be dowsers. I've known a good many water witches, or diviners, or whatever you want to call them. None seemed particularly weird or eccentric. None was a sorcerer, so far as I know.

As a boy I worked part time for an old German farmer who was said to have "the ability"—a means of finding groundwater with a willow switch in a way few others could comprehend. My father once asked him to locate a broken spring line that needed digging up. Which he did.

I never saw him dowse for water, but those who did said that when he felt water, the fork pointed at the ground so hard it tore the skin off his hands. I did see the raw hands from time to time, but I never thought about it much. Until recently....

Dowsing Instruction

He's six-three, a gruff white-haired bear of a man, handsome enough to lower people-noise in a room just by walking through the door. His name is Kerr Sparks, still an athlete, my old ski school boss, and like a father to me. Years ago he told me he could dowse. A few months back, when I called him, he said, "come over."

The next day we were in the woods, looking at a series of ten interconnected springs with a composite total of 300 contamination-free gallons a minute, all feeding a 100,000-gallon, man-made reservoir. He's the only man who knows where everything in the system is. As manager of this waterworks serving a major ski resort, lodges, and a condominium complex, he's in contact with hydrologists, engineers, and government water officials almost daily. And he's the last person in the world you'd expect to be a water witch.

I asked if he thought veins of underground water could be moved, as some dowsers claim they can. He thought not—unless dynamite was used to open new cracks in the bedrock. Sensible.

"So you want to dowse," he said. He went to some bushes, looked a minute, took out his jackknife, and cut a Y from a young basswood tree. Two prongs of the Y were about sixteen inches long, pointed at each end where he'd cut them. The butt, where the two branches met, was a bit shorter, maybe a foot long.

As he walked out of the brush he put his elbows close to his rib cage,

Kerr Sparks, Jr., dowser, spring developer, teacher.

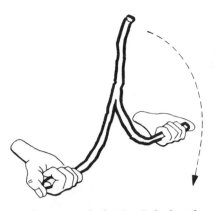

A dowser might hold a forked stick, or Y-rod, like this. Some advocate thumbs on the stick ends, but the American Society of Dowsers insists there is no single "correct grip."

pointed the stick down, grasped both branches with palms up, and placed his thumbs on each of the pointed end cuts. Stepping to a flat place, he pulled outward on the two forks of the stick and pointed it in the air.

I was taken by surprise. The axis of the stick bent visibly toward the ground. Kerr's face grimaced. He looked as if he were hanging on for dear life, trying to restrain a struggling animal. He relaxed, caught his breath, then demonstrated again.

"Try it," he said. "It's very strong here."

Like a golf pro teaching grip he showed me how to hold the yoke. "Elbows in tight, thumbs on the ends, pull out, point it up." He stepped back, then said, "Hang on, baby."

The tip hesitated, then slowly bent downward, as if pulled by a magnet. For the life of me I couldn't hold it back. I strained for maybe fifteen seconds, then dropped my arms, exhausted, thumbs numb.

Kerr didn't seem particularly impressed. "Tough on the thumbs, isn't it?" he said, turning on his heel. "Try it over here." Same reaction, stronger this time.

He shrugged and walked off through the woods, his talk returning to the springs. I followed, holding the stick as shown. Nothing . . . nothing . . . nothing for several steps. Then the stick wanted to pull down . . . two more steps, then nothing again.

"There's water all over the place," I said, more startled than convinced.

"Sure," he said. "We're walking over a big aquifer. A geologist from the university found it a couple of months ago with a magnetometer. But we've always known it was here."

He was showing me another spring that flowed from the same aquifer. I was hardly listening. Standing a few feet above the spring I fought the yoke with all my might trying to hold it upright. The right fork snapped in my hand.

"I just broke the stick."

He laughed, still bending over the spring box. "That just proves the point," he said.

Later he cut me a bigger, heavier yoke, again of basswood. (It's still sitting in my office.) We stood over the first spot we tried, and I tried again. The pull was irresistible.

"Now, if I handed this stick to my wife," he said, "she'd get no reaction. But if I held on to one side. . . ." He took one fork while I held the other, standing beside him. "She could feel this." The pull got stronger. "And if I did this. . . .", he said, laying his free arm across my shoulders. He didn't finish the sentence. The stick plunged downward as though alive.

"Did I feed off your 'ability'?" I asked, in shock.

"We fed off each other," he said. "Anybody can feel it."

He pointed out different shrubbery as we hiked back to the road. "Some of the old guys around here believe a dowsing stick has to be cut from a tree that bears fruit. Applewood is popular. . . . But I don't believe all that stuff."

He pointed to a bush I didn't remember ever seeing before. Its bark was black and the branches wore leaves as big as my hand. "That's called witch hobble," he said. "Some use that too." But he steered clear, and walked way around the bush.

I drove home. Hands and mind burning.

Reading About Dowsing

I bought a copy of Harvey Howells's *Dowsing for Everyone*, an authoritative little book filled with convincing history and anecdotes about dowsers. I

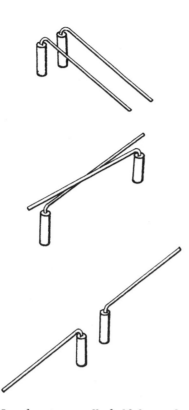

L rods are normally held forward in the "search" position (top). Crossed rods indicate a "no" response (center), while opened rods say "yes," there is water here (bottom). For some dowsers the response is exactly opposite. Believe as you will.

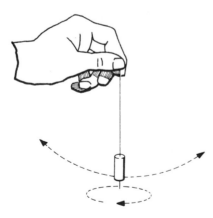

The pendulum is another common dowsing instrument. Back and forth movement may indicate "yes," circular movement, "no."

learned how dowsers have fallen in and out of favor throughout history. I learned of Henry Gross, who sat in his home in Maine and dowsed a gigantic water dome of incomparable quality in Bermuda, an island universally believed to harbor no fresh water at all. He dowsed it from a map.

I learned that a lot of silliness goes on when it comes to finding water, but that dowsing is probably not part of it. I learned about many people who have been saved many well-drilling dollars by dowsers. I learned of suspicion among dowsers that some well diggers go much deeper than necessary to make a well more dollar-profitable, though not necessarily more gallons-per-minute profitable to owners.

I learned about dowsers' instruments: L rods and Y rods, wands, bobbers, pendulums, and bare hands. I learned how some dowsers can move a water vein with a crowbar driven in the ground, then struck sideways with a sledgehammer. I was told dowsers not only find water, but can tell how deep it is, how pure it is, where it's going, and how much is there. But I wasn't quite sold.

I spent several days with a local well driller, an articulate man with at least eleven years' experience, and more than 1,000 good wells to his credit. His assistant was anxious to tell me many stories about water witches. Some were good. Some were bad. When I asked the driller himself, we had to scream at each other over the noise of the drill rig:

"Do you believe in dowsing?"

"No."

"Do you own your own well?"

"Yes."

"Did you have it dowsed?"

(Seriously) "Yes." Then with an eye twinkle, "You never know."

Dowsing Instruction

I called the American Society of Dowsers, Inc., in Danville, Vermont (802-684-3417), "a nonprofit educational and scientific society with an open membership." And, as it turns out, an open mind. Yes, they had a national convention the next month. Yes, they had a dowsers' school for two days preceding the meeting. Yes, I could attend. Yes, they'd get the preregistration material in the mail to me today. Tuition for nonmembers? $50.

Registration was held in the white-clapboard Danville Town Hall, just off the village green. Two hundred and fifty people came, from all over the world. (Six hundred and fifty more showed up for the convention.) They came in rusty old pickups and shiny Jaguars. They seemed like normal, sane, intelligent, curious people from all sorts of backgrounds.

The first meeting started promptly on schedule, at 9 A.M. in the Methodist Church on another side of the green. A bald, elderly, and professorial man stood at the pulpit. His name was Ed Jastram, graduate in physics from MIT; for many years a branch manager of engineering for Texas Instruments. A scientist. Also an accomplished and respected dowser.

"We invite you to partake of a mystery," opened Jastram. Nobody knows yet why dowsing works, he explained, so it's rejected by many scientists and technicians. Much research needs to be done. "But the normal logic of the physical world is very limiting," he continued. "Not everything can be forced into logical patterns. Because there's no logical explanation doesn't mean something doesn't exist. The true scientist is the guy who's willing to investigate everything."

For two days we were lectured to and individually tutored by experienced dowsers, all of whom were confident, yet showed great humility about what we were doing. The messages that came through loud and clear:

anyone can dowse. There are no absolutes and no limits to dowsing. Use any dowsing instrument you're comfortable with. It doesn't matter what the tool is made of. Hold it any way that's comfortable. There is no right or wrong way to use it. Be very specific about what you're dowsing for. The tool may only be an indicator of what your subconscious senses. Trust what you feel. Ask questions.

L rods seem to work for me. So does a Y rod. I feel little from a bobber, nothing from a pendulum. In small groups we dowsed carefully marked plots on Danville Green. We drew maps of what we found. My map of water veins in the plot nearest the town bandstand almost exactly matched the map of my instructor. Everyone in the group felt something; some stronger than others. Sometimes we disagreed. But mostly we agreed. We were all skeptical at times, but we stayed receptive. All of us received a Certificate of Completion for taking the course.

At my home in Stowe, Vermont, the well is 125 feet deep and its yield is eight gallons a minute. Good enough. Unfortunately it contains a lot of iron. My new-found dowsing rods confirm all this, as you'd expect.

But thirty feet from the well, farther down the driveway, the L rods say there are twenty gallons per minute of moving, drinkable water, twelve feet below the surface. I traced the vein down the hill to a wet place I've wanted to turn into a pond. Recently, when a bulldozer and large backhoe came to excavate that same pond, they ran into a big vein of water about where I thought they might. Once they struck it, water ran into the bottom of their big hole, and made life miserable for them. It took two gasoline-powered pumps, each pumping at least ten gallons a minute, to keep up with the inflow. We all figured the vein was thirteen feet or so below the surface.

When and if I need another well, *I'll* call a good dowser. I may call two. And I'll dowse myself. If the three of us, working independently, agree on a spot, that's where we'll dig—or drill. It will be cheaper than drilling a deep, dry hole.

Paul Sevigny, treasurer of the American Society of Dowsers, judge, ex-state legislator, entrepreneur, budding TV personality, and Danville Town health officer, charges 15¢ a mile for dowsing trips, and asks for a $25 contribution to his favorite charity. That's all. He admits he makes mistakes, but quietly confesses he's right about water 90 to 95 percent of the time.

I just don't know. I won't advise what *you* should do.

10. CLUES

Unseen, the mysterious movement of groundwater continues to inspire controversy between the scientific community (namely geologists) and the mildly occult (dowsers). Yet groundwater, stealthy as it is, does leave a few clues about its presence. Land contour and rock structures at the surface often suggest subterranean water routes and aquifers. Wet spots, bogs, and evidences of erosion that seem out of synch with other surface runoff, are all parts of the water picture puzzle. Depth and flow data from neighboring springs and wells may be revealing. The best records come from local well drillers.

The United States Geological Survey, Water Resources Division, has offices in all states. And they often turn out to be good sources of information about rock formations, water tables, and aquifers. They also keep accurate flow records on streams they regard as good indicators of what's going on hydrologically. Remember: brooks that run all summer, even during driest times when there's no surface runoff, must be fed by groundwater. It might be worth looking at the ten-year low flow figures kept on a stream near you.

Vegetation and topography can also provide a lot of information—*if* you know how to read the evidence. Fault lines, small hillside cirques, rough ground among large boulders, ferns, cattails, alders, and other water-loving plants may all be signs of springs. Large fir trees, like hemlocks, will sometimes establish themselves right over a spring. But it's not necessarily a good idea to try to compete for their water. They can quickly fill a man-made spring box with spaghetti-like roots to choke off water *you* want—even if the box is concrete.

Lightning as Indicator

Rural Vermonters have learned something else. It's lightning's usual habit to strike the tallest trees in a stand. But sometimes it picks on shorter ones—consistently. A tree that's particularly battered and charred may be standing on a spring or close to a water vein. Since water is a good ground, lightning may select that tree as the easiest route to earth. Look there.

Phil Wagner, Ph.D., was kind enough to stop by my house. Everybody told me he was the best. He was on his way home from a meeting—about water, naturally—at a large development in town. So he wore a tweed sportscoat and tie. He *looked* like somebody who had taught groundwater geology, called hydrogeology by some, for fifteen years at the University of Vermont. No longer a member of the UVM faculty, he's part of a private engineering firm specializing in water supplies and waste disposal.

He agreed I *might* have saved myself money by digging a shallow well in that vein of water now feeding the pond. "I'd be the last person in the world to say there's nothing to dowsing," he said. I was taken aback. "Though not all geologists would agree with me."

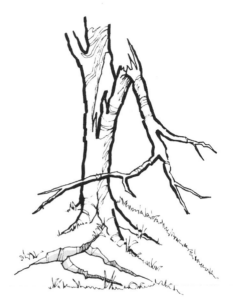

A tree that's consistently struck by lightning might be a good ground to water beneath it.

Aquifers

I asked him about aquifers. "Aquifer," he said, "is too general a term. There are many kinds of aquifers. Understanding the different *types* is the key to good country living." He went on to explain that although geology may be an "elaborate science," specific knowledge about some areas of rural water technology is "woefully lacking." Aquifers differ from place to place. What somebody knows about aquifers in Maine may not help at all in Arizona or Oregon.

The Northeast has several types of groundwater, as Phil Wagner sees it. First is what he calls *interflow*, shallow water that's passing just six inches or more below the surface. "The shallower the water, the more flashy the supply seems to be," he pointed out. "But shallow water supplies also tend to be the most variable."

Next is what he calls *contact water*, water that flows at the interface between soil and impervious bedrock. Third is *bedrock water*, which hides in cracks, and may or may not be under artesian pressure.

Unlike many hydrogeologists, Wagner speaks of water *veins*, as does the dowser. In most parts of the United States, there are clearly definable layers of water, often found in gravel, within the geologic strata. Not so in much of New England, where such layering simply isn't present. Since water here is found in spaces between ledges and within rock fissures, it's appropriate to think in terms of veins.

How would he go about finding water on somebody's property? "First of all," he began, "a full scientific study is out of reach for the average homeowner." There is no way most of us can afford a battery of stream-flow tests and a full statistical analysis of our land's hydrology. So, like anybody else, he would start by looking for places where water comes out of the ground. Almost any ten-acre parcel of land in Vermont, he figures, will have at least one spring. If no surface evidence existed, he would bring in a backhoe and use his educated eye to dig in search of contact water—where soil meets ledge. If none could be found, he'd start to decide where to drill a well. *That* decision might be based on different enchantment. . . .

Sometimes, when he's *not* wearing a tweed jacket, Wagner is studying aerial photographs looking for fault lines, and tramping over the countryside with a box strapped to his back. The box contains a sensor, and is called a "magnetometer." Developed at the University of Pennsylvania, it's an electronic device used for seeking fractures in bedrock, and may be the geologists' equivalent of the dowsing rod.

The magnetometer senses small variations in a magnetic field. Magnetic minerals are often deposited on the walls of cracks, and the instrument picks up these higher magnetic values. These are recorded and plotted on a map to trace fracture lines. Any well that intercepts a fracture is almost sure to have water. Intersections of fractures are even better places to drill. A monstrous artesian well, which overflows more than 100 gallons a minute, was found, using this method, across the valley from me in Stowe, and it now supplies the village's municipal system.

Like crevices in glaciers, cracks in bedrock tend to be widest at the top, becoming tighter and narrower the deeper they go. Below a certain point, pressures are so great there can be little water, and what's there is riddled with briny minerals. To drill deeper than 350 feet in most parts of Vermont is probably fruitless.

But again, you'll get different stories in different places. Scientists, for example, divide the country roughly—*very* roughly—into a number of *physiographic provinces*. What's to be found geologically in the Rocky Mountain Province of Colorado is not likely to match the water patterns in the lava of

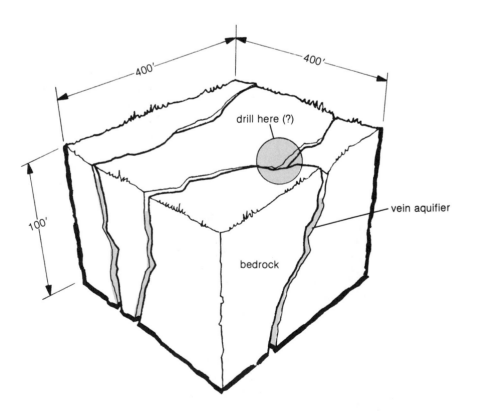

Dr. Phil Wagner's description of bedrock fractures and vein aquifers in many parts of New England. A magnetometer could detect cracks in a 400' by 400' by 100' section of bedrock. Intersections between fractures might be the best places to drill for water.

the Columbia Plateau Province in the Northwest. Studying more specific hydrological maps of those areas will certainly be helpful, but they'll only provide further clues about where to find good drinking water. "Traditional scientific knowledge isn't going to be the only answer," says Wagner, a man who should know. "I'm always amazed at how much the locals know, as opposed to the 'experts'."

To learn the inside scoop on springs in Arkansas, you may have to find Little Rock's version of Kerr Sparks. But while you're at it, call the state geologist's office, and ask if they can send out somebody like Phil Wagner.

11. RUNOFF CATCHMENT

Wherever we have no groundwater, we look upward to our water source. In such places, water must come to us from out of the sky, and we watch weather forecasts hopefully. We keep an ear cocked to precipitation figures. When rain comes, we grab all we can. Almost anyone in Nevada knows what I'm talking about.

A *catchment* can be any surface area that collects runoff during a storm or shower. It might be a paved area or a roof that drains into a rainbarrel or *cistern* in the cellar.

When the weather's been hot and dry, the majority of raindrops at the beginning of a shower evaporate immediately—like a kitchen-faucet dribble hitting a hot frying pan. Still, they say evaporation loss from an asphalt catchment area is less than 10 percent, even in hot climates. Of course, a lot would depend on the pitch of the catchment, and how fast water runs off it. Shingled and gravel roofs, on the average, lose about 15 percent of their water to evaporation. Metal roofs lose much less. General runoff in most areas of the country is estimated at about 75 percent of annual rainfall, according to the EPA. So planning to intercept and control rain water on man-made surface may be well worthwhile.

But another water source will probably be needed. It's difficult to collect and store enough rainwater to supply *all* of a family's needs, in most cases. The only way to know for sure would be to learn about, then juggle, these three factors: the minimum yearly rainfall, the longest period of recorded drought where you are, and the amount of available roof area, or pavement surface you can use. At best, it's a tough proposition.

Catchment experts caution us about overestimating the size of rain-collecting surfaces. Measuring along roof slopes to compute square footage, for instance, may prove to be a disappointing error. It's safer—and easier—to measure the ground surface below the eaves of a roof, computing square footage in the area covered by the building, in other words. Base the potential catchment on that more conservative calculation. (15)

12. PONDS AND LAKES

Our grandparents often piped water to their homes and summer cottages directly from lakes and ponds. That was before we worried so much about water purity. Some of us still take our water from surface supplies, but we're becoming more and more aware that this water *must* be treated.

I remember water in one summer cottage in Vermont that came right out of Lake Champlain. It tasted fine, but once in a while, late in the season, it would have tiny green flecks of algae. If somebody got concerned enough, we'd boil our drinking water for a few days. But after a while we'd forget about it. Today the algae problem in the lake is much worse, and all the cottages in that little summer community are hooked up to a communal chlorination system.

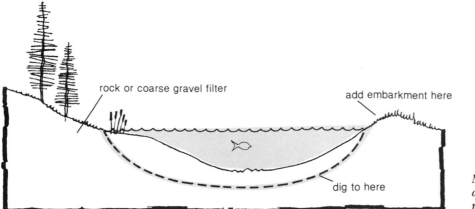

rock or coarse gravel filter

add embarkment here

dig to here

Making a pond may be as simple as excavating an already wet or marshy area.

I've been in far-away corners of the Rockies, Sierras, the White and the Green Mountains, and have drunk water from quick-running streams—even when companions have refused, turning instead to canteens of treated tap water from home. Indeed, harmful pathogens *have* been found at the head-waters of the most "unspoiled" mountain streams, and in high alpine lakes. My companions were right, of course, but they missed a special nectar. . . .

Second Choice

For the most part, surface water should be used only when groundwater is unavailable. That's the way health experts generalize, anyway. Open water is just that—wide open to contamination. Even aerated running water in streams is likely to be turbid during spring runoff and after heavy rains. Water from such sources needs to be filtered and treated in some clean storage area.

If I hike forty minutes to the Pinnacle, a rock outcropping that overlooks Stowe Hollow, 1,500 feet above my home, I'm rewarded with a view Cinerama could never imitate. From that perch, threescore homes in this small mountain valley take on fairy-tale proportions. It's as though the green floor of the glen is scattered with odd-shaped pieces of broken mirror—each a pond. I can count almost twenty, including my own.

A closer look tells me that most of the ponds in Stowe Hollow are clear, clean, and filled, nearly always, to overflowing. In summer, they're also filled with swimmers. In winter, they swarm with skaters. Small boys pull wiggling stocked trout from them each spring. Elderly ladies contemplate October's red and yellow foliage reflected in them. And it's no accident. . . .

These mini-reservoirs, old farm ponds some of them, live in an area rich with water. Each was made with the aid of generations of pond-making expertise. Each has its own story, and there are tales of woe in some: about leaks and washouts, about bulldozers that got mired in mud and sank out of sight, about the "perfect" pond site that eventually produced a puddle costing five times as much as expected. A good pond, you see, is a living organism, a complex thing.

Valuable . . . or Costly

Artificial ponds are attractive. They increase real estate values. They're focal points for recreation. And if they're not properly engineered, they can turn out to be ugly and expensive disasters. Fortunately, help and advice is easy to come by in most rural areas. In many parts of the country the U.S. Soil Conservation Service will help you design and lay out a pond at little or no cost.

Many bitten by the urge to have a pond fail to see that a pond's scope spreads way beyond its shoreline, its underground feeders, and its dam. Land for miles around, acres you can't even see, may shed its water into *your* pond. You hope this watershed will provide the highest quality water. It should *not* provide such a flood during rainy seasons that the pond gets obliterated by an onslaught of unexpected runoff. Emergency overflow provisions must be designed into any good pond.

If it holds enough to supply a farm or homestead with a year's worth of water—beyond what evaporates and leaks out—a pond is thought to be big enough. Its potential is best figured during the driest part of the year—in August or early September in most places. Calculating the pond's *acre footage*, with the help of rectangular measurements at the pond site and sketches on graph paper, is a help in estimating the pond's storage capacity. An *acre foot* is the water needed to cover one acre (43,560 square feet), one foot deep. There are about 325,851 gallons per acre foot. Unless the water table nearby is exceptionally high, each acre foot of pond may receive water from 1½ to 2 acres of watershed. Obviously if the watershed falls short of the pond's needs, the pond never fills.

When you think about it, it's not surprising that natural ponds almost never form in coarse soils that drain well. Yet thousands of attempts at man-made ponds in just such places have proven to be dismal failures. A good pond takes careful research.

Clay is thought to be ideal for a pond bottom. But it's not without its disadvantages. Very waterproof and stable when dry, overly steep clay banks can slide toward flatness when wet. A clay bottom is slippery and soggy, not particularly fun to walk in. When disturbed, it turns water murky. A dock or raft may be needed for swimming, because going in from the shore is unpleasant.

At the opposite extreme, bedrock—or ledge—is next to impossible to excavate without blasting. Besides, it's pierced with cracks and fissures that can leak forever. Ponds can be expensively lined with plastic membranes, high-density concrete, or clay. But the ideal soil condition is somewhere between clay and rock: good digging in predictable earth that may leak a trifle at first, but will eventually seal itself with silt and sediment.

Pond Sites

Topographical depressions, swampy valleys, and wet spots are often good pond sites, just as long as the soil base will hold water. Man-made ponds fall into two basic categories: *excavated* and *embankment* ponds. On the simplest level, an excavated hole can become a water receptacle. A pond with a dam, or embankment, on the other hand, is called an impounded pond in some parts of the country. Either way, if it's dammed or dug out in a place adjacent to a stream, it's called a *bypass pond.*

Dug-out basins made with a bulldozer or large backhoe are allowed to fill with water from surface runoff, groundwater from the water table, from veins, from shallow aquifers, from springs, or even from well overflows. The water level, even in an excavated pond, will fluctuate at different times of year and with severe weather changes. An overflow spillway, perhaps one that's made of concrete, must be worked into the design to take care of excess runoff. The edge of a dug-out pond should be as steep as the soil condi-

A transit is an essential tool in any pond construction. Spillway elevations and "freeboard" must follow U.S. Soil Conservation Service recommendations, and there's no way to do it with the naked eye.

tions will permit. Shallows heat quickly in the sun, breeding cattails, algae, weeds, pollywogs, and mosquitoes.

Embankment ponds, especially those that intercept streams of surface water, are more complicated, more subject to water pressure and seasonal stress. They're also more likely to fail—either because they don't hold water or because they wash out. Attempting to build one without engineering help is all but foolhardy, especially since the soil conservationist in your county is there for just that purpose. Give him a call and have him take a close look at your pond site—before you lift a stone.

He'll be able to tell you if you have enough water *and* enough of the right kind of soil to build the embankment dam. If you have to haul in some different material to build a waterproof foundation at the dam base, your expense may suddenly double or triple.

Dam Dimensions

The soil conservationist will prescribe a specific height for the dam, the amount of *freeboard* above water level, the minimum depth of the pond, and the slope gradient on either side of the embankment. The *water side* is normally the flatter, with a 3:1 slope. The *land side* of the dam can be steeper, usually 2:1. He'll also design an emergency spillway and the drain-piping system.

You may be surprised at the magnitude of the dam once it's staked out. Its width alone takes up a lot of space. For instance: a dam ten feet high should be at least six feet wide at its top, sloping downward only a foot for every three feet of level run (3:1) on the waterside and one foot for every two feet of level run on the land side. All told, this dam would be fifty-six feet wide at its base.

Before you go any further with your pond project, a test hole should be dug—at least eight feet deep. This is to get a reading of the soil profile at the site. If it's not impervious clay, take heart. All is not lost. As already mentioned, there are a number of synthetic membranes that can be used as

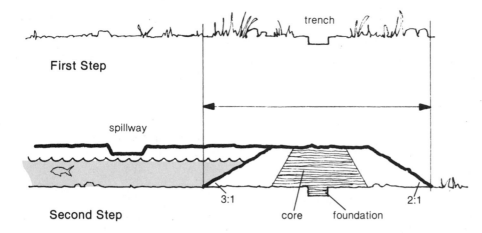

First Step

Second Step

spillway

trench

3:1   core   foundation   2:1

If the soil at the pond site is too poor to hold water, a foundation and core may have to be built into the dam. A trench should be dug at the dam base, at least four feet wide. As the embankment is made, a core of impervious clay should be built in its center.

pond liners. And Bentonite, a natural volcanic clay, can also be used as a sealing compound. The wetter it gets, the more Bentonite expands. The more it swells, the more watertight the pond becomes.

Digging the Pond

"I don't know where they get that magic number of eight feet," spat Wayne through a stream of tobacco. Sitting in the cab of the John Deere 690 backhoe, he was on his way to dig a test hole in the pond site below my house.

"The soil conservationist said an eight-foot hole," I insisted.

Wayne's stomach jiggled as the digger's tracks crept slowly over rough spots in the ground. He spat a second time, then pretended to look neutral on the subject. When he got to the middle of the bog he stopped. And out of orneryness, he dug a hole as deep as the big machine would reach—ten or twelve feet.

We found what we expected: thick, gray clay all the way down. So a future pond should leak little, and no extra material would have to be brought in. "Make your pond deeper'n eight foot," said Wayne, as if to rest his case. He didn't choose to explain his quarrel with the Soil Conservation Service. . . .

All the government literature suggests "eight feet or *more* of depth" for ponds. So the engineers and this backhoe operator seemed to have no conflict that I could see. Vermonters who like deep, cold trout ponds and dislike swampy places with cattails, favor maximum depth.

Again, the government experts seem to concur, recommending that a pond have the majority of its storage capacity below three feet of depth. "Best water," they say, is located twelve to eighteen inches below the surface in a pond or lake. If an intake line is located higher than this, it can take in debris. If it's too near the bottom, it can stir up turbidity. The intake itself, normally flexible tubing, can be attached to a float on the surface, and an anchor at the bottom, to hold it at the right level.

Weed control may be needed in shallower parts of a pond. Copper sulphate and toxic herbicides can do this job, but it's best to consult local health officials before poisoning your weeds—and possibly somebody else's water downstream. In other words, you may need a permit to clear your pond using chemicals; some states require licensed professionals for this work.

Wayne's test hole, by the way, was filled with water the day after he dug it. And it stayed that way for over a year—until the pond was dug. . . .

13. SPRINGS

"If there's magic on this planet," says naturalist Loren Eisley, "it is contained in water." John Pullen may have had Eisley's truth rattling around in his head when he wrote, "Wells are mundane. Springs are magical. There's a sparkling enchantment in their flow of cool, fresh water, sometimes bubbling or boiling from the ground." Indeed.

A spring is any opening where water flows out of the earth, either by gravity or artesian pressure. Some of the finest springs in the world are found high on mountains, meaning that water must come to them from great depths in many cases. A spring atop Mt. Monadnock in New Hampshire is a case in point. Vermont's highest peak, Mt. Mansfield, gushes with springs.

Unfortunately, many of these wounds in the earth's skin "bleed" erratically, and the irregularities are so dramatic that a spring may not always be considered a reliable water source. Geologist Phil Wagner, whose main area of concentration is waste disposal, also warns that springs are easily contaminated, especially in places where there is a lot of contact water.

So not all springs are enchantingly clean, or beautiful. There's one behind my house that I didn't know about until the house was finished. I can depend on *it* only to erupt each November, do its best to flood my driveway all winter, then shut off automatically around the fifteenth of May. I have to make special efforts to drain it, and have even thought about testing the dowsers' contention that water can be "chased" out of a vein. If I get desperate someday, I may try to have this troublesome vein diverted. But in summer I couldn't suck a drop from that spring with a straw.

Study Before Using

It pays to watch a spring for at least a year before you make up your mind to tap it. A neighbor across the valley built his house near a twenty-gallon-per-minute spring. This past August it went dry again, and he's finally decided to drive a well. Observe a spring particularly closely during dry spells.

I grew up on a place that was served by a spring year-round, without fail. My folks finally gave up on it only because the water line running from it rusted out. The spring was so far away it seemed cheaper to find water closer to the house. Besides, this spring was on a neighbor's land.

Spring water in Vermont is always cold, it seems to me. Average well water in this part of the country is around 46° F., and spring water runs about as chilly. In this hilly and stony state there are many *fissure springs* that flow from breaks in rock formations. Fissure springs often deliver water from great depths, which is no guarantee the water is contamination-free.

Tubular springs, known as *bold springs* by some, spew a steady flow of water that has run through caverns and channels in rock. If this water has also been filtered through gravel, sand, or limestone along the way, it's likely to be relatively clean.

Pressure-fed *artesian springs* appear where there's been a rupture in a watertight formation covering an aquifer. Such a break might happen at a fault line. The discharge rate from an artesian spring depends on the elevation of the aquifer's charge point. These tend to be the most dependable springs— *unless* a lot of water is being drawn or pumped from another point in the aquifer. Find out before trying to stake your water claim there.

Gravity springs are *not* so dependable. During the spring runoff they'll produce heavily for weeks, then suddenly go dry as a bone, perhaps in August. As long as the sloping water table stays high enough they'll leak

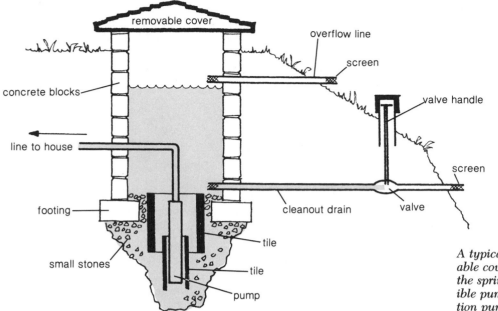

concrete blocks

line to house

footing

small stones

removable cover

overflow line

screen

valve handle

screen

cleanout drain

valve

tile

tile

pump

A typical spring box with removable cover. If the house is above the spring, there may be a submersible pump in the spring, or a suction pump in the house.

groundwater. But once the moving level of saturation gets below the discharge point, the leak is bypassed, and the spring is useless.

I often get my feet wet in open meadows. If I don't pay attention I may step in a *seepage spring.* One of these days I'll learn to look out for them. They're not hard to spot. They're usually in a low place, surrounded by vegetation that's just a bit lusher than the rest of the field. Push back the weeds and you're bound to find water. It's probably unappetizing though, discolored by organic matter, rusty looking scum, or green slime.

Seepage springs are too inconsistent to be serious candidates for the starring role in your water supply. But sometimes, when they're yielding lots of water and are virtually pollution-free, they can play a strong supporting part. During dry periods they won't produce much and are surely vulnerable to all kinds of surface contamination. Forget about them then.

Real Producers

The same day Kerr Sparks cut me a dowsing stick, we were out checking his springs. It was during one of the driest Septembers in memory. He told me one spring was producing its usual quota of thirty gallons a minute, enough to fill a two-inch pipe. I said I didn't believe it.

We drove up a long hill, got out of the car, and wandered through some young trees. It took two of us to lift off the heavy wooden spring cover. I peered into a dark hole and saw nothing. Then my eyes adjusted and I could see that the bottom of the spring, five feet below, was sandy and covered with about eighteen inches of water. The pool was alive with ripples as water pulsated from under the sand. It was the biggest spring I'd ever seen.

It's a "captured spring," as Kerr put it, generous enough to serve a small community. When it was discovered, before the turn of the century, it was a much smaller trickle. But water was needed to feed horses making the long pull up the hill. So it was dug out by hand, and opened further with a small charge of dynamite.

Level footings were poured around the rock fissure, and a concrete box was built on top of them. This was covered by the wooden roof, which needs reshingling about once every two dozen years. A drain and an overflow line were added eventually, but the intake line has been running full and steady since the beginning.

My friend showed me other springs on the same hillside. One was not being used but was flowing strong. "Too hard to keep surface water out of this one," he said. The spring backed up against an almost vertical rock ledge. "One of these days we'll chip back into the rock so we can make a waterproof seal for the cover," Kerr said.

Here the spring box was made of wood, instead of concrete. The outside of the box was covered with heavy metal screening.

"How come?" I asked.

"We built this box one hot summer," he said. "Our hands were sweaty and we must have left salt in the wood. Porcupines would gnaw on it to get at the salt. This is how we protect it."

A third spring with a concrete cover sat in the midst of ferns, marsh grass, and black organic muck. Years before, just two digs with a spade had unearthed pure white beach sand beneath the muck, which spurted water instantly and has never stopped since. This spring was captured and encased like the other two. A dowser's fork had indicated where to dig....

14. WELLS

It's been said that "a well penetrates the past." A modern drill bit boring downward at a foot a minute, streaks through eons of geologic time. The cross section it cuts along the way is of great interest to both scientists and practical men like Jay Hull, whose simply worded driller's log is cited in the next chapter. Available moisture, sought by the drill, may be very old, having accumulated for 50 to 200 years. That's the estimated average age of groundwater found in a newly punctured deep well, anyway.

To be perfectly blunt about it, almost all water wells are driven to *get* water, not to find it. Except in cases of very shallow wells, few of us can afford to drive an exploratory hole just to see if there's water down there. Once you decide where to drill, you're committed. Depth and expense now become the big factors, and the tension mounts.

When I drilled my own well, I was also in the process of building my house. The budget was tight, and the intangible cost of the well created more anxiety than I could bear. I had to leave shortly after the rig was set in place. Whether it's dowsed, located with a magnetometer, or based on the driller's knowledge of the area, a well can be a risky venture.

As well depth varies, so do the many types of wells. Some shallow wells can be dug with a backhoe, and may be only four feet below the surface. Others can be bored, jetted, driven, or drilled for hundreds of feet. The subject of wells, then, makes up a major portion of the discussion in this book.

It doesn't take long to learn that every well is different. The one certainty is that finding deep groundwater is a dirty, noisy job, particularly if a rotary drill is used. Water and air, blasted down the hole, will bring fine drilling particles to the surface in a stream that needs to wash downhill away from the well site itself. It's best to have this job over, done with, and cleaned up *before* a new house is finished, rather than afterward. But this isn't always possible.

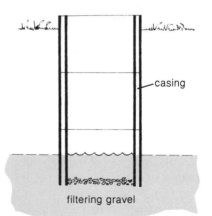

casing

filtering gravel

A dug well is usually excavated by hand, and extends into a shallow water table. This one is lined with three sections of concrete well tile.

Best Place to Drill

The most comforting places to drill are where the water table or aquifer is a known distance below the surface. A *water-table well* reaches water

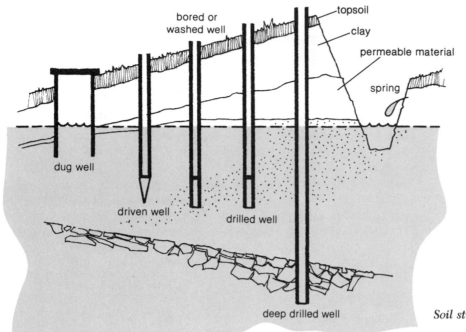

bored or
washed well

topsoil

clay

permeable material

spring

dug well

driven well

drilled well

deep drilled well

Soil strata and various well types.

that's under normal atmospheric pressure—14.7 pounds per square inch at mean sea level. Here water must be pumped to the surface.

An *artesian well* contains water that's confined between impermeable soil layers. When a drill punches through to it, there may be enough pressure to cause water from the aquifer to rise in the newly drilled opening. If the pressure is great enough, water can flow all the way to the surface of an artesian well.

Wells normally poke into a water table or aquifer from directly above. The well should draw water no faster than its aquifer is being replenished. If it *is* pumped too fast, the water level can be lowered and the *safe yield* of the source is being pushed dangerously hard. This is happening today in many places.

Storage Area, Too

It's important to understand that a well is a storage area for water as well as a supply route from the ground. The deeper a well is, the greater its capacity as a reservoir. Stored water can be used as needed, and the well will be depleted—only to recover later as the hole fills with water from its surrounding strata.

A foot-high column of water in a regular six-inch well pipe, called a "casing," contains 1½ gallons. A 200-foot column of water in a six-inch well pipe will hold 300 gallons of water. At a recovery rate of one gallon per minute, another 720 gallons can be added over a twelve-hour period.

In Connecticut, where well regulations are particularly strict, there's a formula for recovery rate as it relates to well depth. In a well with six-inch casing that's 100 feet deep, five gallons per minute or more is acceptable. At 200 feet, just two gallons a minute is fine. At 450 feet the well only needs to produce one-half gallon per minute. Again, more depth means more storage and possibly more yield. Wells *without* enough yield to supply enough water during peak demand times will need holding tanks.

Well Depths and Diameters

Type of Well	Depth	Diameter	Geologic Formation
Dug	0 to 50 feet	3 to 20 feet	**Suitable:** Clay, silt, sand, gravel, boulders soft sandstone, and soft, fractured limestone. **Unsuitable:** Dense igneous rock.
Bored	0 to 100 feet	2 to 30 inches	**Suitable:** Clay, silt, sand, gravel, boulders less than well diameter, soft sandstone, and soft, fractured limestone. **Unsuitable:** Dense igneous rock.
Driven	0 to 50 feet	1¼ to 2 inches	**Suitable:** Clay, silt, sand, fine gravel, and sandstone in thin layers. **Unsuitable:** Cemented gravel, boulders, limestone, and dense igneous rock.
Drilled: Cable tool	0 to 1,000 feet	4 to 18 inches	**Suitable:** Clay, silt, sand, gravel, cemented gravel, boulders (in firm bedding), sandstone, limestone, and dense igneous rock.
Rotary	0 to 1,000 feet	4 to 24 inches	**Suitable:** Clay, silt, sand, gravel, cemented gravel, boulders (difficult), sandstone, limestone, and dense igneous rock.
Jetted	0 to 100 feet	4 to 12 inches	**Suitable:** Clay, silt, sand, ¼-inch pea gravel. **Unsuitable:** Cemented gravel, boulders, sandstone, limestone, and dense igneous rock.

Bored wells are also relatively shallow. The auger is often turned by hand, particularly when the soil is sandy and without rocks.

The biggest myth about wells may be, "The deeper you drill, the better the quality of water." Actually salty water, or "brine," will be found below certain depths in almost all regions. Nor is it true that the deeper you drill, the *colder* the water. Water temperature in most wells hovers around the mean annual air temperature at surface above. In fact, below 100 feet, groundwater gets *hotter*, at a rate of about 1° F. for each 75 to 100 feet of further depth.

Overdrawing from groundwater deposits can cause land above to sink, and can lure seepage of briny water into a well that's close to a body of salt water. But these are only a couple of problems that can develop....

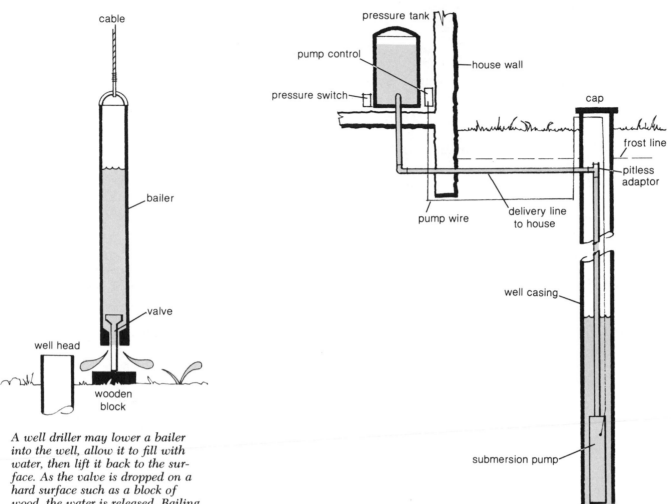

cable

bailer

valve

well head

wooden
block

pressure tank

pump control

pressure switch

house wall

cap

frost line

pitless
adaptor

pump wire

delivery line
to house

well casing

submersion pump

A well driller may lower a bailer
into the well, allow it to fill with
water, then lift it back to the surface. As the valve is dropped on a
hard surface such as a block of
wood, the water is released. Bailing
is one way of measuring the yield
of a drilled well.

The rudiments of a drilled-well system.

3 GETTING WATER

15. CATCHMENT AREAS

From time to time feasts of water shower on parts of the world that otherwise have chronic water famine. With good planning, much of this water can be caught and stored. Runoff that doesn't evaporate or percolate into the ground may gather temporarily in ponds or other natural collection areas. Even there, it's not safe from water loss. Evaporation is still a factor. So is infiltration through the bottom of the pond. *Cisterns* are man-made collection reservoirs—usually covered to make them evaporation-proof—designed to store and protect rainwater from roofs and paved areas called *catchments.*

Before anyone decides to rely totally on catchment areas to supply all the water needs for himself and his family, he should first take a cold, hard look at some numbers. One inch of rainfall over a 1,000-square-foot area can yield 623 gallons of collectable water. That's impressive.

But what is the total annual rainfall in your area? How big a catchment area do you already have, or can you build? How big can the cistern be? Most important: how long is a maximum period of drought likely to be?

If you estimate that each family member needs 75 gallons of water a day (30), and there are four in the family, you need 300 gallons a day. If local weather statistics, which you'll need to check, tell you that the longest average period of time between rainfalls is thirty days, you can calculate that you'll need to store 9,000 gallons of water ($300 \times 30 = 9,000$). A glance at the accompanying chart tells you you'll need a cistern more than eight feet deep and twelve feet square to hold that much. Still not impossible.

Say there's an average twenty inches of rain each year in your region. The second chart says that the per-square-foot yield for catchments in a location with twenty inches of annual rainfall is 8.3 gallons, allowing for leakage, roof washing, and evaporation. At that rate, dividing 9,000 gallons by 8.3, you can determine you need 1,084 square feet of catchment area.

But your two-story house measures 24 by 36 feet beneath the eaves, for a total potential catchment of 864 square feet. Not quite enough. To make it, you'd either have to curb your water needs or look for other sources. (Don't forget that groundwater too full of minerals to be drunk *can* be used in toilets and for irrigation in some cases.)

Roofs are not the only possible catchment areas, of course. Maybe you can supplement what your roof collects by paving an area on a gentle slope nearby. This paved surface should be as smooth as possible, to let water run toward the cistern quickly—before it can evaporate. The area might also be fenced off, to keep animals, people, and other kinds of traffic away. On its upper end there should be a diversion ditch and curbing to move other sur-

Yield of Water Per Square Foot of Catchment Area

Minimum Annual Rainfall	Water Yield (per sq. ft.)
(inches)	(gallons)
10	4.2
15	6.3
20	8.3
25	10.5
30	12.5
35	14.6
40	16.7
45	18.8
50	20.8

Note: Allows for ⅓ of water being wasted to take care of leakage, roof washing, and evaporation. Based on recommendation of Garver, Harry L., "Safe Water for the Farm"; F. B. 1978, 1948.

Capacities of Cisterns

Depth feet	Diameter of Round Type—Length of Sides of Square Type (feet)						
	6	8	10	12	14	16	18
				Round Type (gallons)			
5	1055	1880	2935	4230	5755	7515	9510
6	1266	2256	3522	5076	6906	9018	11412
7	1477	2632	4109	5922	8057	10521	13314
8	1688	3008	4696	6768	9208	12024	15216
9	1899	3384	5283	7614	10359	13527	17118
10	2110	3760	5870	8460	11510	15030	19020
12	2532	4512	7044	10152	13812	18036	22824
14	2954	5264	8218	11844	16114	21042	26628
16	3376	6016	9392	13536	18416	24048	30432
18	3798	6768	10566	15228	20718	27054	24236
20	4220	7530	11740	16920	23020	30060	38040
				Square Type (gallons)			
5	1345	2395	3740	5385	7330	9575	12112
6	1614	2874	4488	6462	8796	11490	14534
7	1883	3353	5236	7539	10262	13405	16956
8	2152	3832	5984	8616	11728	15320	19378
9	2421	4311	6732	9693	13194	17235	21800
10	2690	4790	7480	10770	14660	19150	24222
12	3228	5748	8976	12924	17592	22980	29068
14	3766	6706	10472	15078	20524	26810	33912
16	4204	7664	11968	17232	23456	30640	38756
18	4842	8622	13464	19386	26388	34470	42600
20	5380	9580	14960	21540	29320	38300	48444

face water, which could mix with your clean supply, away in a different direction.

Rainfall collected on a roof or paved catchment should be directed toward a drain that leads to the cistern. During dry weather the catchment may accumulate dust, bird droppings, and grime, and the first water to run off it will be dirty. *Roof washers* are meant to divert this initial water out of drainage, letting it run away as waste or as nonpotable water to be used elsewhere. Once the roof washer closes, either by hand or automatically, cleaner water is sent to the cistern. Sand filters are sometimes used in place of, or in combination with, roof washers. (70)

Cistern

The cistern should be located near or even inside the house, though not in a basement that may flood and allow the water supply to be contaminated with outside surface water. Reinforced concrete tanks, with smooth interior surfaces that are easy to clean, make the best cisterns. Some are made of metal. Others of wood. If a cistern is placed below ground, water inside will be kept cool in summer, but won't freeze in winter. Some cisterns are like huge manholes sitting beneath basement floors, covered with a concrete slab. Some sit *on* the floor. (50)

All cisterns need to be disinfected with chlorine solution—regularly—and inspected for cracks and tree roots that could be inching toward the collected water supply.

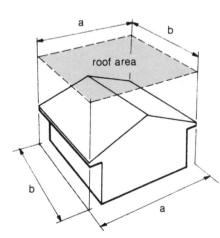

Don't deceive yourself when figuring square footage for rainfall catchment. A roof's potential collecting surface is not the roof area. It's distance A times distance B. Of course these measurements can most easily be measured along the ground.

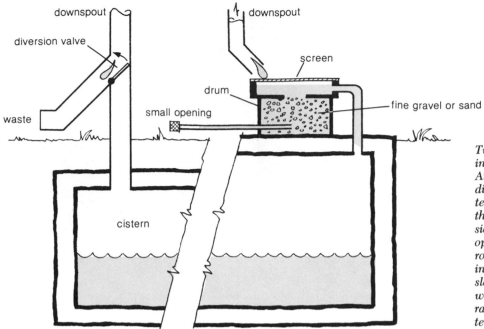

Two ways of ensuring cleanliness in a rain-water catchment system. At left, dirty water from the roof is diverted away from the storage cistern until the roof has been thoroughly washed. At right, diversion valves are usually hand-operated, but here is an automatic roof washer. Initial runoff flows into the gravel-filled drum, and is slowly eliminated through the waste line. Once the drum is full, rain water goes directly to the cistern.

16. STREAMS— INFILTRATION GALLERIES

Sometimes there's no other choice. Surface water may be the only feasible source. Man has always taken water from natural pools, or has dammed streams in an effort to make water pause on its way downhill. Australian aborigines and other primitives who must drink water from lowland bogs, dig pits a few feet from shallow bodies of swamp water. The hole gradually fills with relatively clean water that's filtered as it seeps through the intervening soil.

Some modern men, particularly those who live on heavily forested watersheds in areas of low population density, still take safe water from streams. They protect themselves from some waterborne diseases, turbidity, and floating debris by building a *slow sand filter*. It may be as simple as a small

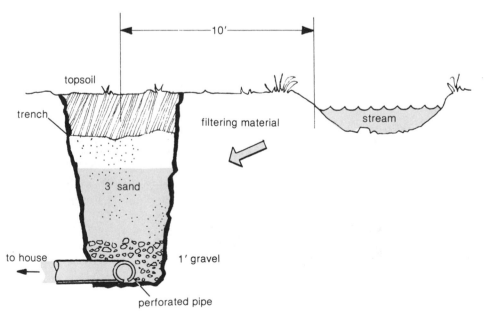

To clean surface water in a stream, dig a trench ten feet away, and allow water to filter through soil before it reaches the perforated intake line. This is far from a perfect filter, but it's better than nothing.

dam, a resulting pool, and an intake pipe, screened on its end, that rests in the quiet water above the dam, covered by at least two feet of sand. The sand cleanses water flowing to the pipe.

Better still is a deep trench dug parallel to the stream. This more sophisticated (and more effective) *infiltration gallery* should be located approximately ten feet away from the stream's high water mark, with its base below the level of the stream bed. It might be three feet wide by as much as ten feet deep. A perforated pipe, or *drain tile*, is laid in the bottom of the trench with its holes facing down. This intake line is covered with a foot of crushed stone or coarse bankrun gravel. On top of this is another three feet of sand. The rest of the trench can be filled with topsoil or some impervious material.

Filtering System

To reach the pipe, water must pass through the soil between the stream and the trench, as well as the gravel and stone *in* the trench. By the time it reaches a watertight concrete holding tank a short way downhill from the intake, the water has been thoroughly filtered, and its lack of turbidity makes it easier to treat. Now it can be chlorinated. (71)

Obviously, an intake tapping into any running surface water should be placed upstream from sewage outlets. Silt buildup in stream water can be high, especially after a storm. And, like all filtering materials, sand must be cleaned or backwashed at some point. Since it's all but impossible to reverse the flow of the stream to remove silt, the filtering material in an infiltration gallery will have to be dug up and replaced periodically. Just how often this must be done depends on the quality of the stream water.

17. PONDS

Building a pond is a big project, and like a well, it involves a certain amount of uncertainty. Maybe the most important pond-making decision has to do with selecting the right excavating equipment. Bringing in the wrong digger is like burying money in the pond bottom forever. Don't be afraid of "overkill". . . .

Unless you're digging in a loose material like gravel—which normally drains too well to hold water anyway—a four-wheel drive, rubber-tired

Where mud is a factor, a bulldozer and large backhoe can work as a team. If one gets stuck, the other can pull it out.

plow, front loader, or backhoe just isn't going to make it. A fair-sized bulldozer or a large backhoe on tracks is a much safer bet. Maybe you'll need both. The day my pond was started, Robby Adams, one of the best bulldozer operators in town, showed up on a D6 Caterpillar. All he intended to do was strip off the top eighteen inches of topsoil and muck, and let the subsoil dry out for two or three days before any serious digging began.

"You're sure you won't get mired down in that stuff?" I asked.

"Nah," he said. "No problem."

Three hours later he'd backed himself into a corner, had severed a neighbor's polyethylene spring line, which we knew ran through the pond site and would have to be replaced, and had buried both his tracks in the mud. Robby appeared at the door with very muddy feet and a red face.

"Well, I found the spring line," he mumbled. "There's a little more water than I expected. I'm going to have to call in the backhoe to pull me out."

After lunch a John Deere 690 and its operator were on the job. They pulled the bulldozer free without any trouble, and stayed for the next several days. Working as a team, the two machines shaped the pond and built the dam quite quickly. The bulldozer worked down low in the hole, while the backhoe stayed high, shaping the embankment with material pushed up to it.

In particularly wet pond sites, like mine, operators may have to trench the area temporarily to let water drain away as they're working there. A dragline on a crane can reach into a new pond—or an old one for that matter—from the shoreline, and may make less mess than a bulldozer. That's another alternative. I guess what I want to say is: if in doubt, don't plunge in with an inexperienced operator on a tractor you've rented from a neighbor. Seek advice from the wisest—maybe the oldest—operator you can find.

If the water-holding quality of the earth to be used in the dam is at all questionable, a dam foundation, already mentioned, will have to be built. A more technical term for this kind of structural insurance is a *cutoff trench*. This long ditch, running along the bottom of the dam, should be at least three feet wide at its base (or as narrow as the excavating machine can make it), should slope upward at a 45° angle from its edges, and should be stuffed with compacted, fairly waterproof fill. The cutoff trench will need to

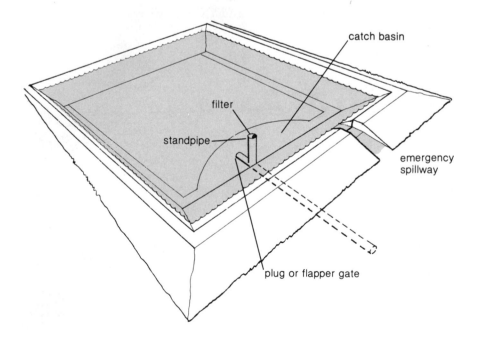

A general view of an embankment pond. The dam should be seeded as soon as it's completed. The emergency spillway, set a foot or so higher than the top of the standpipe, should prevent the dam from washing out during a flood. If the pond should ever need to be drained, the plug on the drain line, near the bottom of the catch basin, can be removed.

be built before material for the remainder of the dam is pushed up and sculpted.

Pond edges that are too steep, as we already know, can erode and cave in. Too-shallow sides admit too much sunlight into the water and encourage weed growth. The Soil Conservation Service specifications calling for a 3:1 slope inside, and a 2:1 outside slope should be followed to the letter, in my opinion. Once the dam is formed, it should be raked, seeded, and mulched immediately, even though the whole thing will settle slightly during the next few months. Be on the lookout for erosion anywhere on the dam at any time. If you spot it, correct it right away.

How to Drain It?

If there's a great pond debate, it rages over which is the better system: an underground drain with a T-riser standpipe, or an open spillway. Tim Matson, a professional pond maker from Thetford Center, Vermont, concedes that a bottom drain allows a pond to be emptied and flushed easily, and that the standpipe maintains a constant water level.

The problem, as Matson sees it, is that the metal T, which is supposed to work more or less like a faucet, often leaks. And because the whole structure is under water, leaks are very hard to locate and fix. He prefers open spillways, despite the fact that the Soil Conservation people, more often than not, recommend just the opposite.

My agent, Carlton Piper, SCS representative in Lamoille County, Vermont, has been "digging ponds," as he puts it, since 1957. By now a "good many" of the older welded, six- and eight-inch galvanized steel standpipes he's seen installed *are* starting to rust out and leak. He believes the heavy PVC plastic tubing, if not a better solution, is probably a longer-lasting one. So that's what we used.

I'm told it should need no maintenance, except that the upper two feet of standpipe should be painted black. The black is to protect the plastic from possible damage by the sun, since PVC, like some other synthetics, gradually deteriorates when exposed to solar radiation.

Spillway height, whether it's at a standpipe or a concrete shelf over which the overflow passes, determines the pond's maximum water-surface

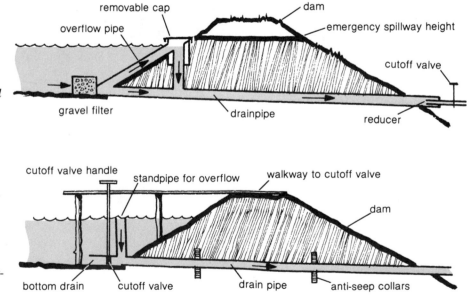

This system is designed for warm-water fish ponds. Cold water is drawn from the bottom of the pond, rather than from the warmer top. The removable cap prevents fish from escaping, while the gravel filter box keeps weeds and debris from entering the drain pipe.

This T-standpipe drainage arrangement allows warm water to leave the pond through the top of the overflow pipe or standpipe. Pond water stays comfortable cool for trout. Anti-seep collars prevent water from migrating along the outside of the drain pipe.

Galvanized standpipes like this are common, but many soil conservationists now prefer plastic. A welder can make the trash guard, shown on top of the pipe.

level. A properly conceived pond will have a secondary earthen spillway 1 to 1½ feet above the level of the primary spillway. This offers an escape route for water during a flood. It shouldn't be needed more than once in twenty-five years. Or less.

The top of the dam should have several feet of "freeboard," meaning that it sticks up at least three feet above the level of the primary spillway. All these heights should be accurately established using a transit level. The size of the spillway is critical. Too big is infinitely better than too small. The spillway will also need a mesh trash guard to keep leaves, sticks, and other debris out of the stand and drain pipes.

The drain pipe, the bottom part of the T riser, may need "anti-seep" collars to block off any water trying to sneak through the dam along the outside of the pipe. These can be installed as the dam is being built, and as the T riser is set in place.

If this piping is to be metal, it should be welded with special care to avoid leaking. The T riser is also an item that's frequently overlooked or underestimated when figuring the cost of a pond. Plan on spending upwards of $1,000 for it. If you use PVC, you'll probably have to spend a little more than that.

When the pond is ready to be filled, the drain pipe can be closed. A lever of some kind, or a chain leading from the plug or "flapper gate" to a float at the pond surface, allows you to "pull the plug" in an emergency or whenever the pond needs to be drained and cleaned.

Beavers and muskrats can cause problems, by the way. It's in a beaver's nature to want to raise the level of any pond in which he resides. My father

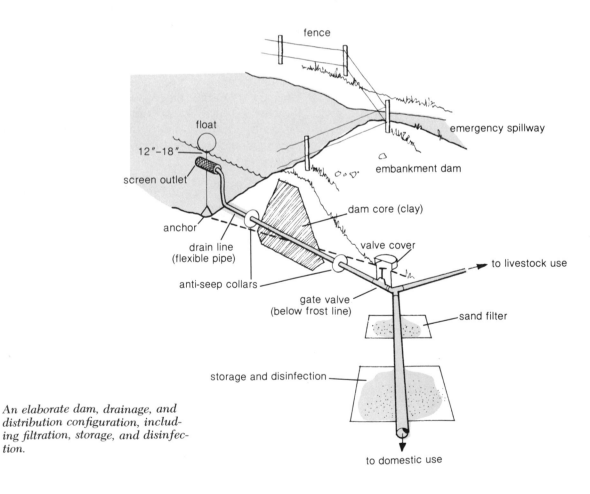

An elaborate dam, drainage, and distribution configuration, including filtration, storage, and disinfection.

THE HOME WATER SUPPLY

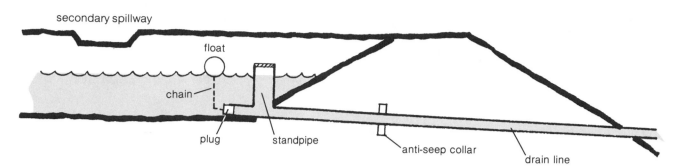

secondary spillway

float

chain

plug standpipe

anti-seep collar

drain line

A simple drainage system with T-standpipe. Normally the bottom of the secondary spillway is 1 to 1½ feet above the level of the primary spillway, and the top of the dam is at least 3' above the level of the primary spillway.

nature to want to raise the level of any pond in which he resides. My father has waged a sometimes more-, sometimes less-friendly battle with a long line of beavers at the concrete spillway of his pond. He enjoys having them as neighbors, so rather than trap them or run them off, he tolerates their periodic efforts to take over, and rips out any and all of their attempts to raise the dam.

Whenever they're in a building mood, their new spillway has to be wrecked each morning. And sometimes this goes on for days before they're discouraged. Allowed to take shape at all, a beaver dam can become an intricate engineering marvel that can be removed with nothing short of a large bulldozer or dynamite. Seriously.

Thousands Built

I was staggered to learn that almost 50,000 new ponds are built in this country each year. A few fail, but again, most of those that are properly designed do fine. Owners get into trouble when they lose sight of the fact that a pond is a mini-ecological system that's in a constant state of change. Like any other living thing, it begins to die the instant it's created. It may leak in the beginning, until settling silt seals its bottom. But this process also seals its doom.

Left alone, the pond will fill with sediment, turn swampy, and eventually dry up. An "old" pond is one that's approaching this state. A deeper pond stores water better and has a greater life expectancy than a shallow one. And deep and small in area, as opposed to large and shallow, means less water loss through evaporation. Redredging a pond after a number of years also breathes new life into it.

When the water level in either a dug-out or dammed pond gets too low for too long, toxic conditions start to develop in the water. *Eutrophication* is the natural process that threatens the life of all lakes and ponds. Growing algae that thrive on pollution, particularly nitrogen and phosphorus, strangle the oxygen supply to the point where little life can exist.

That's why it's important to look after the pond's watershed as well, to insure the basin is being fed enough clean water. The EPA recommends that a watershed should be: 1. Kept clean and well grassed to protect the ground from erosion, 2. Be free of barns, animal sheds, septic tanks, and leach fields, 3. Be protected against drainage from heavily fertilized fields and livestock areas, 4. And be fenced in to keep livestock *out*.

A pond can be excavated in a wet spot, but the quality of the dam material is critical, as is the slope of the dam.

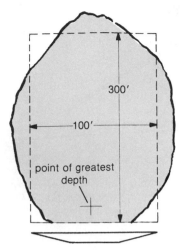

To estimate the capacity of a pond or lake, measure a rectangular area that approximates the surface area of the pond. Multiply length times width to figure the square footage. Measure the point of greatest depth. Compute the average depth at .4 times the greatest depth and calculate cubic feet of water (1 cubic foot = 7.5 gallons). Take 80% of that figure to find the pond's realistic storage capacity.

A PVC T-riser is set in place within the pond's dam. Once the drain line, lower left, is capped, the water level begins to rise. Later the top of the standpipe will be cut off, to determine the depth of the water in the pond.

Water in any pond will be polluted to a certain extent, some of the time. So any water it holds should be considered a secondary source, rather than a primary supply, if that's at all possible.

The amount of water stored in the pond should be estimated. Since a pond offers excellent fire protection, (30) the local fire department should be told its storage capacity.

Storage Capacity

The U.S. Department of Agriculture gives us a simple formula for figuring how much is there:

1. Measure a rectangular area that approximates the surface area of the pond.
2. Determine the square footage by multiplying length times width.
3. Measure the point of maximum depth in the pond.
4. Then compute the *average* depth at .4 times the greatest depth.
5. Now calculate the number of cubic feet of water. (Each cubic foot contains about 7.5 gallons of water.)
6. Realize that the actual volume of water in the pond is probably closer to 80 percent of its full capacity at any given time, than it is to 100 percent.

Any pond water that's to be used in the household system should be filtered to screen out turbidity and bacteria. This filtered water should then be disinfected when it's in storage. (71)

Raising Fish

D. J. Young, another pond expert, suggests that a stocked pond can provide over 50 percent of a farm family's fish needs. He says trout want a pond that's at least an acre in size and eight to ten feet deep. Water temperature is the most critical factor in raising fish. Trout like cold, and can't exist for long in water outside a range between 33° and 75° F. Young also claims that trout will not breed in a pond, and that the pond must be restocked each year. Those that are not fished out will live no longer than three years.

Bass, bluegills, and catfish are comfortable in warm water ponds, smaller than an acre in size, which have temperatures as high as 80° or 90° F. Trash fish, or wild-water fish as they're sometimes called, must be removed from a pond before game fish can be stocked. The U.S. Fish and Wildlife Services and local Fish and Game Services are always available to give the complete information needed on fish ponds.

I don't know if my pond will prove an exception to Mr. Young's rules or not. It's certainly smaller than an acre in size. During its excavation by Robby Adams, Gene Fellows, the other half of Lamoille County's Soil Conservation team, showed up to check the dam height. He took one look at the big vein of groundwater already starting to fill the pond.

"You're sure not going to have any problem getting water," he offered. "The pond's going to be cold though. Not so good for swimmin' but good for fishin'."

I wondered out loud if the pond would get too warm for trout.

"Not with *that* much cold water feeding it," said Fellows. "Stock it and see. Trout might even spawn here. All they need is enough cold running water to keep sediment off their eggs. You might be lucky...."

We'll have to wait and see.

18. IRRIGATION WATER

Water that's drawn from irrigation canals to be used for domestic purposes should be regarded as surface water at its most polluted, and should be treated as such. Return irrigation water, or *tail water*, as the Water Supply Division of the Environmental Protection Agency points out, is not only very silty and turbid, it's likely to contain high concentrations of fertilizer, herbicides, pesticides, and coliform bacteria.

Water purification chemists insist that even the worst water can be made drinkable and safe, *if* it's processed enough. Irrigation water offers a challenge to that contention, and it should be used only as a last resort. Even after it's treated, this water should be subjected to chemical analysis on a regular basis. (Chapter on Treating Water)

19. SPRINGS

A good, steady spring deserves tender attention. A spring *without* consistent flow is more than an unreliable source, it can also be a health hazard. To be considered truly dependable, a spring should yield at least twice a family's maximum needs—twenty-four hours a day, 365 days a year. (30)

A spring on a hillside will provide water pressure to a home below. In fact, for every two feet of elevation, one pound of pressure will be developed. The pressure will always be there as long as the spring is productive enough to keep the intake pipe filled, regardless of how much water is being used. In this case, the spring functions like an elevated reservoir. (49)

If the spring's yield is inconsistent, or in any way doubtful, a *hydropneumatic system*, made up of a storage tank, pump, and pressure tank will be needed to pressurize the home's internal plumbing. (56) If the spring is located *below* the house, it's a whole different story. Here you will have to determine the distance water must be lifted, and calculate *head loss*, before designing a pumping system that's sure to be adequate. (80) If the distance in elevation between the spring and the house is much more than twenty feet, it may be just as easy to find another water source.

Developing a spring, to increase and protect its flow, can be a touchy business. Too much blasting, digging, and tampering can ruin it by diverting the veins that feed it. And trying to seduce water from a dry spring that's

A spring would flow at the foot of this boulder—but only in winter. Careful digging with a backhoe was one way to develop this spring. Two feet down, the water table was found.

located higher than the dry-weather water table is a complete waste of time.

The main goals of spring development are to gather as much water as you can, to clean out the spring hole, to surround it enough to keep it from getting plugged in any way, and to prevent whatever water is there from draining away into the surrounding soil or neighboring springs and wells.

Once it's developed, a spring will have at least five components: the spring box itself, which is a basin that's watertight above, yet open enough below grade to let groundwater flow into it freely, a cover or housing, clean-out access, an overflow, and an intake line that connects to the distribution system of the house.

A weak spring will need a particularly good storage basin, located far enough below it to accept as much flow as possible. Sometimes, rather than being concentrated in one spot, a spring's output will be dispersed. Perforated drain tile, fanning out from the spring box, can collect water seeping from a large area of ground, and direct it toward the basin. The tile must slope toward the box, and should be laid in at least four feet of gravel. The gravel is then covered with impervious clay to discourage surface water from mixing with water from the spring.

Spring Box

A spring box can be round or square. The best ones are made of concrete, either precast—such as round *well tile* that's hauled to the site—or concrete that's formed and cast in place. If the box is set directly over the spring, it may need footings but may also be bottomless. If it's collecting water from above, on the other hand, it *may* have a concrete bottom. The base of the

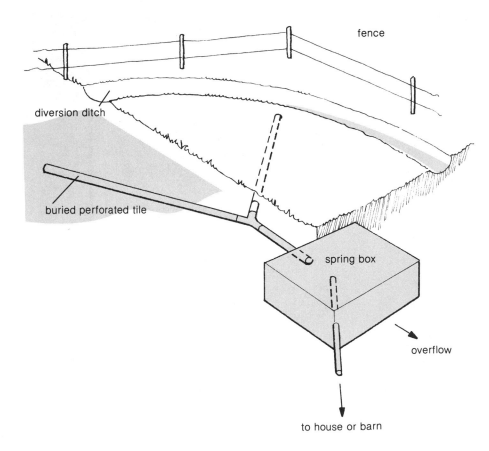

To increase a spring's flow, bury porous tile uphill from the spring itself. The perforated tile will collect water and direct it toward the reservoir. The fence is to keep livestock out; the diversion ditch prevents surface water contamination.

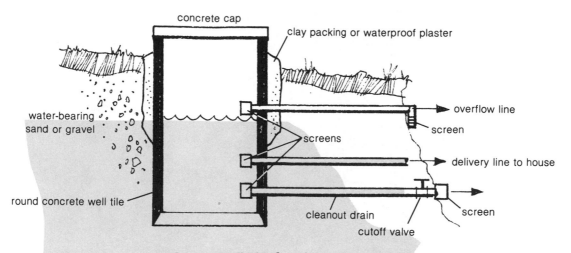

concrete cap

clay packing or waterproof plaster

water-bearing sand or gravel

round concrete well tile

overflow line

screen

screens

delivery line to house

cleanout drain

cutoff valve

screen

Concrete well tiles three feet in diameter make great spring boxes. Cut holes for pipes with a cold chisel, then pack them with a waterproof plaster, such as roofing cement.

uphill wall can be built out of concrete blocks set on edge, or of field-stone—both of which allow groundwater to enter the collection chamber.

Spring boxes are often set in gravel that surround their uphill sides, but are packed with tamped clay above ground and around their downhill sides. Again, the clay is to keep the box watertight. The objective is to keep surface water out, and to keep water *inside* from leaking and leaching away.

Spring covers can be made of wood and shingles, metal, fiberglass, or concrete. Precast concrete caps are the heaviest and most difficult to move. The concrete may not be completely waterproof, but it can be made so if it's covered with black polyethylene. Clear "poly" will disintegrate after a few months. The ultraviolet rays in sunlight eventually destroy it.

Some authorities say a spring cover should be made of metal or fiberglass, reminding us that wood rots. That's correct, but I know that a sloping cover with cedar shingles, set on a concrete foundation, and kept clear of brush and undergrowth, will outlive us all. However it's made, the cover should come off easily, to permit cleaning, maintenance, and regular inspection of the spring.

The encasement should have an overflow pipe for those times when the water table is high and there's too *much* water. It should be set at the maximum desired water level inside the spring box, and it should discharge onto an apron of rocks far enough away from the spring to prevent any erosion of the clay packing. Small creatures like frogs, mice, and snakes like to creep into cool spring housings to escape the heat of summer. So do spiders and certain insects. Once they find their way in, they can't always find their way out, and end up dying in the spring. To keep them out, the overflow pipe must be screened at its outer end.

Drain System

The spring will also need a drain, and the line leading from *it* should be screened as well. Once every few years you'll want to open the drain valve and let water out of the spring box long enough to clean away sediment that's bound to gather inside. Naturally, this drain outlet must be set in the lowest point of the box.

Round concrete well tile is used to encase a spring. Because the cover is so heavy, a tripod and chain are used to raise it.

The end of the intake line, which delivers water to the house, should also be covered with screening—in this case to keep debris from getting into the line. This intake will need to be cleaned periodically too. It should be located six inches or more above the drain outlet. This height difference allows sediment to build up in the bottom of the spring box, without entering the intake line. All piping leading to and from the collection basin should be carefully fitted through holes in the concrete sides of the box, and grouted with waterproof compound so there can be no leakage.

Ideally, the intake feeds a line that runs downhill to the house or barn. Plastic tubing, which doesn't corrode, should be laid as straight as possible so there's little friction in the line. It should be buried deep enough to be below frost level. Needless to say, a frozen spring line makes the spring worthless. Spring lines *can* be dug and backfilled by hand, but if the frost level reaches down to 4½ or 5 feet as it does in a place like Minnesota, a hired backhoe makes the job a lot more fun.

Be sure to use tubing that's the right size. A ¾-inch line is standard in most situations, but a larger diameter (and more expensive) line may be needed if hydrostatic pressure from the spring will be used to deliver water all the way to faucets through the house plumbing. *Too* big a line, of course, can drain the spring too quickly.

Gathering boxes are sometimes built at intervals on spring lines that drop great distances on their way to storage reservoirs below. These way stations collect some water, making the supply more consistent, but their main purpose is to *relieve* pressure buildup by reducing head. (80)

Don't forget: springs are exceptionally vulnerable to contamination. A swale or diversion ditch should be dug above the spring box to redirect surface water away from the spring. Build a fence to keep livestock away, and disinfect the spring every several months. (71)

System Still Works

I lived for many years in an old and crooked farmhouse in Duxbury, Vermont. The house had no well. My good friend, my ex-wife who still lives there, has altered the dilapidated water system little if at all—though she's upgraded other parts of the house.

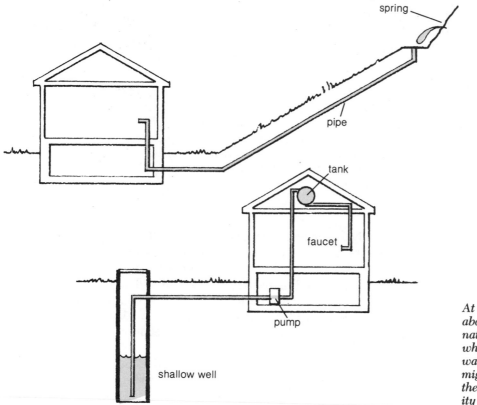

spring

pipe

tank

faucet

pump

shallow well

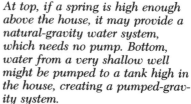

At top, if a spring is high enough above the house, it may provide a natural-gravity water system, which needs no pump. Bottom, water from a very shallow well might be pumped to a tank high in the house, creating a pumped-gravity system.

Two ¾-inch polyethylene water lines came into the cellar. One led underground, up the hill behind the house to our primary water source—a rock-lined spring, maybe forty-five feet above the elevation of the wooden storage tank, pump, and pressure tank in the cellar. The second plastic line led to a spring somewhere on another part of our hill. To be honest, I never located this second source in all the years I lived there. The previous owner didn't know where it was either. "I guess I'm too old to remember," was all he said.

Only once, during a wickedly dry August, did the main spring fail to deliver us all the water we could use. That year we opened the back-up line to the mystery spring and were able to fill the nearly dry storage tank in a few hours. This wooden storage tank, which we called a cistern, was connected to the rickety pump, whose leather gaskets needed to be replaced with an irregularity nobody could ever explain to me. The pump sat on top of the pressure tank that boosted water to a shower, two sinks, and a clothes washer upstairs.

From time to time each summer, we'd use enough water to drop the spring level below the intake line. At first worried the spring had gone dry, I'd always trudge up the hill, lift off the corrugated metal cover, and look inside, only to find plenty of water in the spring.

The first time this happened, hurried consultation with a wise neighbor taught me the line was "prob'ly airlocked." An air bubble *had* gotten in the line as we'd drawn water below the intake. And it blocked any waterflow, even after the spring recovered. My neighbor explained how to fix it.

And whenever it happened again, it became a routine matter to attach the cellar end of the line to the extra fitting on the pressure tank, open the valve and allow hydropneumatic pressure to force water back up through the plastic line. There would be an immediate "blurp!" in the spring as the bubble was blown out of the line, and water would flow, with a vengeance, back into the house.

In winter, ice would form on the intake every once in a while. This would happen only when there was too little snow to insulate the spring and when the temperature would drop below −10° F. and stay there for many days. The same procedure would work then. By forcing water up the line, ice could be moved away from the intake. After a while I got so good at this I never even bothered to go up the hill to check the results.

I can't even count the number of my neighbors who still have similar funky water systems, each with its own set of idiosyncrasies. You'll have your own, no doubt.

20. WELLS

Because groundwater moves in so many ways, at different speeds and at different depths, the general term "well" is about as useful as the word "aircraft." To say a well is any pit or hole in the ground used to extract water, is a misleading oversimplification. There are wells and there are wells. Some shallow wells, like light training airplanes, venture only a short distance from the ground surface. Elsewhere deep wells, like rockets and missiles, penetrate deep into subterranean space. The range between these extremes is practically infinite.

Wells and well technology, like groundwater, are complex and largely misunderstood by the public. And there's considerable disagreement even among experts, including well drillers, about what's down there. Inconsistencies in attitude and know-how can be explained by the fact that geologic strata, particularly as they involve water, vary greatly throughout the world. The phrase "artesian well," for example, is often used incorrectly, at least according to the geologists' explanation of the concept. When I asked one experienced well driller about "aquifers," he looked blank, and confessed he wasn't familiar with that term.

Paul Sevigny, the high-credibility dowser mentioned earlier, has had outstanding success at finding what he calls "shallow" wells in northern New England. (9) He defines shallow as two to ten feet in depth, and maintains

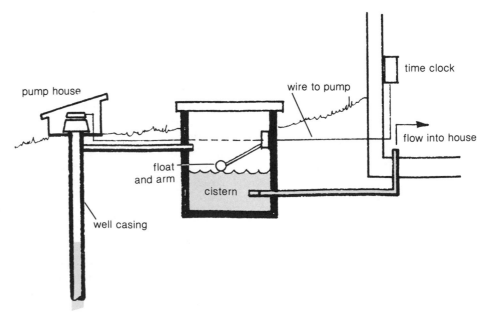

To ensure enough water from a weak well, an intermediate holding tank may be used. A timer inside the house instructs the pump to run periodically—often enough to keep a fairly consistent supply of water in the cistern. Water is drawn, on demand, from the cistern. When the water level there is high enough, the float switch shuts the pump off.

that the vast majority of such sources are not only very dependable, but often have a better chemical quality than deeper wells where water tends to be "hard." (61)

In Sevigny's eyes, a vein of water that runs year-round at a rate of three gallons per minute (gpm) or more is satisfactory for a family of four. When he locates a vein of water like this with the help of dowsing rods, he uses a backhoe to intercept the vein and confirm the flow. He insists that the machine dig *across* the direction of water movement in the vein, rather than with it, for fear the vein will be obstructed or diverted by the intruding backhoe bucket.

If the amount and quality of water are acceptable, the machine excavates farther—to a depth one or two feet below the vein. Crushed stone or clean gravel is dumped in this hole, and a section of cylindrical concrete well tile, three feet in diameter, is placed on the stone, with its base six to twelve inches below the bottom of the water vein.

The tile is capped with a round precast slab, perhaps packed with clay on its outside, and backfilled as soon as an overflow and intake line can be tapped into the captured vein. In this case, the well is more like a developed spring than what we'd normally expect a "well" to be.

Sevigny cautions that shallow wells like this are illegal in some states. In Oregon and California, for instance, a well must be at least forty feet deep. The rationale in those western states is that wells too near the surface are easily contaminated with runoff. Check groundwater statistics near you, as well as state regulations and local ordinances before you dig. (98)

Ready to Drill

Less than thirty miles from Paul Sevigny's home, Jay Hull was the picture of concentration—even though it was just another day. That morning the $300,000 mobile drilling rig—one of several owned by the H.A. Manosh Corporation of Morrisville, Vermont—had been jockeyed into place on the Pinzer property. Bob, Jay's assistant for the past six years, had moved the flatbed truck, carrying a 1,000-gallon water tank, into position beside the drill.

The rig was leveled on its hydraulic pads and organized quickly. The men worked wordlessly, like surgeon and operating-room nurse, speaking only to answer questions from the stranger with the camera. Half an hour after their arrival, a hole had been started, drilled to a depth of four or five feet, then stopped. The bit had run into slanting ledge at such shallow depth that it wanted to deflect sideways. A glance from Jay communicated that the rig would have to be moved. The bit was pulled up, the pads raised, everything was made fast, the drill truck was started and moved forward four feet. Fifteen minutes later a new hole was started.

Jay stayed all day at his post next to the control panel at the rear of the truck, smoking, drinking coffee, eating a sandwich, but mostly watching, listening, *feeling* the motion of the rig, and always making slight adjustments. Every few minutes he'd put his shovel next to the well hole and collect some of the water-and-grit mixture blown up from the depths by 200 or more pounds per square inch of compressed air the machine was forcing *down* the hole through the hollow drilling rod. He'd examine this slurry like a prospector looking in his gold pan. Sometimes he explained what was going on to the visitor. Sometimes he made notes in a small notebook he kept in his breast pocket.

Bob kept drill water flowing from the tank on the second truck, shoveled and trenched the slurry, making sure it ran downhill away from the rig, pre-

Jay Hull, a driller for the H.A. Manosh Corp., at the controls of his rig.

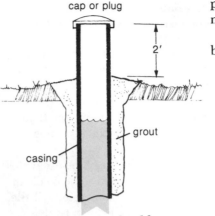

A well head, as completed by a driller.

By collecting and timing the overflow of a well, the driller can determine its capacity.

pared the well casing, welded the couplings, and assisted whenever a bit needed to be changed, or another length of drilling rod added.

By day's end the well was finished and capped. Jay handed me his notebook with a grin. This is what it said:

Sept. 9, 1981		Stowe Hollow
8″ bit 19′		Casing 20′ 4″
	Pinzer	
0–9		Dirt
9–25		Light gray
25–35		Brown
35–50		Gray
50–52		Brown vein 1 gal.
52–77		Medium gray
77–78		Quartz 3 gal.
78–119		Dark and medium gray
119–135		Brown and rotten quartz 11 gal.
135–145		Light gray

Total: 145
Bit size: 5 5/16
GPM: 15

Later a more complete well *log,* taken from Jay's cryptic notes, would be done. One copy would be kept on file in the Manosh Corporation office, one copy would be submitted to the state, to assist the State Geologist's office in its efforts to chart statewide geologic strata, and one copy would go to the Pinzers, owners of the property.

The Pinzer well was 145 feet deep and yielded fifteen gallons per minute—a fine well. The first drilling rod to enter the hole, called the *starter rod,* was twenty feet long. Attached to its end was an eight-inch drill bit with tungsten-carbide buttons on its cutting face. By nineteen feet the bit was far into ledge, and a 20′ 4″ length of steel well casing, with a *well shoe* on *its* end, was driven into the eight-inch hole.

Once the casing was in place a smaller, six-inch bit was used—its actual diameter: 5 5/16 inches. After the starter rod, all other drilling rods were twenty-five feet in length.

By monitoring the cuttings coming·from the hole, and by keeping close track of his depth, Jay developed a profile of the well. On its way down the drill passed through gray and brown strata, as well as through quartz, a material that often holds water. Between fifty and fifty-two feet the bit passed through a vein yielding one gallon per minute. (The driller knows exactly how much drilling water—as well as air—he's blowing down the hole. The amount of water coming back *out* of the well, less the amount he's putting in, equals the yield.)

At seventy-eight feet the drill passed through a second vein, this one with three gallons a minute. Since Mr. Pinzer had specified at least ten gpm, Jay kept going. Between 119 and 135 feet the bit found a much bigger vein— eleven gallons per minute, which was doublechecked with a gallon bucket filled with overflow from the well. Jay drilled another ten feet beyond the vein—standard practice to allow room for the pump and additional storage. (42)

The drill was then retracted and the casing was driven an eighth of an inch deeper to seat the drive shoe in the ledge, making the base of the casing watertight and preventing any surface water from running into the well by passing down the outside of the pipe. Sixteen inches of casing was left above ground, and the cap was placed on its top to await a Manosh hook-up crew that would move in a day later.... (47)

THE HOME WATER SUPPLY

21. WELL CONTRACTORS

A deep well, particularly one that's drilled or driven, should be left in the hands of a reputable well contractor—preferably one that's licensed by your state. Ask for a written contract.

A well-drilling contract should describe all the work to be done, prices, and terms, including:

- A statement that all work is to comply with any and all local and state codes.
- The size of the well hole and methods of eliminating surface contamination.
- Casing specifications. For instance: the casing is to be at least four inches in diameter and extend at least twenty feet below the ground surface. (A hole with a diameter larger than four inches may be needed to accommodate a bigger pump.)
- The type of well seal and grout seal around the casing, and the type of well development to be done—if necessary.
- The type of screen to be installed—where needed.
- The test-pumping procedure to be used.
- A date for completion of the well, and delivery of the well log and test-pumping report.
- A guarantee of materials and workmanship.
- Costs: an itemized list including the cost of drilling per foot, charges for any other materials per unit (including casing), and any other charges for grouting, developing, and test pumping.
- Liability insurance for both owner and driller.

Standard well-drilling, estimating, and contract forms are available from most established contractors or from the National Well Water Association, 500 W. Wilson Bridge Road, Worthington, OH 43085. This association certifies well drillers, and will happily provide lists of local qualified contractors.

Minimum Depth Fee

Keep in mind that some drilling companies have a minimum depth fee. In other words, they'll charge you for at least 100 feet (standard), even if they strike water at 50. Once water *has* been struck, it's normally part of the contractor's responsibility to pump the well free of all sand and drilling particles and to disinfect it.

The well log that describes depth and strata, aside from being a valuable record, is used to determine the size of the pump that will be installed. It's also in the owner's best interest, I believe, to have the drilling company hook up to the well head, and install piping that will bring water as far as the house. From that point on, the internal plumbing may be handled by someone else.

22. LOCATION

Modern wells tend to be placed where it's most convenient for the drilling contractor to move his rig into position. That's fine, in many instances, as long as a little time is spent recognizing where a well should *not* be located. For instance, a rural well should never be too close to a septic tank or leach field. A typical regulation states that a well be at least 75 feet from such a source of pollution. In Ohio it's 50 feet. In Vermont the minimum is 100. A few states insist on 150. To avoid problems, talk with the local health officer, before drilling, regarding codes, permits required, and proper distances.

Our geologist friend, Dr. Phil Wagner, contends that most local codes are inadequate on distances required. The reason, as he explains it, is that disease-causing viruses often contained in human sewage can travel great distances from a leach field in moving groundwater. This is particularly true in areas where bedrock is not far beneath the surface. Further, he says, in too many cases water sanitation tests don't *include* tests for viruses, even though they do seek coliform bacteria.

The well location should be an integral part of the master plan for any homesite, along with the house, outbuildings, roadways, and septic system. It should not be an afterthought. The closer it can be to the house, the shorter the plumbing needed to deliver water from the well. It should be away from livestock, clear of dumping sites, and removed from oil deposits and any other potential source of contamination. It's also wise to locate a well at least two feet beyond the dripline below the eaves of any building. In fact, *any* roof or land grading that encourages surface water toward the well casing should be avoided.

For what it's worth, a dowser who locates a well may mark a very specific spot on the ground, drive a stake there, and expect the driller to bore straight down from that point. A modern drill rig, such as the one operated by Jay Hull, has a "pretty accurate" bubble level near its control panel. If the truck is properly leveled before drilling begins, the hole theoretically should be plumb.

Old Story

Like all partisans, members of the American Society of Dowsers are fond of "war stories," as they call them. A favorite is about the skeptical driller

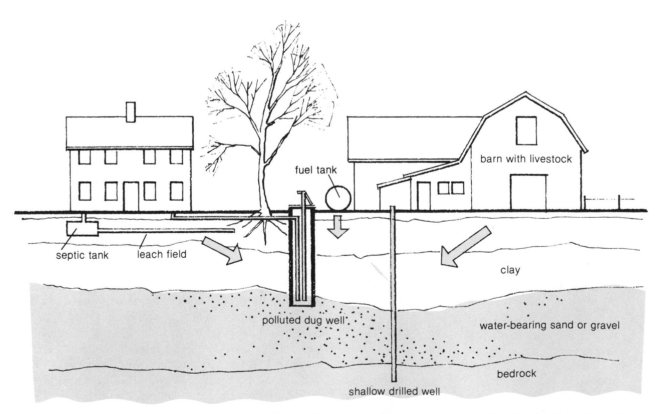

Shallow wells can be threatened by many sources of contamination. Water drawn from wells at greater depth is more likely to be thoroughly filtered.

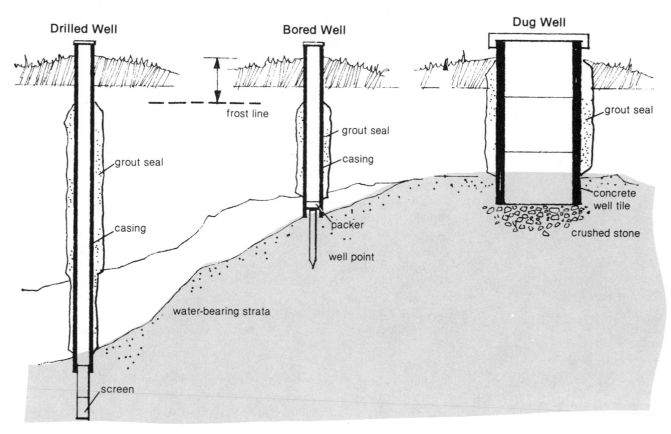

Several methods of protecting wells from surface contamination. (A) drilled well, (B) Bored or driven well, (C) dug well.

who "missed" the water vein sensed by the shrewd dowser. The time, setting, and exact cast of characters changes as this story gets retold, but the gist of the scenario goes something like this:

The driller fails to find water. The dowser is called back to witness the dry hole.

Driller (gloating): "You were wrong. There's no water at 80 feet like you said. We're down to 300 feet, and there's still nothing."

Dowser: "Did you drill straight down?"

Driller: "Sure I did."

Dowser: "You're sure?"

Driller: "Positive."

The dowser drops a pebble down the center of the well casing. There's silence for a split second, then they hear a ping-ping-ping as the stone bounces off the metal pipe. Obviously it's either crooked or out of plumb.

The embarrassed driller is forced to admit that well holes aren't always *perfectly* straight and vertical, and the dowser can now reiterate that there *is* water at 80 feet. It's just been missed by a drilling inaccuracy.

In some versions of this tale the dowser then "chases" the vein into the well. In others "development" by the driller frees up the nearly missed water and the well is made productive. (52) Sometimes it's a stand-off. Again, you can draw your own conclusions.

An interesting footnote: the American Society of Dowsers, at this writing, claims fifty-seven professional well drillers among its membership.

23. CONE OF DEPRESSION

It's worth knowing what happens down below whenever water is pumped from a well. Water coming up the discharge line from the base of the well is either sucked from above or pushed upward from below by the submersible pump. The *drawdown* is the distance the water table immediately next to the well is lowered during pumping. Naturally, the intake at the bottom of the discharge line accepts water closest to it first, and water farther away gradually seeps toward the intake.

When a significant amount of water is removed from the water table, a relatively dry, funnel-shaped area, called the *cone of depression*, develops between the static water level and the pumping level. We can imagine, as someone has suggested, that the cone of depression resembles the indentation we'd make if we pushed a finger into an inflated balloon.

This cone will begin to resaturate, of course, the moment pumping stops. But the shape and width of this inverted cone, and how rapidly it refills, depends on the consistency of material at the well base. Shallow, wide cones tend to form in aquifers of very permeable sand and gravel. Where water moves more slowly through less permeable strata, steeper, narrower cones are more likely.

Drawdown and the cone of depression have a direct bearing on the well's recovery rate, *and* on pumping costs. If the pump must work overtime to pull water from the surrounding strata, more energy must be used.

24. RADIUS OF INFLUENCE

A well's *radius of influence* is the horizontal distance from the well hole to the top of the cone of depression. Although we can't see it, we must realize that the radius of influence expands with more and more pumping. It *is* easy to see why several wells drilled too close together—so the radius of one overlaps the radius of the other—can yield an unsatisfactory amount of

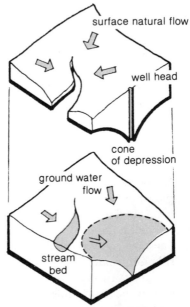

Pumping from a well can affect the surrounding water table, diverting water away from a stream bed, for instance.

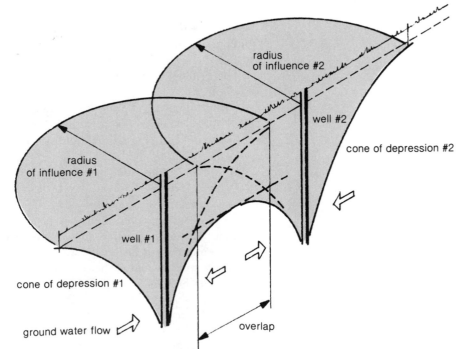

Wells located too close together interfere with each other, as cones of depression overlap.

water for everybody concerned. The wells are just pumping each other dry. That's why it's imperative, if you're considering a densely populated neighborhood, to learn both the nature and location of other wells in the area.

When too many wells are drawing water from the same aquifer, the permanent water table is lowered, and wells begin to go dry. Drilling deeper ones is only a stop-gap measure. In coastal regions, where salt water is nearby, briny water can be drawn into dwindling supplies of fresh groundwater. Such problems already exist in many parts of the United States. Avoid adding to them.

25. DUG WELLS

Grandma's well, with its stone-wall top we could just see over, its little roof, and the bucket on a windlass, was almost certainly a dug well. We might remember it as a "wishing well"—the type our mothers worried we'd fall into. It's likely to be abandoned by now, replaced by a much deeper well with an automatic pump. And if it's still there, it's probably just for show. Because it penetrated just a short distance into the water table, its water may have been polluted—even in our grandparents' time. A very high percentage of today's dug wells *are* contaminated.

Dug wells are generally thought to be undependable as well as unclean. They're often known to fail during dry times. Still, in places where the water table remains pretty constant and groundwater quality is high, dug wells are common. Compared to drilled wells, they're shallow, for the most

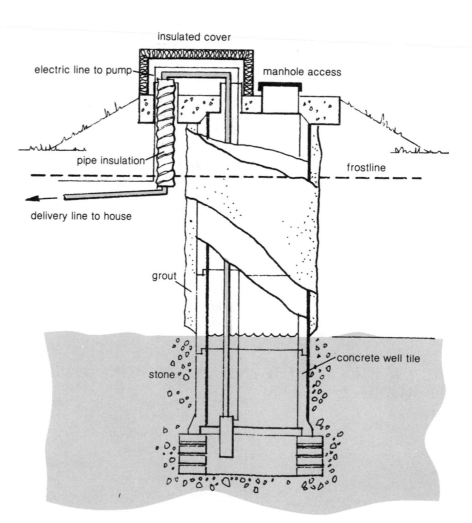

In many places, older, dug wells still yield water from shallow water tables. Before the invention of the pitless adapter (see section 47), delivery lines had to be brought above frost line, turned, and redirected underground. They also had to be insulated to prevent freezing.

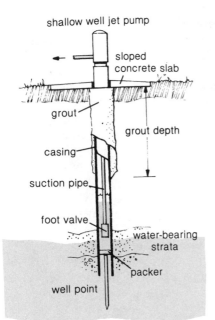

shallow well jet pump

sloped concrete slab

grout

grout depth

casing

suction pipe

foot valve

water-bearing strata

packer

well point

A hand-driven shallow well showing the well point packed within the casing. The jet pump sucks water from below.

part—rarely more than 50 feet deep—reaching just a few feet below the water table into soaked sand and gravel.

Digging the well hole, which may range from three to twenty feet in diameter, is normally a tedious hand-excavated, pick-and-shovel operation. Dug-out material is hauled to the surface in a pail on a rope. A clam-shell bucket on a crane *can* be used if the earth is very soft.

The stone wall around the top of Gramy's well was actually the upper end of the lining. Today fieldstone is still used to keep the well walls from caving in, but brick and mortar or concrete blocks are easier to work with. More often, dug wells are cased with sections of three-foot wide, precast well tile that fit together at tongue-and-groove joints. Whatever the material, this well lining should be as well sealed and watertight as possible.

The roof over the wishing well was an attempt to keep rainwater out of water below. A more modern dug well should have a sanitary seal at the ground surface, which does this job more effectively. It will keep surface water from contaminating the water table; space between the well liner and the surrounding earth should be backfilled with clean sand, and the top ten feet or so should be plugged with a waterproof cement grout.

Power-operated pumps may be needed to remove water temporarily as the digging gets into saturated soil below the water table. The base of the hole may be packed with clean crushed stone to act as a filter for water entering the well. In very dry periods, if the water table lowers, there may be need to clean out the well bottom and dig it deeper still.

26. BORED WELLS

A *bored well* is essentially a dug well, made with an earth auger instead of a shovel. If the auger is turned by hand, the hole will be between eight and fourteen inches in diameter. Power-driven augers bore wider holes—up to three feet in diameter. A bored well might be somewhat deeper than an ordinary dug well, but rarely can it be expected to reach a water table that's lower than 100 feet in the ground.

Earth augers work only in very consistent soils, such as clay. If there are boulders, or if the earth tends to cave in, a different digging tool will be necessary. If a bored well passes through impervious hardpan into a pressurized aquifer, it *could* be artesian—though most bored wells simply draw water from a static water table.

Vitrified tile, steel, and plastic are the lining materials used most often. In some instances this casing is perforated where the pipe extends into water-bearing gravel and sand. These perforations receive water from the surrounding strata, and may need to be covered with screening to keep silt from entering the discharge line. This screening will need to be cleaned out from time to time. (52)

Like all wells, a bored well head must be sealed and protected from surface drainage.

27. JETTED OR WASHED WELLS

When and if conditions are right, a well can be *jetted* or *washed*. The two most important ingredients in this kind of operation—aside from soil with reasonably uniform texture—are a nearby water source and a pressure pump. A protective casing is driven into an augered hole, and a *riser pipe*, fitted with a special washing point on its lower end, is inserted inside the casing. A stream of water is forced down this riser pipe and the jet from the wash point dislodges sand and soil below. As the point is pushed deeper and deeper, the muddy mixture is carried back to the surface in the space between the center pipe and the casing, and is discharged into a settling vat.

Later, when the wash point is removed, the riser pipe becomes the suction line for water being pumped out of the well from above, and the top few feet of space between the two pipes are grouted to make it watertight.

Mail-order advertising that touts do-it-yourself power augers or "hydro-drills" for jetting relatively shallow well holes should be studied cautiously. Be skeptical unless you have ideal soil conditions, a very high water table, and an abundance of muscle. Recent lawsuits brought against some manufacturers of this type of equipment, filed on grounds that the machinery was ineffective, dangerous—or both—have caused some of these products to be taken off the market.

28. DRIVEN WELLS

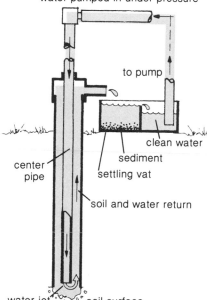

water pumped in under pressure

to pump

clean water

center pipe

sediment

settling vat

soil and water return

water jet   soil surface

A jetted or washed well can be dug in soft, consistent soil. Water is forced down a center pipe within a larger casing. Pressure at the jet loosens the sand or earth, forcing it back toward the surface. The soil particles are removed in the settling vat, and the cleansed water is recirculated through the system.

Percussion-type drilling rigs hammer through earth and rock. Rotary units drill downward, the tungsten-carbide buttons on the bit grinding away with the help of water and compressed air.

The perfect place for a *driven well?* According to a friend of mine who lives there, the southern tip of Indiana may be the richest and most efficient farm land in the world. Near the junction of the Wabash and Ohio Rivers, two large bodies of surface water flowing to the Mississippi, huge "rivers" of groundwater also run just a few feet below a thick layer of fertile topsoil.

Here wells can be driven almost anywhere, I'm told. And they'll provide an infinite supply of water for homes, towns, and crops. The climate's right, water and down-river transportation is cheap, and the soil can grow enough corn and hogs to feed many nations. You and I, even if we were totally inexperienced, could probably drive a successful well there. We couldn't miss.

A *driven well*, however, and a *drilled well* are *not* the same thing, despite the fact the two terms are interchanged from time to time. A driven well is quick, relatively inexpensive, and, unless there's an unlimited water supply near the surface as just described, relatively undependable when compared to its deeper relative, the drilled well. In places where well driving is easy, but the water table fluctuates, homeowners hedge their bets by driving a number of wells and connecting them to one pump to insure enough water throughout the year.

Driven wells can be anywhere from 25 to 100 feet deep, though most draw water from 50 to 60 feet. A *well point*, made or forged of cast steel, is connected to several lengths of threaded pipe, and forced into the ground by blows on the pipe from above. This is the simplest and most direct way to reach groundwater, as long as there are no rocks in the soil to damage the wire-mesh jacket of the well point. Professionals are apt to dig a pilot hole first, using an earth auger, to be sure there are no obstructions. In some cases wells are driven from the bottoms of already bored or dug wells that have gone dry.

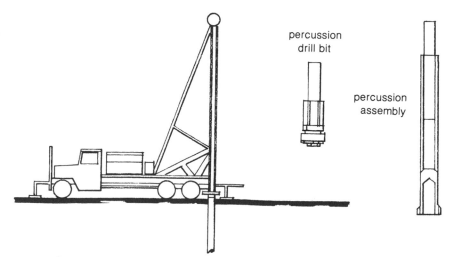

percussion drill bit

percussion assembly

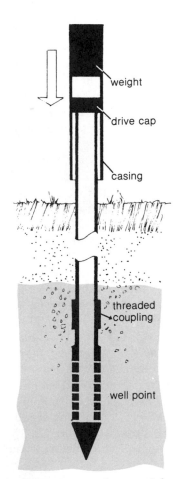

A weight slips over the top of the drive well casing, and is repeatedly dropped on the drive cap, pounding the point into the ground. As the well goes deeper, new sections of casing are added.

The section of drive pipe to be struck is fitted with a *drive cap* to protect its threaded upper end, which will receive a coupling when another section is added. The cap is then driven with a maul, sledge hammer, or a *drive head*—a weight and sleeve mechanism that is lifted and dropped over and over again. As it's being hit, the drive pipe should be continually turned so there's not too much stress on the threads on any one side.

Penetrates Easily

The drive point itself is only 1¼ to 2 inches in diameter, so it has little resistance as it penetrates. Of course the necessarily small riser pipe limits a driven well's yield to about thirty gallons a minute at the most. But if it's driven deep enough, the well may have twenty feet of available drawdown. Maybe more.

Different points have different mesh configurations, and an appropriate point should be chosen according to the type and coarseness of material in the aquifer. There are slotted well points, with larger openings for water, and points with smaller perforations. Too large a mesh will take in silt and other fine material once suction is applied, making the well what's affectionately known in the trade as a *sand pumper*.

The EPA, in its *Manual of Individual Water Supply Systems*, makes some technical observations about drive points: "Well-drive points can be obtained in a variety of designs and materials. In general, the serviceability and efficiency of each is related to its basic design. The continuous-slot, wire-wound type is more resistant to corrosion and can usually be treated with chemicals to correct problems of incrustation. It is more efficient because of its greater open area, and is easier to develop (52) because its design permits easy access to the formation for cleanup.

"Another type has metal gauze wrapped around a perforated steel pipe base and covered by a perforated jacket; if it contains dissimilar metals, electrolytic corrosion is likely to shorten its life—especially in corrosive waters.

"Wherever maximum capacity is required, well-drive points of good design are a worthwhile investment. The manufacturer should be consulted for his recommendation of the metal alloy best suited to the particular situation."

29. DRILLED WELLS

Maybe the best argument for a deep (and probably more expensive) *drilled well* is that it's less likely to be polluted. Second, it's *more* likely to produce greater yield, simply because of its immense drawdown potential. Third, professional well drillers on the whole are well trained, well organized, and fairly well controlled politically. These are just some of the reasons drilled wells have become increasingly popular as private water sources for individual families in the United States.

In many districts, law demands that wells be drilled *only* by licensed drillers. There may be other local regulations about well location (22), construction (20), capacity (31), disinfection methods (71), and water quality standards. (98) Maybe a drilling permit is needed. Maybe not. Rules vary from place to place. So do per-foot drilling and casing costs.

Even if you're reconciled to the idea that your well will cost $2,000 or more, drilling is *still* a gamble. Emmett Morton, my contractor's representative, was as poker-faced as a casino dealer when he stepped out of his company car on my lot. I noted his license plate read "H₂O."

"I need a well—cheap!" I joked as we shook hands for the first time.

"There's no such thing as a cheap well," he growled in warning. So we were off to a great start. But he proved to be helpful and thoughtful, and his suggestions about where and how things should be set up no doubt saved money over the long haul. "We're in a tough position," Emmett admitted later. "When we have to drill deep, we don't make many friends."

Two Drilling Methods

Drilled wells are done in one of two ways: with a *percussion-type* cable tool that beats and punches its way into the ground, or with a *rotary* bit that grinds, bites, and crushes its way through rock. Both are mounted on portable derricks with self-contained hoists.

The cable tool—or *pounder*—is somewhat slower, certainly the louder of the two, but effective. A heavy bit and stem are raised, then slammed into the earth. The advantage of this reciprocating action is that it fractures whatever is in its path. The hard shock is meant to free water in rock fissures and soft formations near the hole. Proponents of percussion drilling argue that rotary bits tend to close rather than open water veins as they pass through strata.

Rock cuttings are mixed with water trucked to the job site, and the resulting slurry is lifted to the surface in a *bailer*, a ten- to twenty-foot length of pipe with a valve at its lower end. Bailing gives the drillers an indication of the formations the drill is breaking through. By constantly monitoring the consistency of the slurry and the speed with which water enters the hole, they also know when they've reached a sufficient supply of groundwater.

Hydraulics Used

Rotary drilling is done with the help of hydraulics. Sometimes water is used as a drilling fluid, sometimes air, sometimes both. A rig like the one run by Jay Hull has an air compressor *and* a water pump. It combines the advantages of both percussion and rotary, can drill as fast as sixty feet an hour, and will drive casing.

I asked Jay how long a drilling bit with carbide buttons would last in hard ledge. "They'll go about 2,000 feet, if you're lucky," he said. Once the bit is well into bedrock, the rig works more or less automatically. But cave-in problems can develop before that—in topsoil and subsoil. Before the casing is driven, special detergent is pumped down the hole with the drilling water. This creates a muddy foam that firms up the sides of the well hole.

A flat-faced *drive bit*, which isn't a bit at all, is then mounted on the end of the starter rod, to pound the casing into place. The drive bit beats against the *headache ball* which fits in the top of the casing to protect its threads. As soon as the casing is firmly installed in the bedrock, drilling continues with a smaller bit. Where the hole passes through solid rock, no casing is needed.

The *drive shoe*, mentioned earlier, is a tapered, hardened-steel fitting that's fastened to the bottom of the well casing. It's driven and wedged into the rock to prevent surface water from seeping along the outside of the casing into the well. In Vermont it's not necessary to grout casing unless the well is to be used for commercial purposes. But in some other states grouting is required by law in *any* drilled well.

A few pertinent facts: six-inch drill bits are used most commonly, once the casing—also usually six inches—is in place. As you may recall, the starter bit is normally eight inches in diameter, to make a hole large enough to accept casing with a six-inch *inside* dimension. Between one and two gallons a minute of drilling water are pumped down the drilling rod, along with 100 to 250 pounds per square inch of compressed air. This air pressure blows cuttings and water out of the hole, even from great depths, at a speed of 3,000 feet a minute. If you can stand the tension of not knowing when water will be struck, stick around. A well drilling is a great show.

Four-inch casing is not unusual. In fact, the need for any casing larger than six inches is uncommon. Sections of casing are often connected by threaded couplings, then welded because they must be driven into the ground with such great force.

Different sizes, types, and thicknesses of well casing are available, as are a number of different connections to join lengths of casing pipe. The thicker the casing, the stronger and better. It's more resistant to corrosion, too, as any drilling company salesman will be happy to tell you. Further, it's more expensive, which he'll mention more reluctantly.

The bottom of the well casing, if it extends all the way into an aquifer, may be slotted. Otherwise the well pipe may have a screened intake fixture at its lower end, to permit sand-free water to flow into the well as it's pumped.

The slot or screening size is determined by the grain size of the aquifer's sand-and-stone aggregate, based on sieve samples taken from the well. If they're too small, the slots will naturally plug. If they're too big, they may inhale sand that can be pumped into the water system where it can cause all sorts of unnecessary wear and tear. Manufacturers have excellent tables to make the selection of proper screen size easy. . . .

4   *MOVING WATER*

30. CALCULATING NEEDS

Water consumption in the United States is on the upswing, and has been for some time. Estimates of water usage vary, of course, but if we use seventy-five gallons of water per person per day, as some conservative guesstimates suggest, that's about four times what our grandparents consumed at the turn of the century. Other experts calculate that each and every one of us requires 100 gallons a day, including what we use in the kitchen, the laundry, for bathing, drinking, and our sanitary needs.

As water requirements are figured, it's helpful to formulate a picture of your system's overall water budget. There will be receipts and disbursements, as well as water on hand in storage. Snow and rain, along with water from the spring or well, can be placed in the credits column. Debits will show up as general use, runoff, seepage into the ground, evaporation, and transpiration. Weigh your needs against the supply from existing water sources. These supplies must be estimated as accurately as possible, and their total must exceed projected use.

At 100 gallons per day for each member of a household, the average family of four, living in a conventional, single-family, suburban home, will consume 146,000 gallons of water in a year's time. Of this 146,000 gallons, 45 percent will be used in toilets (one flush takes as much as 6 gallons), bathing and shaving will use another 30 percent, laundry 20 percent, and cooking and drinking only 5 percent.

To get an even clearer idea of your water needs, it's important to look beyond per-person family use *within* the home. Outside there will be garden needs, livestock and pet needs, irrigation, recreation, and fire protection to consider. The feasibility of supplying each of these uses will depend not only on local rainfall figures, but on local soil conditions and evaporation rates as well.

In arid areas, prospective homeowners might do well to consider at least two separate water systems. One would provide potable water for the family, with sources of lesser quality taking care of livestock, irrigation, maybe even laundry.

Calculating the Supply

Water supplies are normally calculated on the basis of *flow*. Flow from a water source is measured, not in gallons per day, but in gallons per hour (abbreviated: gph) or in gallons per minute (gpm). Because we've grown fond of washing machines and dishwashers, garbage disposers, big lawns, perpetually clean automobiles, and all the other trappings that seem indispensable to our late 20th century lifestyle, today's modern home sometimes

Water Needs

Needed by	Gallons per day
Each person	75–100
Each milk cow, drinking and sanitation	35
Each horse, dry cow, or beef animal	6–12
100 chickens	3–7
100 turkeys	7–18
Each hog	2–4
Each sheep	2

Home Fixtures	Gallons needed	Rate of Flow (gals. per minute)
Filling ordinary washbowl	2	4
Filling average bathtub	30	5
Flushing toilet	6	4
Each shower bath	up to 30	5
Automatic dishwasher	per load 20	2
Automatic clothes washer	per load up to 40	5

Yard Fixtures		
½-inch hose with nozzle		3
¾-inch hose with nozzle		6
Lawn watering	600°	3–7

° Watering a lawn or garden with 1 inch of water on 1,000 square feet requires about 600 gallons of water.

requires as much as ten gpm, provided at thirty to fifty pounds per square inch (abbreviated: psi) of pressure.

As a group, we in this country use the most water at meal times, when we do our laundry (usually around midmorning), and before the late evening news, as we're brushing teeth and otherwise getting ready to turn in for the night. These are times of peak demand. To have a satisfactory water system we have to anticipate these times of maximum water use—just in case somebody flushes a toilet, while the dishwasher's running, as is the lawn sprinkler, right in the middle of *your* shower. Without good planning, everything could slow to a dribble. (32)

Surveys show that we cherish our lawns almost as much as we love clean cars. Both are considered signs of our affluence and prestige, either real or imagined, and both use plenty of water. Lawns appear in the driest, most infertile, and otherwise unsuitable places, and are one of the biggest water (and energy) sinks we have. Yet we continue to indulge ourselves.

A half-inch of water sprinkled on a 1,000-square-foot lawn requires 300 gallons of water. Make your lawn-need calculations on that basis. You'll probably be using 500 to 600 gallons per day at a minimum, with the flow at 180–360 gallons per hour.

Maintaining another luxury item, a swimming pool with the same surface area, actually takes *less* water than 1,000 square feet of lawn. On the average, 300 gallons a day should keep the pool full, given normal circumstances. Sprinkling 1,000 feet of garden space with an inch of water consumes twice that much—600 gallons each time you do it.

Livestock Use

Animals also use a lot of water. Livestock, especially dairy cattle, should be permitted to drink at will and should not have their water rationed. A cow producing 14,000 to 15,000 pounds of milk a year may need as much as thirty-five gallons of water each day. Laying hens demand an equally regular water supply—three to seven gallons a day for every 100 birds. Sheep and goats need two gallons per head, horses twelve gallons each, swine two to four gallons a day, and a flock of turkeys, geese, or ducks seven to eighteen gallons per 100. Keeping a milk room or dairy parlor sanitary takes at least 500 gallons of water each day, floor flushing in a barn uses ten gallons per 100 square feet of space, and a sanitary hog wallow an additional 100 gallons a day.

Any farmer will tell you that production of eggs, milk, and beef are all increased by a steady, dependable water supply. Limited water limits weight gain in hogs. Vegetable production can be increased one to three times with an abundance of water, applied in the right way. (100)

Believe-it-or-not water-use statistics, starting to show up regularly in national magazine features, are enough to make Ripley sit up and take notice. *Newsweek* says, "The water that goes into a 1,000-pound steer would float a destroyer . . . 14,935 gallons are needed to produce a bushel of wheat . . . 25 gallons for one ear of corn." Water expenditure is unbelievable. Adding things up will be a vital part of your decision-making as you plan your water system.

Fire protection is another consideration. As the EPA points out, a typical home water system yielding 3.5 gpm (210 gph) provides sufficient flow to fill one garden hose with a steady stream of water. That's hardly enough to quench a major fire that's already under way.

Minimum Needs

To be adequately protected, you should be able to count on at least ten gallons a minute at 30 to 40 psi, for at least a two-hour time period, even during the driest weeks of the year. (Some fire officials double these estimates, claiming a need for twenty gpm at 60 psi.) As you design your plumbing layout, (77) you may be smart to locate outdoor water outlets—called *sillcocks* by some—with an eye to fire protection as well as convenience. The USDA likes to see hose outlets at 100-foot intervals.

It's also wise to wire your pump and other water system controls to be independent of—even separated from—the rest of the home's circuitry. To have the pump fail as you're trying to extinguish your own fire would be embarrassing at the very least, possibly tragic. That's just part of the excellent advice offered by the National Fire Protection Association in a report called *Water Supply Systems for Rural Fire Protection*. It's part of the *National Fire Codes*, volume 8, published in Boston in 1969. Your local fire department probably has a copy.

31. DETERMINING YIELD

The numbers game approaches its moment of truth when we finally face up to the big question: exactly how much water is available to you? There's little point in planning to move it if there's not enough to begin with. The yield of a particular ground or surface water source can be measured quite accurately. In the case of catchments, where rainwater is trapped and stored, intelligent speculation, based mainly on past weather records, is the best you can hope for. (15)

A well driller will measure the approximate yield of his drilled or driven hole before he dismantles his rig, caps the well, and moves out. Jay Hull built an earth dam in the stream flowing from the Pinzer well, stuck an eighteen-inch section of plastic tubing through the dam to act as an over-

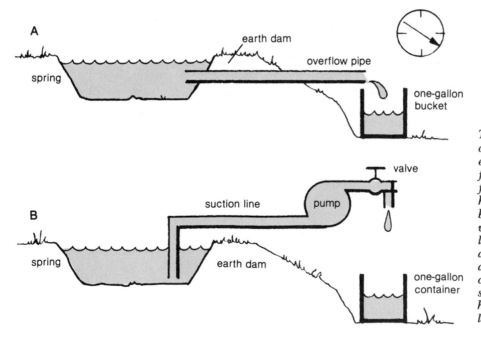

Two ways of measuring a spring's capacity: Above, build a temporary earth dam to collect water running from the ground, and run an overflow pipe through the dam. Time how long it takes to fill a gallon bucket. If it takes 20 seconds, divide 20 into 60, for a yield of 3 gallons per minute. Below, you might also use a pump. Adjust the valve at the pump outlet until the machine pumps at the same speed the spring is producing. Now record how long it takes to fill the one-gallon container.

flow pipe, and filled a one-gallon bucket with water from the tubing. He timed how long it took to fill his container.

If it takes four seconds to fill the bucket, he divides four into sixty seconds, for a gross yield of fifteen gallons per minute. If he knows he's pumping three gallons of drilling water per minute into the well, he must subtract this three gallons from the gross. Fifteen minus three equals twelve gpm net yield.

Springs and small streams can be measured the same way, so long as the flow can be dammed long enough to capture all overflow. A spring's yield can also be determined by test pumping. A *centrifugal pump* works best. (39) The suction line to the pump is placed in the spring, and the pump's discharge line is adjusted with a valve until the pump is pumping the same amount the spring is yielding. The water level in the spring will stay at the same level when this is the case. Water from the pump can be caught in buckets of known size while the filling time is recorded. Measuring stream or spring flow just once may be a mistake. To get a more complete understanding of the yield, readings should be taken several times during the course of a year. Don't forget that an inconsistent spring is a potential health hazard as well as an unreliable water source.

Measuring Stream Flow

A weir may be used to measure stream flow or spring capacity. The baffles in the metal box calm the water that enters. The height of water exiting through the V indicates the flow volume.

Kerr Sparks once showed me a *weir*. By dictionary definition a weir is just a dam, but in rural New England it can be more than that. It's a device that, once in place, allows you to measure a stream's flow at any time. Kerr's is a large box made of welded steel plating, maybe four feet square and three feet high. This particular box was placed in a stream bed, but a weir could also sit at the end of an overflow line from a spring.

Water is allowed to flow into the upper end of the weir. All of the water's movement and bubbling is controlled by a number of baffles within the box. The downstream end of the box, technically the weir itself, is notched with a large "V" through which the water exits. Horizontal markings, at ¼-inch gradients, are scratched in the metal surface beside the triangular opening. The height of water flowing through the "V" can be quickly converted to gallons per minute. For a more precise reading the flow can be timed as it is collected in a fifty-five gallon drum.

A formula for figuring the storage capacity of a pond or small lake has already been outlined. (17) But don't be lulled into complacency by the knowledge that you have X-number of acre feet of water in that sort of reservoir. The critical factor is the pond's overflow at its spillway—again a quantity that can be measured.

Overflow should equal the pond's intake, less evaporation loss, less seepage and leakage. Obviously if the pond has no overflow at any time of year, more water is being drawn out of the pond than it's taking in. And a stagnant water situation may be developing. (48)

Jay Hull's way of determining well capacity is more or less standard among well drillers. But it's only a rough estimate. Measuring *drawdown*, the distance water level lowers as a well is pumped, comes later, and offers a more error-free assessment of how much the well can produce. Drawdown is measured in a number of ways, as we'll see. (33)

32. PEAK DEMANDS

The total quantity of water you and your family use during a twenty-four-hour day will most likely be delivered during relatively few hours—the times of peak demand. Other periods can be thought of as *recovery times* for the well, spring, cistern, or storage tanks. This is when they refill.

Seven-Minute Peak Demand Period Usage

Outlets	Flow Rate GPM	Total Usage Gallons	Bathrooms in Home			
			1	1½	2–2½	3–4
Shower or Bath Tub	5	35	35	35	53	70
Lavatory	4	2	2	4	6	8
Toilet	4	5	5	10	15	20
Kitchen Sink	5	3	3	3	3	3
Automatic Washer	5	35	—	18	18	18
Dishwasher	2	14	—	—	3	3
Normal seven-minute[*] peak demand (gallons)			45	70	98	122
Minimum sized pump required to meet peak without supplemental supply			7 GPM (420 GPH)	10 GPM (600 GPH)	14 GPM (840 GPH)	17 GPM (1020 GPH)

NOTE: Values given are average and do not include higher or lower extremes.
[*] Peak demand can occur several times during morning and evening hours.

It's easy enough to understand why any individual water system has to move the most water during peak demands. *"How* much?" is the important question. The extent of your peak demands will have a direct impact on the plumbing, specifically the size of the tubing (81), the amount of pressure loss generated within the system (80), pump sizing (44), and how much storage capacity will be needed to keep you comfortably supplied during dry times. (53)

Scare yourself beforehand by imagining that all the fixtures in your plumbing plan (77) were opened at the same time. Water consumption would soar. In a minute's time, if a bathroom basin faucet were turned on (flowing at a rate of 2 gallons per minute), along with a standard ⅜- or ½-inch sink faucet (4.5 gpm), a tub faucet in one bathroom (6 gpm), a shower in another (5 gpm), a washing machine is started (5 gpm), a toilet is flushed (another 5 gpm), while a ¾-inch garden hose is running (5 gpm), an astounding sum of 32.5 gallons per *minute* would be used. Rest assured that this situation isn't likely to happen, but a critical combination *could* develop. Base your plumbing plans on that possibility.

A generally accepted rule of thumb for predicting peak demand is to divide your estimated total daily requirement in half, and see *it* as your maximum hourly need. If total usage for a farm or rural home is figured at 2,000 gallons a day, for example, at peak periods the water system should provide at least 1,000 gallons per hour, or just under 17 gallons per minute.

33. MEASURING WELL CAPACITY

A well's capacity depends a lot on the geological formations it penetrates. Wells in bedrock are hardest to predict. My own well in Stowe is 125 feet deep, and is fairly typical of others in the neighborhood. It yields eight gpm of water, and, before we did something about it, enough iron to stain bathroom fixtures and insure that lady houseguests would complain whenever they washed their hair. (60)

My father's artesian well, a little more than 100 miles away, went 275 feet deep in very similar bedrock, but it supplies at least forty gallons a minute, probably more. There was so much water nobody ever bothered to measure it. What *has* been measured is seven gpm of pristine water that gushes to the surface, around the clock all year long, without the aid of any pump. He has so much extra water he needs an elaborate piping system just to draw it off.

Hydrogeologists are more comfortable forecasting well production in regions where the earth is not so solid. They find that wells poking into predictably layered aquifers yield fairly predictable amounts of water. Fine sand, for example, will produce two to ten gallons a minute. Coarse gravel, on the other hand, might give up as much as ten to thirty gpm.

When a well is pumped, the water level at its base is lowered, even though the larger area of the water table may stay the same. The distance water drops near, and in, the well during pumping—in the midst of what we already know as the cone of depression—is called the *drawdown*. A well's yield is expressed in *gallons per minute per foot of drawdown.*

Testing for yield and drawdown involves measuring a volume of water (such as the contents of a driller's *bailer*), ability to measure the change in water level over a specific period of time, and observing the recovery rate of the water level. A well drilling company can probably do all this in a matter of a few hours—in a small fraction of the time you and I could do it with lines, floats, weights, and a tape measure. It's best, as with most aspects of well drilling, to leave it in the hands of the pros. . . .

A driller's bailer, on a cable tool, may be the simplest and most direct way of measuring the amount of water a well is producing. The bailer is a long tube with a valve at its bottom end. It's lowered into a well, filled with water, lifted to the surface, and emptied. The driller knows, of course, exactly how much the bailer holds.

He will mark the cable at the point the bailer first hits water, draw a measured amount of water for a specified time, then mark the cable again. The distance between the two marks—whatever distance the bailer has lowered—is the drawdown.

Test Pumping

Test pumping, though, is probably the most *accurate* way to measure yield. Water is pumped from the well for several hours—sometimes as long as twenty-four hours—at a rate higher than the calculated daily needs of the family. This way the true story of the well can be written.

Every hour, pumped water is collected in containers, usually for five minutes. If twenty-five gallons are collected in that time (five gpm), this number multiplied by twelve will be the well's per-hour yield. ($25 \times 12 = 300$ gph) Averaging these numbers over many hours will give a very accurate accounting of the well's capacity.

In a deeper well, drawdown might be measured most easily with a pressure gauge or vacuum gauge—hardly common household items. It *is* common knowledge (to any ex-student of basic physics, anyway) that a column of water 2.3 feet high will generate one pound of pressure. The calibrated pressure difference in a well, before and after pumping, multiplied by 2.3 will equal the drawdown.

The American Association for Vocational Instructional Materials (AAVIM) publishes a fine book called *Planning for an Individual Water System*, which offers exceptionally clear directions on how to measure drawdown. It suggests three techniques to be used, depending on the type of well. Here's what it says about wells of large diameter—dug wells, for instance:

> If there is room to drop a weighted float on string down into the well, drawdown can be checked very simply and easily. Proceed as follows:
>
> 1. *Lower weighted float on string until it reaches water level.*
> 2. *Tie knot on string at surface level before starting the pump.*
> 3. *Repeat steps 1 and 2 at end of pumping period.*
> 4. *Measure the difference between the upper and lower knots.*

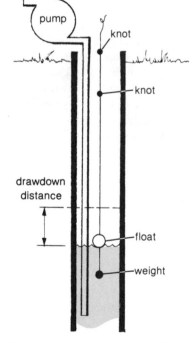

To measure drawdown in wells of large diameter: (1) Lower weighted float on string until it reaches water level. (2) Tie knot on string at surface level before starting pump. (3) Repeat steps 1 and 2 at end of pumping period. (4) Measure the difference between the upper and lower knots. The difference is the drawdown during the pumping period.

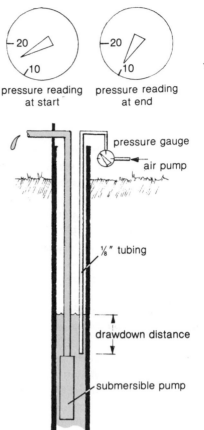

pressure reading   pressure reading
at start   at end

¹⁄₈″ tubing

drawdown distance

submersible pump

Air pressure can also be used to measure drawdown in wells of small diameter. An air pump and a length of ⅛″ tubing are needed. The difference in pressure before the submersible pump is started, and after it's stopped, multiplied by 2.3 equals the drawdown (in feet).

The distance between the two knots represents the drawdown during the pumping period.

The AAVIM goes on to elaborate on how to determine drawdown first with a pressure gauge, then a vacuum gauge.

If your well is too small in diameter to check drawdown with a string and float, you will have to use a water-level indicator. It consists of plastic and copper tubing—⅛ inch diameter—attached to a pressure-gauge and an air pump. Proceed as follows:

1. *Drop the open end of the tube into the well to a position below the water level.*
It is important that the end of the tube not be closer than two feet above the intake of the pump, and that it should never be below it. If the end of the tube is too close to the intake, your pressure-gauge reading will be wrong because of pump suction.
2. *Pump air into the tube until the pressure-gauge reading remains constant.*
If the pressure-gauge pointer returns to zero, there may be a small leak in the tube or at the connections. Check for leaks and then replenish the air until the pressure-gauge pointer remains constant.
3. *Record pressure-gauge reading.*
4. *Start the pump.*
5. *Check pressure-gauge reading at end of pumping but while the pump is still running.*
6. *Subtract the lower reading from the higher reading.*
7. *Multiply the reading (in pounds) by 2.3.*

A column of water that is 2.3 feet high will develop a pressure of one pound. Consequently, by multiplying 2.3 times five pounds (example from step 5), you have the total number of feet of drawdown.

Reading at Start . . . 15 pounds
Reading at End . . . 10 pounds
DIFFERENCE . . . 5 pounds

5 pounds × 2.3 (feet per pound) = 11.5 FEET DRAWDOWN

If you have a small-diameter jetted or driven well, the pump suction line may be the only means you can use to check drawdown. In this case you will need to use a vacuum gauge. Use a piston pump for testing—one that is in good condition. It will lift water by suction as much as 25 feet, under most conditions. Proceed as follows:

1. *Connect suction side of pump to well drive pipe.*
2. *Insert gauge in suction line.*
3. *Start pumping operation.*
4. *Check gauge reading immediately and record.*
5. *Check gauge reading at end of test period.*
6. *Subtract lower reading from higher reading.*

Most vacuum gauges are *calibrated in feet.* If yours indicates calibration in feet, you have the feet of drawdown already determined.

Reading at End . . . 20 feet
Reading at Start . . . 10 feet
DRAWDOWN . . . 10 feet

Some vacuum gauges are *calibrated in inches of mercury.* If yours is that type, multiply your reading by 1.13 to get the feet of drawdown.
One precaution—in checking drawdown by this method, it is necessary that all pipe connections be airtight. Otherwise, your reading will not be accurate.

34. SUCTION

Gravity is the prime mover of water in its liquid state. If a water source, in a hillside spring, for instance, is located above where we are, we can move the liquid downhill, through aqueducts or tubes, using gravity. Transporting water this way involves only a few, relatively simple problems. More often than not, unfortunately, water we need has found its way to a place *below* where we live, meaning we have to raise it back up to us.

Pumps, as everybody knows, are machines for elevating water. Keep in mind that "pump" refers to both the water-moving mechanism *and* the power source that operates it, be it a windmill, electric motor, gasoline- or diesel-driven engine, or muscles in the arm that operates a hand pump. Remember, too, that pumps come in a variety of sizes and in various types. Proper selection and sizing are vital, and the range of choices is wide. There are piston pumps, centrifugal pumps, jet pumps, turbine pumps, and submersible pumps. It's worth spending the time to know a little about each.

When thinking about your own need to move water, realize that suction pulls and pressure pushes. It's fundamentally easier to push water upward than it is to pull it, though it's not always as convenient. Somewhere between fifteen and twenty-five feet straight up is the maximum distance water may be lifted through suction. This is why:

We live beneath an ocean of air that's about twenty-five miles deep. The weight of all the air above us constantly presses down, everywhere, at a rate of 14.7 pounds per square inch of surface area. This 14.7 psi is considered normal atmospheric pressure at sea level. A suction pump works by drawing air out of a pipe that's been lowered into a well or other low-lying water source. It's like sucking on a drinking straw. Pulling air from the pipe lowers the atmospheric pressure within it. A partial vacuum, say 10 psi of pressure, is created there. This low-pressure area becomes a very attractive space for water below that's being pushed down by normal atmospheric pressure.

Water Rises

Because the suction pipe offers pressure relief, water rises in it. But only to a height of 22 to 25 feet, regardless of how much power is applied from the pump's motor. Water has weight like any other matter—in its case a pound per square inch for every 2.3 feet of height, as you'll recall. Theoretically, atmospheric pressure alone should lift water 33.8 feet (14.7 × 2.3 = 33.8) at sea level, *if* a perfect vacuum could be created, and *if* there were no friction in that pipe. But suction pumps aren't efficient enough to remove all the air. So you can't count on using suction to lift water any more than 25 feet at the most.

If there's a leak in the suction pipe, the vacuum will be reduced or destroyed, and the pump's ability to move water up is diminished. If the water level in the suction pipe falls all the way back to the level in the water source, the pump is said to have "lost its prime."

What's more, suction lift is reduced about 1 foot for every 1,000 feet above sea level, since atmospheric pressure lowers with increases in altitude.

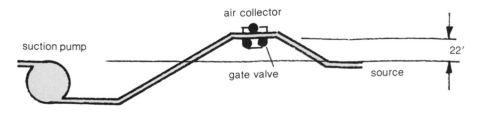

A siphon-gravity system can be used to move water over a hill, as long as the rise is not greater than 22 feet above the source. The suction pump must be sound, and the tubing airtight.

If you live on a 3,000-foot mountain, your suction pump can't be expected to lift water higher than 22 feet. So a pump's lifting capacity is limited not only by its elevation, but by water friction in the well pipe as well. (36)

Shallow-well pumps lift water from above, using suction. *Deep-well pumps* are lowered, or parts of them are lowered, into the well itself where they become water *pushers*. Pushing pumps lift water to heights many times greater than twenty-five feet because they develop so much more power. The line of demarcation between shallow-well and deep-well pumps, not coincidentally, is twenty-five feet.

35. PRESSURE AND HEAD

When water is pushed, and this push is described in *pounds*, it's called *pressure*. But when this pressure is expressed in *height*, as it often is in the lingo of water, it's called *head*. If you're a layman confused by this distinction, don't fret. You're not the first.

One pound of pressure will produce 2.3 feet of head. (Looking at it another way: one *foot* of head takes .434 psi.) Either way, it should take 100 pounds of pressure to elevate water 231 feet in a tube one inch square. Whether the tube is perfectly vertical or slanted at an angle doesn't matter. It's total vertical feet that counts.

If no water moved in the tube, this 231 feet of still water would be called *static head*. Head below a pump's intake is called *static suction lift*. Pressure at the point where water leaves a pump is known as *static discharge head*. *Total static head* is a combination of these two. In other words, the total elevation, in feet, from the water level in a well to the highest fixture in the house is the system's total static head.

In most individual water systems, pressure developed by a pump is stored in a hydropneumatic tank. (56) The pump and the pressure tank operate as a team. We know water can't be compressed. But air can be. As water is pumped into the pressure tank, air, also in the tank, is squeezed into a

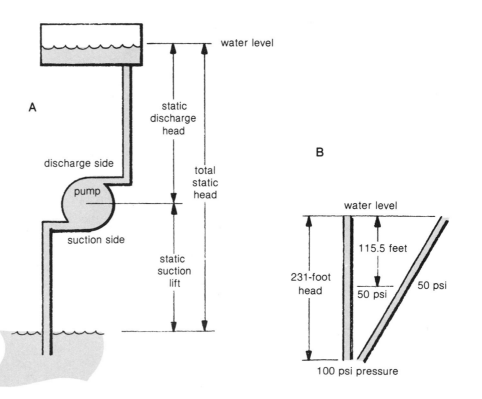

(A) *Static suction lift is the distance water must be raised to the suction side of a pump. From the discharge side of the pump to the uppermost water level is called the static discharge head. Total static head is the sum of these two distances.*
(B) *Whether or not a column of water is vertical or tilted doesn't matter. If it's 231 feet high, it will always exert 100 pounds per square inch of pressure.*

smaller space, and reacts like a coiled spring, pushing back against the incoming water.

Many modern pumps are set to stop when pressure in the tank amounts to 40 psi. (A pressure switch [89] actually instructs the pump to stop.) As water is used in the house it's taken from the pressure tank. And as the water level drops, so does the pressure there. When it reaches 20 psi, the pump starts again. Air pressure then, is really controlling water pressure and creating head within the system.

This twenty- to forty-pound pressure range is considered standard by the American pump industry, incidentally. Pump manufacturers are represented collectively by an organization called the Water Systems Council. The WSC has a certification program to insure pump quality. (Look for their sticker on new pumps, promising "Certified Performance.")

We'll probably see higher pressure ranges—possibly thirty to fifty psi, maybe even forty to sixty psi—in the near future, because washing machines and water conditioning units (common equipment in many households already) tend to reduce pressure in the average system.

But back to terminology:

36. FLOW

Reduced pressure, just mentioned, is another important factor in water dynamics. Obviously water is *not* static in the system. As it moves through pipes or tubing it has "flow." Flow is defined as the *amount* of water, expressed as gpm or gph, that's on its way somewhere. Along its route it meets resistance in the form of friction inside the pipes. It also gets slowed down by its own turbulence wherever it turns corners, passes through jagged fittings, or encounters rough, crusty corrosion.

The farther water travels, the greater the friction, hence the greater the head. The higher the flow, the more pressure will drop. All of these things are accurately measured and can be easily calculated from friction-loss tables that take pipe diameter, tubing material, and the age of piping into consideration. There are even friction-loss tables for fittings.

Any plumber will tell you, for example, that "when flow doubles, pressure drop increases four times." Naturally, the smaller the pipe, the more friction there is. A system's *total head* is the sum of its *friction head*—described as loss of head in feet per hundred feet of pipe—and its total static head.

Power from the pump and discharge pressure from the tank must be enough to push water to a height equivalent to the system's total static head, *plus* the pipe friction, calculated in feet, which is determined by flow. All of these items are considered when choosing a pump. Obviously consulting with an experienced plumber will have its advantages.

37. TOTAL LIFT

As long as the vertical distance between the level of a shallow-well pump and the highest fixture in the house—the total elevation head—is twenty feet or less, the pump, operating in the normal twenty to forty psi range, should supply the whole system with adequate pressure. That's assuming the piping is properly sized, and installed to keep friction at a minimum. To put it another way, a well designed two-story home should have plenty of water pressure, even upstairs, with a normal pump placed in the basement.

If the elevation head is more than twenty feet, a standard shallow-well pump *may* deliver a trickle to the upstairs shower. But it may deliver nothing. In this case, a heavy-duty shallow-well pump—either centrifugal or piston type—may be needed to provide higher discharge pressure. Pumps like these are easy to find, but, of course, more expensive.

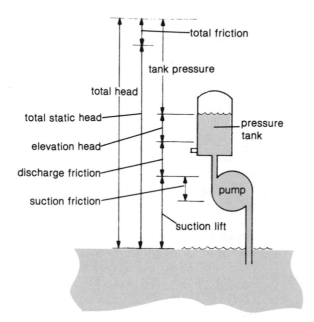

Total head and its various components.

When a deep-well pump, pushing water from below the well's point of lowest drawdown, is asked to supply water to outlets more than 20 feet above the level of its pressure tank, *total lift* must be computed. Total lift is the well depth (120 feet, for instance) added to the elevation head (say 30 feet). In this particular example, the pump must be capable of a total lift of 150 feet, if twenty psi of tank pressure is expected at the highest point of delivery. Better, as they say, to be safe than sorry. Consult several pump manufacturer's specification charts beforehand, to be sure the pump you buy will lift water this high.

Again, twenty to forty psi is the standard pressure range for most pumps. So that's normal pressure in most modern homes. But to repeat: some types of water-conditioning equipment will reduce pressure by as much as fifteen

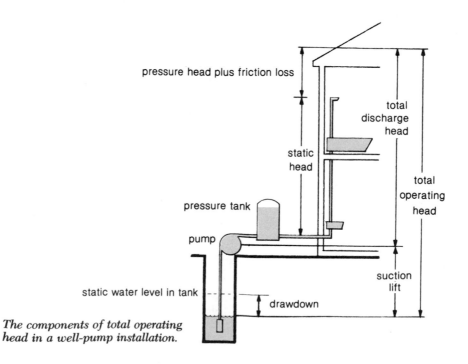

The components of total operating head in a well-pump installation.

to twenty pounds as water passes through it. You may have other needs, such as barn flushing, which require thirty-five to fifty-five psi.

Fire Protection

Pressure for fire protection is another consideration. Forty to sixty psi is ideal. If you feel you need this kind of pressure, a special high-pressure pump, a high-pressure storage tank, and larger-than-normal plumbing should be permanently installed. Portable high-pressure pumps that develop up to eighty psi can be moved around to outlets supplying sufficient amounts of water, and used for cleaning jobs that require a strong spray.

The "dream" system is one in which the source supplies water at a faster rate than the household can use it—even at times of peak demand. In most real-life situations like mine, however, the rate of supply is below the peak-demand requirement. In such cases the hydropneumatic tank takes up the slack, by storing forty-two or eighty-two gallons of water until it's needed.(56)

Sometimes the capacity of the source is so low, two separate pumps are needed. Here a well pump lifts water to an open-air tank. (Non-pressurized tanks like this may have covers, but they're not airtight. In the trade they're known as *atmospheric tanks*.) The first pump shuts off when a float switch— exactly like the one in any toilet tank—indicates the tank is full.

A second shallow-well pump then sucks water from the atmospheric tank, and charges a hydropneumatic tank. From there water is passed on to the rest of the system, under pressure.

38. PISTON PUMPS

That first pump in the two-pump system just described, by the way, should run for at least two minutes each time it turns on. So the float valve should be adjusted accordingly—to prevent the pump motor from turning off and on constantly. *No* pump, for that matter, should stop and start more often

Friction Loss

Allowance in Equivalent Length of Pipe for Friction Loss in Valves and Threaded Fittings

Diameter of Fitting	90° Std. Ell	45° Std. Ell	90° Side Tee	Coupling or Straight Run	Gate Valve	Globe Valve	Angle Valve
Inches	Feet	Feet	Feet	Feet	Feet	Feet	Feet
⅜	1	0.6	1.5	0.3	0.2	8	4
½	2	1.2	3	0.6	0.4	15	8
¾	2.5	1.5	4	0.8	0.5	20	12
1	3	1.8	5	0.9	0.6	25	15
1¼	4	2.4	6	1.2	0.8	35	18
1½	5	3	7	1.5	1.0	45	22
2	7	4	10	2	1.3	55	28
2½	8	5	12	2.5	1.6	65	34
3	10	6	15	3	2	80	40
3½	12	7	18	3.6	2.4	100	50
4	14	8	21	4	2.7	125	55
5	17	10	25	5	3.3	140	70
6	20	12	30	6	4	165	80

NOTE: The figures in the columns under "feet" indicate the allowance in equivalent length of pipe that should be given for friction loss for valves and threaded fittings.
SOURCE: Environmental Protection Agency

than necessary. It only makes the pump overheat, and wears out the motor's starting switch.

A pump's "cycle rate" is the number of times it starts and stops in an hour's time. When it does so too often, the pump is said to be *short-cycling*. Normally the storage tank, with its pressure switch, prevents short cycling by allowing the pump to work until it's built forty pounds of pressure, then telling it to quit. The pump now rests until the tank's pressure drops to twenty psi.

This is as good a time as any to remind you that proper pump wiring can't be neglected. The electrical current needed when a pump motor *starts* is many times greater than when it's running. The wiring must be heavy enough to handle this high start-up voltage. Motor overheating is the number-one cause of pump failure. And overheating is usually caused either by electrical overloading or by short-cycling.

The oldest of automatic pumps is the piston pump. There are *single-action* and *double-action* piston pumps, but both are called *positive-action* pumps because each stroke moves a constant amount of water. Like other pumps, it should remain sealed to prevent air from entering its mechanism.

Grandfather's Explanation

When I was about nine my grandfather, a science teacher, taught me about the hand piston pump at his cabin in the Adirondacks. He had an old bathroom plunger that looked like a giant suction cup—nicknamed a "plumber's helper"—with a hole poked in it. The plunger fit tight in a tin can he just happened to have handy.

When he let me push the plunger into the can filled with water, water squirted up through the hole. The demonstration was so vivid, I've always remembered that water can't be squashed into a smaller space.

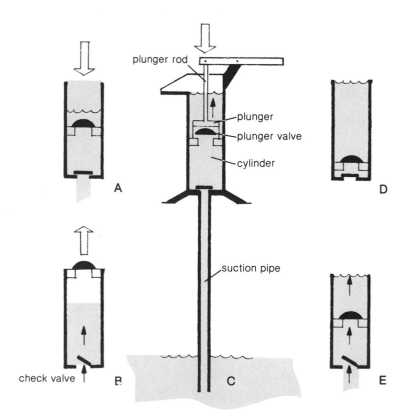

Operations of a hand piston pump: (A) The pump is primed. (B) As the plunger rod moves up, water is pulled up the suction line, opening the check valve. (C) As the plunger rod pushes down, the check valve closes and the plunger valve opens, letting water pass above the plunger. (D) As the plunger reaches the lower end of the cylinder, both valves are closed. (E) While the plunger moves back up, water is forced out the spout, and more water is raised in the suction line.

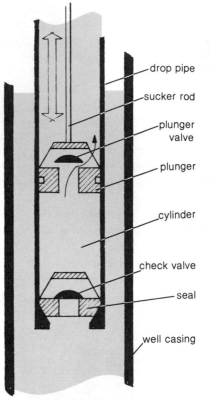

drop pipe

sucker rod

plunger valve

plunger

cylinder

check valve

seal

well casing

The motor for a deep-well piston pump may be at the well head, but the pumping mechanism is located below water line within the well casing. The two vital components are connected by the sucker rod.

He then took me to the pump in the kitchen. Push down on the pump handle, he said, and the plunger inside the can-like cylinder comes up, pushing water out the spout. While this is happening, a partial vacuum builds beneath the plunger, pulling water up the suction pipe. He even made me understand about vacuums and atmospheric pressure. I learned that a *check valve*, which allows water to travel in only one direction—in this case up, but not down—opens when water presses against it from below. It lets water into the cylinder.

Lift the handle up, and the plunger pushes down. The check valve won't let any water back into the suction line, so the cylinder becomes like the can, sealed at the bottom. The noncompressible water has to go somewhere. The *plunger valve*, which blocks the plunger's opening, is now forced open, much like the hole in my grandfather's plunger, letting water reach the plunger's upper side. *This* water is then discharged as the pump handle is pushed back down. This is a single-action piston pump.

A motorized shallow-well piston pump is similar, but more efficient. It works faster and more continuously not only because it's power-driven, but because it has two chambers instead of just one cylinder. This is also why it's called a double-action pump.

In a hand pump the plunger moves up and down. But in a double-action pump the plunger moves from side to side on a piston rod. As it moves right, it forces water out of the right chamber and at the same time sucks water into the left. When it moves back to the left, it does just the opposite, forcing the valve near the left discharge chamber open as water is pushed out. Meanwhile, back at the suction inlet, the valve to the right chamber is opened, letting the right side fill.

A deep-well piston pump works more like a single-action hand pump. The motor may be at the top of the well casing, but the plunger and cylinder are dropped down into the well. The plunger connects to the motor via the *sucker rod*, which moves up and down, or *reciprocates* as they say, at between forty-five and sixty-five strokes a minute. On its up-stroke the plunger forces water up the "drop pipe," similar to a suction line. Simple.

A double-action piston pump is more efficient. (A) As the plunger moves right, well water is pulled into the left chamber of the pump. At the same time water is forced from the right chamber, out the discharge outlet. (B) When the plunger moves left, a different set of valves opens, while the others are forced to close. In this phase water is drawn into the right chamber, and pushed out the left.

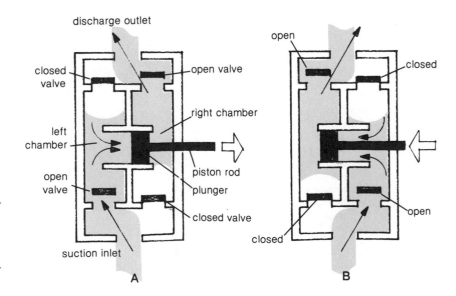

discharge outlet

closed valve

left chamber

open valve

open valve

right chamber

piston rod

plunger

closed valve

suction inlet

A

open

closed

open

closed

B

39. CENTRIFUGAL PUMPS

If a child's hollow metal top had holes drilled around its greatest circumference, could be filled with water to the height of these holes, then spun, it would shoot water out in all directions. As the top turned faster, water would be thrown farther and with more force, in proportion to the speed increase. Imagine that the toy top also had a hole in its base and could be spun as it sat in a pan of water. As water was shot from the upper holes, an equal amount of water would be sucked into the bottom. A centrifugal pump works much the same way.

Within every centrifugal pump is at least one rotating *impeller*, which spins water outward across its curved vanes at ever-increasing speed. The water is accelerated enough to create a partial vacuum, causing more water to be drawn into the eye of the impeller. The impeller itself sits in a precisely machined *wearing ring* which allows the impeller to turn independent of the suction pipe.

Unlike a positive-acting piston pump, a centrifugal pump does not displace a constant quantity of water. Increases in water pressure will slow it down, and it will pump less water as the water level in a well lowers. A shallow-well centrifugal pump can't be called upon to lift water more than fifteen to twenty feet.

Some centrifugal pumps have more than one impeller—or stage from which water can be pushed and pressure generated. A deep-well *submersible pump* (42) has several impellers, stacked on top of each other like pancakes, and is classified as a multi-stage pump. The motor and pump are usually connected, and are designed for long-term, maintenance-free, underwater operation. The whole unit is lowered into the well.

Pumping action in any centrifugal pump depends on there being no air in the mechanism. In fact, any air leak in a suction line will cause the pump to quit moving water. So all submersibles must be perfectly sealed. More on that shortly. . . .

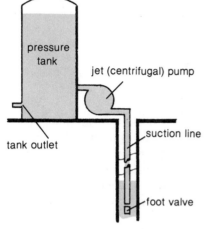

A shallow-well jet pump can deliver water from a depth of 15–20 feet.

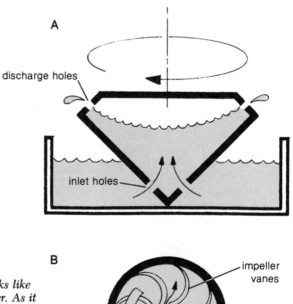

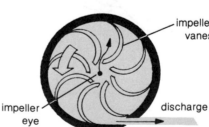

(A) A centrifugal pump works like a child's top filled with water. As it spins, water is squirted out the sides, and sucked into the bottom holes. (B) The impeller vanes in a real centrifugal pump spin water outward, causing more water to be drawn into the impeller eye.

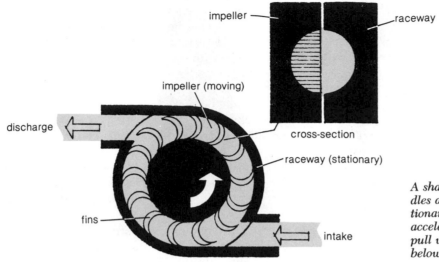

impeller — raceway

impeller (moving)

discharge

cross-section

raceway (stationary)

fins

intake

A shallow-well turbine pump paddles and spins water round its stationary raceway. As the water is accelerated, suction is generated to pull water into the pump from below.

40. TURBINE AND HELICAL PUMPS

It looks much like a regular centrifugal pump, but it's not. A *regenerative turbine pump,* in a way, is a cross between a centrifugal pump and a positive-displacement piston pump. It has just one impeller, but that single moving part generates greater pressure than a conventional centrifugal pump. The turbine-type impeller both spins *and* pushes water around its curved housing, known as a *raceway.* The water circles the track several times before it's forced from the pump outlet.

The constant paddling action of the turbine's fins—sometimes called *buckets*—sets up a spiraling action in the water, generating and regenerating enough suction to lift water twenty-five feet or more in a shallow-well situation. Deep-well turbine pumps are submersible. Multi-stage impellers are connected to the motor at the top of the well through a vertical drive shaft.

A *helical rotor pump* is still another type of shallow-well positive-acting water lifter. A screw-like rotor, mounted inside a moulded rubber *stator,* traps water in its continuous spiral, forcing it ahead toward the pump's discharge. If it has an advantage, a helical rotor pump provides a very uniform water flow. But it must be installed directly over the well head.

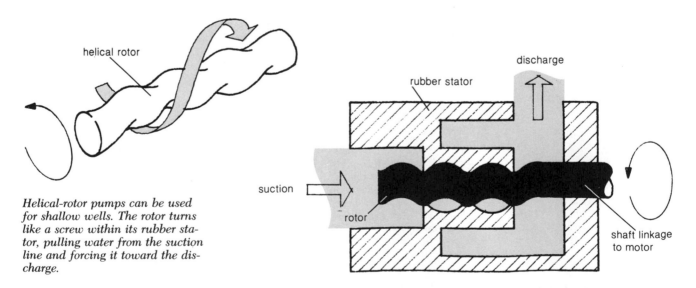

helical rotor

rubber stator

discharge

suction

rotor

shaft linkage to motor

Helical-rotor pumps can be used for shallow wells. The rotor turns like a screw within its rubber stator, pulling water from the suction line and forcing it toward the discharge.

41. JET (EJECTOR) PUMPS

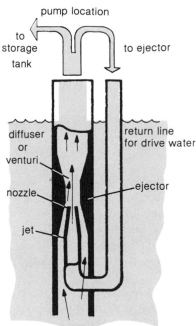

Pump (at location of arrows, top of drawing) pushes part of water into return line. Flow of this water is speeded up at jet, lifting water from the well into the stream, and forcing it high enough so that pump can lift it by suction.

When water under pressure is jetting through a small opening like a garden hose "nozzle," it accelerates and squirts. As it speeds up, a low-pressure zone is created at the very spot where the squirt begins. Any fluid near the squirt, even though it's not part of the squirt to begin with, tends to get drawn into the jet stream. Naturally this additional fluid contributes to the overall flow. It's easy to see that a jet of water, blown into other water, could move a large volume of liquid.

If all of this happens in a confined space, such as a well pipe, all of the original water, plus the extra, can be slowed down again in a gradually widening venturi called a *diffuser*. Low-pressure water diffused of its velocity, develops strong force which can be carried forward. In other words, high-speed water, blown into the point of a hollow cone, will slow down and be converted into pressure.

An *ejector* is a metal plumbing assembly that contains just such a nozzle and a diffuser. The combination of an ejector and a centrifugal pump—called a centrifugal jet pump—is a powerful and efficient one.

Most Common Pump

The centrifugal jet is by far the most common pump for domestic water systems, making up roughly 50 percent of the total market. It requires little maintenance, is quiet, and because of its simple design (the ejector has no moving parts), it's economical to own and operate.

It works this way: a small amount of water is diverted from the outlet of the pump and is sent to the ejector. This is called *drive water*. Drive water is discharged through the ejector nozzle, where it speeds up and creates a partial vacuum. Atmospheric pressure then forces water from the well into this vacuum. The new water is called *pumped water*. Now the diffuser applies the brakes and recreates water pressure, which can then be picked up by the pump's impellers. The invested drive water has come full cycle, bringing along an abundance of pumped water in return.

The ejector for a shallow-well pump is mounted on or near the pump itself—again at the top of the well casing. Deep-well ejectors (and sometimes the pumps themselves) are submerged about ten feet below the deep end of

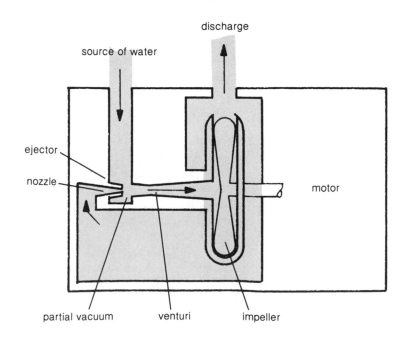

The ejector for a shallow-well jet pump may be mounted right in the pump body, rather than in the well itself.

the well's drawdown. Drive water is brought down the *drive pipe*, a tube within the well casing, toward the nozzle. Once the vacuum helps *drive water* pick up *pumped water*, it's all forced up a second tube, called the *suction line*, through the pump impellers into the pressure tank, where we'll pick it up in the next chapter. (56)

42. SUBMERSIBLE PUMPS

It's odd that submersible pumps, developed in Europe at the end of the last century, were first used to pump petroleum from the Texas oil fields in the 1920s, but weren't generally accepted for water use until the late 1940s. Now they're everywhere.

Today's sophisticated units are slender enough to pass down a six-inch, four-inch, in some cases even a two-inch well casing, and are dependable enough to stay there for years without major servicing. This is made possible by excellent mechanical seals.

A typical submersible pump is operated by a ½-horsepower electric motor, and has as many as fourteen teams of impellers and diffusers, one above the other. It's suspended on a drop line attached to the well seal above. The pump motor is filled with lubricating oil, but depends on the water that surrounds it for cooling. The motor must of course be totally wet proof to prevent water from shorting it out, and the motor windings must also be hermetically sealed.

Troubleshooting and servicing are usually easy and uncomplicated. Most maintenance checks are done with the help of ammeters, voltmeters, ohm-meters, and pressure-vacuum gauges—all without ever removing the pump from the well. The biggest danger to the pump is motor burnout, which can happen if the water level in the well gets too low, or when the intake screen becomes clogged. Low-water cut-off switches have been developed to shut down submersible pumps whenever the water level gets dangerously low.

Yet the few problems that exist with submersible pumps are usually electrical, not mechanical. It's particularly important that the pump have adequate power at all times, and that it be protected from abnormal voltage and current conditions which sometimes occur on power supply lines. Both the control box (91) and the submersible motor should have built-in lightning arresters (93) that are correctly grounded.

Submersible motors come in three basic types: (1) single-phase with three-wire cable, (2) single-phase with two-wire cable, and (3) three-phase with three-wire cable. *The Water Systems Handbook*, published by the Water Systems Council, insists that anyone installing a submersible pump be sure the motor, control, and power source are all of the same voltage, phase, and cycle as that stamped on the motor nameplate. Proper wiring, carefully checked and double-checked, is essential. All electrical work should conform to local and national electric codes.

Multi-stage submersible pumps are powerful enough to develop high pressure heads, sometimes higher than the holding ability of a home system's pressure tank. The tank's pressure switch is designed to protect the tank from overload, but a pressure relief valve (92) should be installed as an added precaution.

Once a submersible pump is wired and running, the well should be test pumped and the water checked for clarity. If it's murky, the pump should keep running until the water clears. Stopping it too early could cause abrasive sand particles to lock up the motor. If the water fails to clear up in a reasonable amount of time, and it looks as though the water may be permanently gritty, the normal life expectancy of the pump will be threatened. (In

Workman prepares to lower submersible pump, with drop line attached.

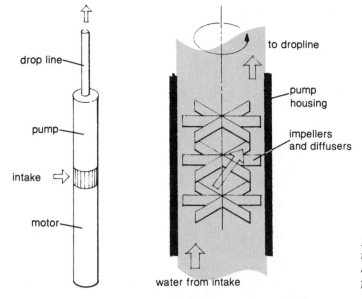

drop line

pump

intake

motor

to dropline

pump housing

impellers and diffusers

water from intake

In a slender submersible pump, teams of impellers and diffusers are stacked on top of each other like pancakes.

fact, the manufacturer's warranty may not cover repair or replacement if the pump's been operated in dirty water continuously. Read the fine print on the guarantee.) A different screen may be needed at the foot of the well to filter out sand particles.

43. PUMP SELECTION

Once you've studied the basic operation of each type pump just described, mapped out the yield of your water source and weighed it against your daily needs, and figured total head and lift in your proposed system, you approach another moment of truth—the selection of your pump.

If the lift from source to pressure tank is never greater than fifteen to twenty-five feet—even when the well is at its lowest—a shallow-well pump offers the best bargain. Shallow-well pumps are cheaper to buy and they're easier to install. All you do is drop a suction line down the well.

Don't forget that a shallow-well pump should have either a foot valve at the base of its suction line, or a check valve *in* the suction line to keep it

To pull water from a shallow water table (left), a centrifugal pump and ejector might work from above. Pushing water from an ejector below (right), even if the pump sits at the surface, lifts water to greater heights.

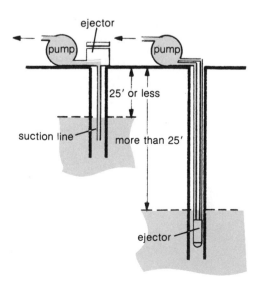

ejector

pump

pump

25' or less

suction line

more than 25'

ejector

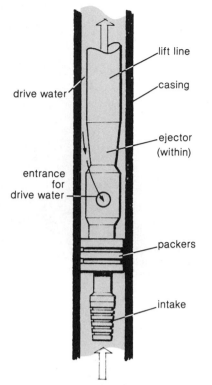

Jet-ejectors are even made for well casings of very small diameter (2 to 4 inches). Drive water is returned to the ejector in the casing itself, instead of through a return line. Gasket-like packers prevent the drive water from escaping out the bottom of the casing.

filled. This way the pump will always keep its prime. One thing more: obviously a nonsubmersible pump should never freeze. So it must be sheltered in a warm, dry place, where you can get at it easily.

If the lift is more than twenty-five feet, you'll have to explore the many deep-well pump possibilities. The size of the well casing will influence your decision, particularly if it's smaller than four inches in diameter. There are a number of deep-well piston pumps for casings as small as two inches. These include a closed-type single-action cylinder, a packer-type Eureka cylinder that needs no drop line, and a double-action cylinder, which probably has the greatest capacity since it pumps on both its up- and down-strokes. But plan ahead. Each of these may need to be specially ordered by your dealer.

Jet pumps for two-inch casings are also available, believe it or not. The ejector in these skinny pumps is enclosed in a rubber *packer* that jams against the inside of the casing to form a watertight seal. The packer keeps water in the upper section of pipe from leaking out the bottom of the casing, while the intake is located below this fat gasket.

Before you sign on the dotted line, get good advice from plumbing contractors and several reputable dealers. Ask tough questions about reliability, initial cost, economy, efficiency, servicing, and the availability of replacement parts. There's no reason for a good supplier to offer bad advice, or give you a bum steer on any product. Any dealer who sells you the wrong pump knows he's only going to end up with service and warranty problems later on.

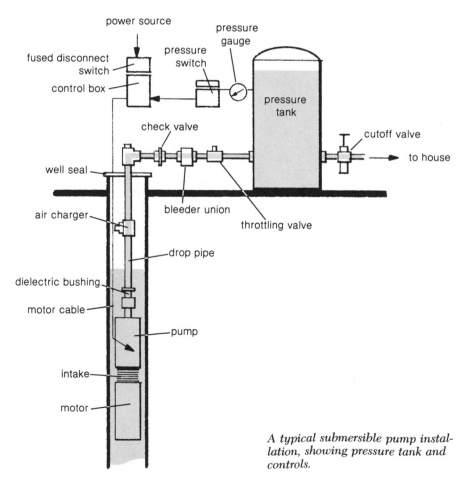

A typical submersible pump installation, showing pressure tank and controls.

Pumps

Type of Pump	Practical Suction Lift*	Usual Well-Pumping Depth	Usual Pressure Heads	Advantages	Disadvantages	Remarks
Reciprocating: Shallow well Deep well	22–25 ft. 22–25 ft.	22–25 ft. Up to 600 ft.	100–200 ft. Up to 600 ft. above cylinder.	1. Positive action. 2. Discharge against variable heads. 3. Pumps water containing sand and silt. 4. Especially adapted to low capacity and high lifts.	1. Pulsating discharge. 2. Subject to vibration and noise. 3. Maintenance cost may be high. 4. May cause destructive pressure if operated against closed valve.	1. Best suited for capacities of 5–25 gpm against moderate to high heads. 2. Adaptable to hand operation. 3. Can be installed in very small diameter wells (2″ casing). 4. Pump must be set directly over well (deep well only).
Centrifugal: Shallow well Straight centrifugal (single stage)	20 ft. max.	10–20 ft.	100–150 ft.	1. Smooth, even flow. 2. Pumps water containing sand and silt. 3. Pressure on system is even and free from shock. 4. Low-starting torque. 5. Usually reliable and good service life.	1. Loses prime easily. 2. Efficiency depends on operating under design heads and speed.	1. Very efficient pump for capacities above 60 gpm and heads up to about 150 ft.
Regenerative vane turbine type (single impeller)	28 ft. max.	28 ft.	100–200 ft.	1. Same as straight centrifugal except not suitable for pumping water containing sand or silt. 2. They are self-priming.	1. Same as straight centrifugal except maintains priming easily.	1. Reduction in pressure with increased capacity not as severe as straight centrifugal.

* Practical suction lift at sea level. Reduce lift 1 foot for each 1,000 ft. above sea level.

Type of Pump	Practical Suc-tion Lift°	Usual Well-Pumping Depth	Usual Pressure Heads	Advantages	Dis-advantages	Remarks
Deep well Vertical line shaft turbine (multi-stage)	Impellers sub-merged.	50–300 ft.	100–800 ft.	1. Same as shallow well turbine. 2. All electrical components are accessible, above ground.	1. Efficiency depends on operating under design head and speed. 2. Requires straight well large enough for turbine bowls and housing. 3. Lubrication and alignment of shaft critical. 4. Abrasion from sand.	
Submersible turbine (multi-stage)	Pump and motor submerged.	50–400 ft.	50–400 ft.	1. Same as shallow well turbine. 2. Easy to frost-proof installation. 3. Short pump shaft to motor. 4. Quiet operation. 5. Well straightness not critical.	1. Repair to motor or pump requires pulling from well. 2. Sealing of electrical equipment from water vapor critical. 3. Abrasion from sand.	1. 3500 RPM models, while popular because of smaller diameters or greater capacities, are more vulnerable to wear and failure from sand and other causes.
Jet: Shallow well	15–20 ft. below ejector.	Up to 15–20 ft. below ejector.	80–150 ft.	1. High capacity at low heads. 2. Simple in operation. 3. Does not have to be installed over the well. 4. No moving parts in the well.	1. Capacity reduces as lift increases. 2. Air in suction or return line will stop pumping.	
Deep well	15–20 ft. below ejector.	25–120 ft. 200 ft. max.	80–150 ft.	1. Same as shallow well jet. 2. Well straightness not critical.	1. Same as shallow well jet. 2. Lower efficiency, especially at greater lifts.	1. The amount of water returned to ejector increases with increased lift—50% of total water pumped at

Type of Pump	Practical Suction Lift*	Usual Well-Pumping Depth	Usual Pressure Heads	Advantages	Dis-advantages	Remarks
						50-ft. lift and 75% at 100-ft. lift.
Rotary: Shallow well (gear type)	22 ft.	22 ft.	50–250 ft.	1. Positive action. 2. Discharge constant under variable heads. 3. Efficient operation.	1. Subject to rapid wear if water contains sand or silt. 2. Wear of gears reduces efficiency.	
Deep well (helical rotary type)	Usually submerged.	50–500 ft.	100–500 ft.	1. Same as shallow well rotary. 2. Only one moving pump device in well.	1. Same as shallow well rotary except no gear wear.	1. A cutless rubber stator increases life of pump. Flexible drive coupling has been weak point in pump. Best adapted for low capacity and high heads.

44. PUMP SIZING

The size of your pump must be estimated on the basis of peak demand, not average use during the course of the day. One simple formula suggests that the pump's capacity, in gallons per minute, should equal the number of fixtures in the home. So a house with two bathrooms, three outlets in each (shower/tub, lavatory, and toilet), plus a kitchen sink, clothes washer, dishwasher, and one outdoor sillcock, should have a capacity of at least ten gallons per minute.

Here's a list of considerations for pump selection, summarized nicely by the Water Systems Council:

1. The pump should have adequate capacity for present and future uses. (Ten gpm is probably adequate in most instances.)
2. It should provide adequate pressure for the present and future use, considering the possibility of a lower water level in the well.
3. Cost of the pump.
4. Cost of labor to install the pump.
5. Cost of materials to install the pump (fittings, piping, accessories, well pit, etc.).
6. Area needed to install pump. Is enough space available?
7. Reliability of pump.
8. Cost of servicing pump.
9. Ease of servicing pump. Can it be repaired in the field or in the dealer's repair shop, or does it have to go back to the factory?
10. Cost of operating the pump (power *plus* replacement parts).
11. Flexibility of the pump for various types of installations.

Remember that *no* pump, no matter how powerful, can deliver more water than the source can supply. It would be ridiculous to buy a pump that was too big, and a storage tank that was too small. When it's set up, the entire water system, including the properly installed pump, should be expected to last at least eleven years. Maybe as long as twenty-five.

45. CASINGS

The shaft of a well is enclosed by its casing. We already know casings can take several forms, from large-diameter precast concrete pipes set in dug wells (25), to much smaller 1¼-inch metal pipes in a driven well. (28) Between these size extremes might be sections of ceramic tile, often used in augered or bored wells (26), and the type of metal casing best suited for jetted wells (27), which may be as large as fourteen inches across. Most drilled wells, however, are cased with steel.

Standard pipe, line pipe, drive pipe, reamed and drifted pipe ("R and D") are all used for drilled well casing, as is standard, threaded water-well casing, normally four to six inches in diameter. The casing's wall thickness may range from .145 of an inch for 1½-inch pipe, to .375 inch for one that's twelve inches in diameter.

"Extra strong" grade casing should be used in a well to be drilled with a cable tool or other rig that will drive the tube into the earth with great force. In general, thicker is better when it comes to casing selection, particularly in areas where the soil and subsoil is known to be corrosive. Beefier casing simply lasts longer.

Top Above Ground Level

The top of a well casing should extend eight to twenty-four inches above ground level, according to most health officers. Protecting the well from surface-water contamination is their main worry. Pollutants can enter a well in one of three ways: directly through the unprotected top of a well, from seepage below ground level, or through the space between the casing and the surrounding soil. Health experts will worry less if they know any surface water finding its way to the base of your casing has been filtered through at least ten vertical feet of porous material.

Any soil next to the casing top should be graded to coax surface water away from the wellhead. And unless the casing is driven into bedrock and thus sealed (29), the space between the casing and the earth at the surface should be "grouted" with a waterproof cement mixture. Wherever a casing intercepts the surface on a slope or hillside, a diversion ditch, dug fifty feet

Storage Capacity of Well Casing or Pipe

Well Diameter (inches)	Storage per Foot of Depth (gallons)	Well Diameter (feet)	Storage per Foot of Depth (gallons)
2	0.163	1	5.87
3	0.367	2	23.50
4	0.653	3	52.87
5	1.02	4	94.00
6	1.47	5	146.87
8	2.61	7	287.86
10	4.08	9	475.86

or so uphill from the well, may be needed to shoo surface water away from the well itself.

The top of the casing should have a removable cap, allowing access to the well below. A vent in such a cap *might* be used to measure well depth, but its number-one function is to prevent a vacuum from developing in the casing whenever the water level is lowered. Where pump connections enter the casing (46), there must be *sanitary well seals.* These are usually soft rubber gaskets—often made of neoprene—squeezed between two metal plates that are tightened down on them.

Slotted casing is installed in the bottom of some wells, to allow sand-free water to enter the tube. The size of the slots is determined by the average size of the water-bearing gravel aggregate in the aquifer. In most instances, though, screening is placed over the bottom of the casing, or a screened intake device is held in place at the lower end of the casing by a waterproof packer. (52)

46. OFFSETS

Only rarely is a well located directly beneath the house it's meant to serve. Water moved straight upward in a well needs to be turned sideways somewhere near the ground surface so it can be directed to the pressure tank, and eventually to the house. The vertical-to-horizontal direction change, including the run to storage, is called the *offset.* The length of offset will influence the size and location of both the pump and the pressure tank.

It seems like a simple problem—to turn water ninety degrees—and the plumbing solution is easy—except for two factors: the frost line and the possibility of surface water shorting out wiring and contaminating the well. In the old days well pits, often covered by pump houses, were used for access to lateral pipe connections near the top of the well. The purpose of the pit was to get the junction between casing and the main water line to the house all below frost level.

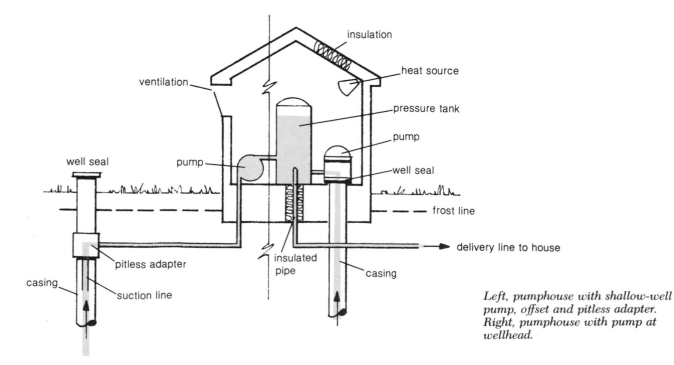

Left, pumphouse with shallow-well pump, offset and pitless adapter. Right, pumphouse with pump at wellhead.

Some systems are still installed with a pump, offset plumbing, and sometimes the pressure tank at the top of the well, and pump houses still decorate the rural landscape here and there. The very best pump houses are easy to reach, easy to clean, watertight, well drained, heated, insulated, and well lit. Some are even connected to an auxiliary power source, to insure heat during an electrical failure.

The trouble with any well pit is that it invites contaminating water into the well. So they're labeled unsanitary and outlawed in many parts of the United States. *Pitless adapters*, underground diverting connections that fasten permanently to the casing, are modern technology's answer to the offset puzzle. They are normally buried below temperature extremes, have sanitary seals, still allow the well casing to end well above ground, and cost a good deal less than old-fashioned pump houses.

47. PITLESS ADAPTERS

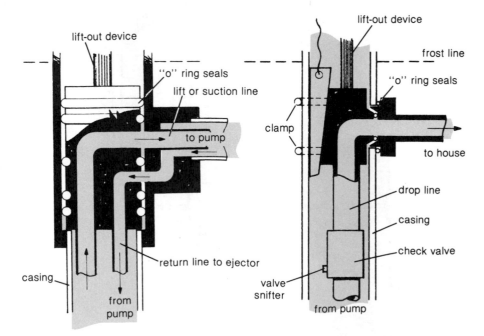

Pitless adapter

Sealed pitless adapters keep surface water and near-surface water out of both the well casing and the potable water line to the house. The Water Systems Council lists three basic designs: adapter, unit, and above-ground discharge types.

Adapters first: at the appropriate offset point below frost level, a hole is cut in the casing for the discharge line leading to the pressure tank. The portion of the adapter inside the casing is connected to the drop line, then clamped or welded to the casing's inner wall.

The second type, adapter units, are factory-assembled and ready to be threaded or compression-gasketed into the casing.

Third, above-ground discharge adapters fit into the top of the well casing and send water by gravity flow to the potable water line below. Naturally it's important that the discharge line in this last type of system run downhill at a steep enough angle to move water away from the well head quickly, before it can freeze.

To keep water pressure in the discharge line of any offset, a check valve is often placed beneath the adapter. When the pump, either pushing or pulling, stops moving water into the line, the check valve closes, preventing any backflow, and water above it is held there under pressure. Many pitless

A pitless adapter (left) allows water to make a 90-degree turn below the frost line. It must have a perfect sanitary seal. This is a jet-pump installation.

A clamp-on pitless adapter (right) installed above a submersible pump. Check valve may be placed in the drop line to keep water from running backwards toward the pump.

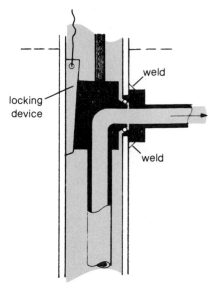

Some pitless adapters are welded in place. In this case, the adapter allows an offset for a shallow-well pump installation.

adapter units have built-in check valves, making this extra installation unnecessary. Pitless adapters are an integral part of any individual water system. And professional hook-up crews have their installation down pat.

Hooking Up the Well

At 9:30 A.M. they were still having coffee. Earlier their dispatcher told me where they were going, and said it would be okay if I went too. I spotted the blue Manosh Company pickup at a roadside restaurant, and pulled in beside it.

It looked like a twentieth century tinker's wagon—more like a mobile workshop than a vehicle. Racks behind the cab held spools of wire and coils of polyethylene tubing, and side boxes held a full inventory of electrical components, tools, and plumbing fixtures. In the bed I could see welding tanks, a brand new pressure tank still in its box, a Gould submersible pump, and many buckets filled with brass plumbing parts. A plumber's vise was attached to the back bumper. The vise sat under a mounted light which would allow men to work there at night.

In the cafe Bill Gabaree, master plumber and head of this hook-up team, seemed to be in no big rush. His young apprentice, Stuart Manosh, third son of the company owner, was restless and wanted to get going.

"Will you get it all done today?" I asked.

"This well's only got an eighty-foot drop," said Bill, assessing the stranger. "This is an easy day. We'll be out of there this afternoon."

I followed their truck through a maze of back roads in Panton, Vermont. We got lost twice. By 10:15 we arrived at a comfortable summer cottage owned by a wealthy local contractor. It sat on a pretty point of land jutting into Lake Champlain.

For years this house had been served by water taken from the lake and run through an automatic chlorinator. But now the cottage was being renovated, replumbed, and rewired. A new well was part of the updating scheme, and there was already a freshly dug ditch running from the well casing to one corner of the house.

This truck is the company's portable workshop.

Stuart uncapped the well while Bill went to talk to the electricians working inside.

Unwanted Water

"The static level is only about three feet below the top of the casing," said a surprised Stuart when his boss came back. The ditch also had at least a foot of water in its bottom, a fact that would make the day messy for Stuart, who had to work there.

Together they concluded that water in the well—*and* in the ditch—was coming from the lake, and was seeking the lake level. I asked if that was bad. "It's a lot better than taking water straight out of the lake," said Bill, less suspicious of me. "At least the well water's being filtered through a few hundred feet of gravel and sand. . . . Let's get to work."

Stuart unpackaged the ⅓ hp Gould pump, and chained it in the vise on the back bumper. Then he unrolled and measured out eighty feet of one-inch plastic tubing, cutting it off with a hacksaw. He was obviously more than competent.

One end of the pipe was clamped to a fitting on the upper end of the pump. Next he unrolled about ninety feet of three-strand wire. One strand was red, one black, and one yellow, exactly matching the three strands coming off the three-wire pump motor. It would have been all but impossible to attach the wires incorrectly.

Bill produced some round nylon objects that looked like overgrown ski pole baskets. "These are torque stops," he said, anticipating my question. "Every time the pump starts, it wants to twist a little in the casing—just like an electric drill in your hand. Torque stops steady the pump and keep the wires from slapping against the sides of the casing and wearing out."

Both the wiring and the tubing were threaded through the stops, spaced every twenty feet or so along the plastic drop line.

How Strong?

I *asked* about the strength of plastic drop lines, and Bill said they were common in wells less than 200 feet deep, and in situations where the pump was not exceptionally heavy.

The ends of the drop-wire strands were fastened to the pump wires. Bill cut a six-inch section of 3/16-inch copper tubing, slipped it over the ends of wires to be spliced, and carefully crimped both ends of the tubing onto copper wire stripped bare of insulation. Each splice was then examined critically, before it was wrapped with electrical tape. Then the entire length of drop wire was taped to the drop line, with wrappings every eight feet or so.

"Naturally we don't want to lose a $500 pump in the bottom of a well," Bill explained. "And we don't want to come back on a service call unless we have to. It's no fun pulling a pump in the middle of January. That's why we work slowly now, why all of our mechanical connections get double-clamped, and why we pay special attention to our wire splices."

After lunch Stuart pulled on rubber boots and jumped into the muddly ditch with a cutting torch. Bill set up a hand pump that would draw the well level down to a point below the pitless adapter location. Stuart cut a neat hole in the casing near the bottom of the ditch—well below frost line.

The interior half of the "pitless," as they called it, and its gasket, was threaded temporarily on a length of galvanized pipe and lowered into the casing. The exterior portion was then threaded into the inside half, through

Before the pitless adapter can be installed, a hole must be burned through the steel casing.

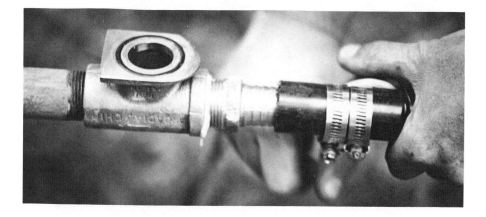

The inside half of the pitless is threaded, temporarily, to a length of galvanized pipe (left end), while the drop line is double-clamped to the adapter's base (right end). It's then lowered into the casing, the exterior half of the pitless adapter is installed, and the galvanized pipe is removed.

Stuart's hole, and both gaskets were drawn tight with the help of a pipe wrench. Installing the pitless didn't take more than ten minutes.

The pump, wiring, and drop line were lowered into the well, and the flanged fitting at the top of the drop-line slipped neatly into the pitless adapter. The galvanized holding pipe was then removed, leaving only wire sticking out the top of the well.

"And that pitless setup is perfectly watertight?" I said.

"Perfectly watertight," said Bill.

"Sanitarily sealed?" I said.

"Sanitary," said Bill, dropping a handful of chlorine tablets into the well to disinfect it.

Bleeder Valve

Stuart stayed in the ditch, fastening a nipple to the outside of the pitless adapter, while Bill went to hook up his wiring to the electrician's. Because this was a summer home and the water system would have to be drained each winter, Stuart installed a "bleed-down" by placing a "curb valve" on this nipple next to the well. This would be the system's lowest point. Once the ditch was backfilled, the bleeder valve could be opened in the fall, through a long handle that reached above grade, and all water would drain out of the unit.

Stuart worked with great skill and confidence. But before he buried his work he called, "The arrow of the curb valve points toward the well, right?"

"Nope, it points with the water flow," came the answer, "*away* from the well."

Stuart grumbled considerably, as Bill left his work and stepped to the edge of the ditch. "You didn't put it in *back*wards, did you?" He laughed. Stuart got hotter and mumbled more. "Do you want *me* to do it?" said Bill.

"I started it. I'll *finish* it," snapped Stuart from the mud. And Bill's wink at me ended another in an ageless line of confrontations between master and apprentice.

From there it was all routine. Stuart corrected the backwards valve. Bill had already installed a circuit-breaker box—just for the pump—in the house. Even though the pump had built-in lightning protection, Bill fastened a second lightning arrestor to the breaker box. Electrical surges from lightning are a submersible pump's nemesis.

Wire was laid in the ditch from the wellhead to the house, and the water

Once the pitless adapter is in place, the corner to the offset has been turned. In this instance, because water rose high in the casing, there was overflow through the adapter before the offset line was installed.

line, also of plastic, was run beside it. Stuart was careful to keep both the water main and the cable from resting on any sharp rocks that could sever them during backfilling. Stuart then spliced the cable to the drop wire at the wellhead, and replaced the well cap.

Bill plumbed the pressure tank, using a check valve on the intake side of the "T," and a pressure gauge, drain valve, and ball valve on the discharge side. All of this was done before the tank was jockeyed into position in the house. He also installed a pressure switch near the T.

I asked if it was a twenty- to forty-pound pressure switch.

"This is a thirty to fifty," he said. "The pressure switch should always match the air charge in the pressure tank. We like to use tanks with low-end pressure of thirty psi to give the system a little more punch. But twenty to forty is still standard in most places." He then connected the well to the tank, and the tank to the system in the house.

By now the truck was almost loaded. At the last Stuart went inside the house to wire the pump control, and the pump was tested. The gauge told us that pressure in the tank quickly rose to fifty pounds. All tidy. No leaks anywhere.

They made the whole thing look ridiculously easy. And were headed home by 5 o'clock. . . .

5   *HOLDING WATER*

48. PONDS   The historic moment came unexpectedly. After a hot baseball practice on the first of June, nine months after the pond was dug, Greg Campbell, age 10, announced, "I'm going in, Dad."

He stripped to his underpants, leaving a trail of grimy clothes across the lawn, stepped to the rock at the water's edge, and stuck in his foot.

"Warm," he lied.

"Dive, dive!" prodded his older sister.

Assured that newly stocked fingerling trout would not attack him, he launched his body toward previously unexplored waters. It was an heroic gesture, since the water had only started to lose its murkiness a couple of weeks before. But the entry of our pond's first swimmer was less than magnificent. As his head went under, Greg's legs splayed awkwardly, looking much like those of the frogs already living in shallow places along the shore.

The pond was low then, its level having dropped six inches or so below the spillway on the T-riser standpipe. It had filled completely during the late fall and winter, only to recede again throughout a dry spring. Robby Adams had been out earlier that day to inspect the rough earth below the dam he'd been unable to clean up with his bulldozer the previous fall. It had been too *wet* then.

"Pond's down," he said. I agreed.

"A lot of them don't stay full the first year," he said. "The bottom has to silt up more, so it won't seep so bad."

He'd already walked the base of the dam, and had found no major leaks there, even though the area outside the dam was still too wet to work with a heavy excavating machine. So he brought in a regular backhoe to trench the wet spots and drain them. And the *backhoe* almost got stuck.

"Do you think the wetness below is leaking out of the pond?" I asked.

"Don't think so," said Robby. "You can usually spot a leak. It makes a big muddy hole near the foot of the dam. I think this water is from springs in the ground down there."

Since that day many of us have followed Gregory into this vast open storehouse of very cold water. The pond immediately became home for a splendid array of flying, hopping, and swimming creatures, all of whom just seemed to show up. To be honest, the pond is there mostly to be seen, to be a corral for the young herd of rainbow and brook trout bought at a local hatchery, and to cool us on hot summer afternoons.

Knowing we have plenty of water for emergencies is reassuring, and we watch the up-and-down movements of the water with great interest, a bit surprised that it varies so much. Its height is a continuous indicator of the adjacent water table, a barometer of groundwater movements and pressures, and a rough gauge of the tremendous evaporation that takes place there during a sunny day.

The silt lining in our new pond could probably be heavier, as Robbie Adams suggests, but that will come in time. In most ponds too *much* silt inevitably becomes a problem, and ours will be no different.

Silt buildup can be averted in a bypass pond or any other that has a definite intake point, where surface water enters. A silt basin can be dug just above the mouth of the feeder stream. Here the inflow will be slowed, giving suspended matter in the water a chance to settle out. A hole like this will need to be dredged from time to time as it fills.

Fence Needed

Any farm pond that's not directly intended as a watering hole for domestic animals should be fenced off, to keep livestock from trampling the shoreline, muddying the water, and otherwise polluting the pond. Cattle, unfortunately, make no effort to leave the water before they defecate.

When the waters *do* get muddied, turbidity can be reduced by spreading gypsum or alum (aluminum sulfate) on the pond surface. The AAVIM describes how this open-pond treatment works:

> *Coagulation and sedimentation* is a process that causes fine sediment in the water to be collected into larger particles and settle to the bottom of the pond, before the water reaches a filter. This can be accomplished with *powdered gypsum.* It can be spread by hand over the surface of the pond at a rate of about 12 pounds per 7000 gallons of estimated water storage in the pond. The powdered gypsum causes the turbidity particles to collect in clusters (coagulate) and settle to the bottom (sedimentation).... Powdered gypsum is safe for both marine life and humans if applied in the quantity recommended for this purpose.

Other authorities recommend spreading gypsum at a rate of twenty-five pounds per 1000 square feet of water surface—a formula that may be easier to calculate than the AAVIM's. Alum should be applied at a rate of forty pounds for each acre foot of water.

Weeds and algae thrive in pond water that contains too many nutrients and receives an abundance of sunshine. These can be treated with a wide variety of chemicals, some of which may have an adverse effect on water downstream. In some places, strong herbicides for ponds are forbidden. Check with the nearest health department before using *any* poisonous chemicals.

Pull Cattails

The safest way to control cattails and other large weeds in pond shallows is to put on a pair of waders, step into the water, and pull them out with your bare hands. The USDA warns about smaller forms of vegetation, however, "Algae in the pond should be controlled, particularly the blue-green types that produce scum and objectionable odors and that, in unusual instances, may harm livestock."

Colonies of these one-celled plants become ugly in a pond, especially when they congregate to form a flotilla of green slime.

Algae is an umbrella term that includes thousands of identified single-cell water plants. The name undoubtedly embraces many other varieties no one has ever taken the time to find or label.

Once in a while pond owners are tempted to remove algae with strong swimming pool algicides. But the Environmental Protection Agency discourages this, saying, "Commercial algicides for use in swimming pools are widely available. Until competent advice of the local health authorities is obtained and correct dosage is determined, swimming pool chemicals should not be used in water intended for human, livestock, or poultry consumption."

For those who see ponds as both the source *and* major storage depot for their drinking water, the EPA also offers elaborate advice on how pond water should be treated before it's consumed.

They say the intake line from the pond should be suspended on a string between a float above it and an anchor below. Twelve to eighteen inches below the surface is the best location for this screened intake. The idea is to draw only water "of the highest possible quality." (It's interesting that an Ohio Agricultural Experiment Station study, done in 1962, revealed that this twelve- to eighteen-inch depth was the level of *least* turbidity in most of the ponds examined.)

Gate Valve Needed

The EPA also suggests that wherever a water line passes through a dam on its way to a home, it should be equipped with a gate valve, so that discharge flow from the pond can be regulated. Once out of the pond, the water should be run through a settling basin where it can be mixed with alum, and coagulation-sedimentation can take place. (The alum feeder in this settling basin will have to be filled at least once every two weeks, by the way.)

Next, the water should pass through a sand filter. As turbidity is removed further, a film of silt will gradually collect on the filter. The greater the silt buildup there, the slower water passes through the filter. (So the filter will have to be cleaned regularly too.) Finally, the water should end up in a clear-water storage area. This clear well, as it's called, is nothing more than a concrete cistern. (50)

From the clear well, water may be pumped through an automatic chlorinator to be disinfected (71), then into a hydropneumatic pressure tank. (56) (Any algae tastes or odors still in the water might be removed by passing the pond water through still another filter, this time an activated-carbon filter.) Even then, according to the EPA, no water should be drunk or used

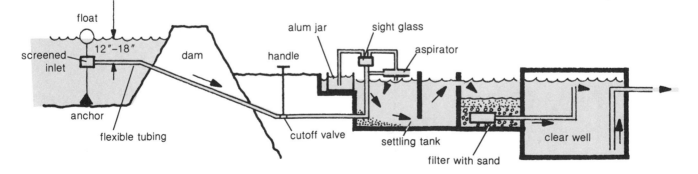

An elaborate system for removing turbidity from pond water, as recommended by the Environmental Protection Agency. Alum is added in the settling tank, where coagulation and sedimentation take place. After most suspended particles have been removed, the water passes through a sand filter for further clarification. Clean water is then stored in the clear well.

for cooking until a water sample is properly taken (59) and a bacteriological examination has been made. (62)

This sort of private pond-water treatment facility will probably produce very safe water. Though thorough, systems like this would be expensive to build and a nightmare to maintain. All components would have to be protected from wintertime freezing (57), the chlorinator would have to be carefully monitored, and filters would have to be backwashed or changed. As you read further you'll probably discover you only need *some* of these headaches. You should also see shortcuts that suit *your* situation.

49. INDIVIDUAL RESERVOIRS

Anyone can see that a pond is a source and a storage reservoir all rolled into one. To a much lesser extent wells, and even spring boxes, are capable of storing small amounts of water. Still, other reserves must be an integral part of any water-supply system for a home or farm. Water to be stored for later use may be collected in one of three primary ways:

First, ground-level or below-ground reservoirs, called "cisterns," need to be covered and protected. Sometimes made of steel, sometimes concrete, sometimes constructed of wood such as redwood or cypress, these tanks deserve vigilant maintenance. Some individual reservoirs are served by windmills that pump water to the surface from shallow aquifers. Some require a second pump to move water from the stopover point to a pressure tank.

Second, elevated storage tanks, called *gravity tanks*, provide gravity-flow pressure to systems below. They're usually designed to hold enough to supply a family with at least two days' worth of water.

Pressure tanks, already discussed, and *elastic storage cells*, which *will* be discussed, constitute the third type of storage. Although they generally have a small capacity, hydropneumatic tanks and storage cells are considered the most sanitary way to keep water on hand. Their additional function is to keep a steady push of water against the plumbing. (*Lack* of constant pressure is what causes noisy and sometimes dangerous plumbing irritations like "water hammer.")

A ground-level reservoir is often called an *intermediate storage tank*. It's located on the same level as a pressure pump, but since it holds no more than normal atmospheric pressure, in itself it supplies no pressure to the

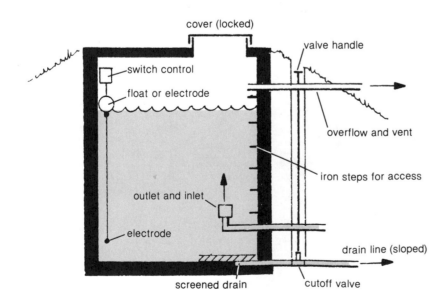

cover (locked)

valve handle

switch control

float or electrode

overflow and vent

iron steps for access

outlet and inlet

electrode

drain line (sloped)

screened drain

cutoff valve

An individual reservoir may be a concrete cistern partially buried in the ground. It should have an overflow and drain line. A float switch might be used to control the amount of water entering the tank. Or a system of electrodes could indicate the high-water mark, as well as a dangerously low water level.

96

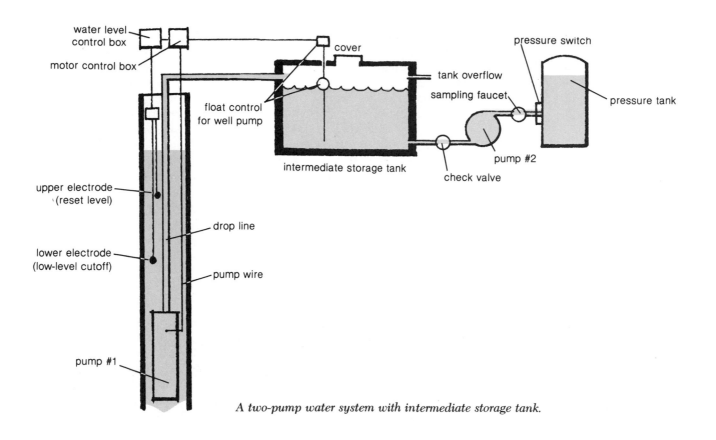

A two-pump water system with intermediate storage tank.

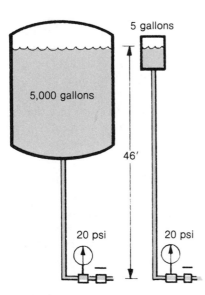

It's height *of the water level in the elevated storage tank that determines the amount of pressure* below, *not the quantity of water stored.*

piping farther on. Its only job is to accept water from the source, possibly from another well pump located below it, and to store this water for times of peak demand. You may remember earlier mention of such a two-pump system.

In this situation the well pump might be controlled by water-level sensors in the intermediate storage tank. Pump #2, the pressure pump, would receive its commands from the pressure switch at the hydropneumatic tank.

An intermediate storage tank in a two-pump system may need to hold as much as 2,000 or 2,400 gallons of water. Here's how to arrive at that figure: If the well or other source has a limited yield, the well pump may have a smaller capacity than the pressure pump. Say it only pumps five gallons per minute from the well. The pressure pump, on the other hand, may need a capacity of twenty-five gpm. The difference between the two (25 − 5 = 20 gpm), in this case twenty gpm, helps determine the need for storage.

Figuring Tank Size

To compute storage tank size, figure on at least two hours (120 minutes) of net pump capacity to insure enough water during peak demands.

20 gpm × 120 minutes = 2,400 gallons

For excellent fire protection you may want twice as much storage capacity, as much as 5,000 gallons.

An elevated storage facility, a gravity tank, can provide pressure to a system without any need for a pressure tank—*if* it's located high enough above the uppermost outlets in the house. As always, 2.3 feet of elevation will produce one pound of pressure. If the system needs twenty psi, the tank must be at least forty-six feet above any faucet (2.3 feet × 20 psi = 46 ft.). This can be accomplished easily enough if the tank is placed on a hill well above the house.

Large spring boxes often function as gravity tanks when they're located much higher than the home they serve. Yet, in spite of what we may think, the amount of water stored in a gravity tank has nothing to do with the amount of pressure it will produce. As the AAVIM says, "Water-level height is what causes pressure." A 5,000-gallon gravity tank can't push water downward with any more force than can five gallons in a spring box—assuming they're both at the same elevation.

Both gravity tanks and ground-level reservoirs should have vents, to allow air in as the water level within them is lowered, and to let air *out* as water is pumped in. Screening should cover these vents to keep insects and small animals from getting in. Contaminating groundwater should also be kept out of any storage reservoir that's placed below ground level. If the tank is made of concrete, it should be waterproofed, and be built well enough so that its walls or base won't crack.

50. CISTERNS

House, barn, and shed roofs are fine rainfall catchments. So is a parking lot or any other sloping paved surface. In fact, water that runs off asphalt, metal, slate, tile, or terra-cotta roofing is probably drinkable. Asbestos, on the other hand, has been linked to cancer, as you've no doubt heard, so drinking water taken from an asbestos-shingled roof is probably not a healthy prospect.

An inch of rainfall should provide .42 gallons of water per square foot of catchment surface, but it's important that you not overestimate square footage. (15) A cistern, which collects and stores rainwater, can be expected to gather as much as ⅔ to ¾ of the annual rainfall on the catchment. Some homes have cisterns just for emergency storage, others use rainwater for garden water, cleaning, toilet flushing, and other nonpotable uses. Because rainwater is soft, water in a cistern can also be used for bathing, laundry, and dishwashing.

Many Victorian houses had rainwater cisterns in attic rooms. This kind of elevated storage tank would provide gravity pressure to all the fixtures in the house. If such an arrangement sounds appealing, slow down long enough to consider the massive weight of this kind of water-filled container. Most modern homes, constructed as they are, would not support a raised cistern. But provisions *could* be made as a new house was being designed. In older buildings, though, massive retrofitting would probably be necessary.

Location of Cistern

A cistern should be placed as close as possible to wherever the water will be used. The tank might be buried to prevent its contents from freezing and to keep its water cool, but it's better buried in high ground than in a low, wet spot where it could be flooded. Cisterns should be carefully covered, and their sidewalls should stick out of the ground at least four inches. The wall tops might then be surrounded with a concrete curbing of about the same height.

Covers must be accessible, of course, and they should be locked to keep unwanted visitors and substances from getting in. Manhole covers also make great cistern covers, keeping out dust, light, and surface water. It's best if the cover overlaps the curbing by about two inches all the way around.

Cisterns should be disinfected with a chlorine solution on a regular basis.

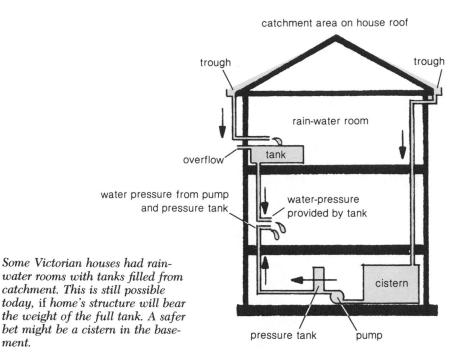

catchment area on house roof

trough — trough

rain-water room

overflow

tank

water pressure from pump and pressure tank

water-pressure provided by tank

cistern

pressure tank — pump

Some Victorian houses had rainwater rooms with tanks filled from catchment. This is still possible today, if home's structure will bear the weight of the full tank. A safer bet might be a cistern in the basement.

An initial run of rainwater coming off a roof or catchment should be diverted away from the cistern for the first few minutes—via a roof washer (15)—until the catchment has been thoroughly rinsed. Every so often a cistern will need to be drained, and a proper drain valve should be provided. Water being drained *from* the storage tank should not be directed into sewage lines leading to the septic tank and leach field, however. The septic system would simply be overrun with more water than it could handle.

Constructing a good cistern is not a project to be taken lightly. Brick or stone masonry is sometimes used, but high-density concrete, vibrated as it's cast in place, is far better. The concrete should be allowed to *wet cure* before the cistern is used.

Wooden cisterns may leak at first, but once filled for a day or two, the wood will swell like planking in a boat, and the tank will be watertight. Concrete tanks can be waterproofed on the *outside* with asphalt foundation sealer, waterproofing clay such as Bentonite, or with a rubberized, reinforced polyethylene membrane like bituthane.

The EPA also has more to say about masonry cisterns:

If used, brick or stone must be low in permeability and laid with full portland cement mortar joints. Brick should be wet before laying. *High-quality workmanship is required, and the use of unskilled labor for laying brick or stone is not advisable.* Two ½-inch plaster coats of 1:3 portland cement mortar on the interior surface will aid in providing waterproofing. A hard impervious surface can be made by troweling the final coat before it is hardened. . . .

Asphalt or tar for waterproofing the interior of storage units is not recommended because of the objectionable taste imparted to the water and the possibility of undesirable chemical reaction with the materials used for treatment. Specifications covering the painting of water tanks are available from the American Water Works Association (17 Battery Place, New York, NY 10016). Appropriate federal, state, and local health agencies should be consulted relative to approved paint coatings for interior tank use.

51. SPRING PROTECTION

A spring box with a concrete cover is virtually childproof.

Springs are especially vulnerable to pollution. Septic tanks and livestock housed or allowed to graze nearby can infect a spring with pathogenic bacteria. It's a particular problem in areas of limestone where groundwater moves to and fro fairly readily. Obviously protecting the sanitary quality of any spring used as a potable water source is of paramount importance.

A spring ought to have a removable cover, but the cover should be a heavy one, and perhaps be locked in place. I've never known a child who could resist exploring a spring once he's found one. It's best to fence in a spring—to keep both children and livestock *out.*

Terrain above a spring should be bermed or swaled to divert surface drainage away from this source of relatively pure groundwater. If spring water looks turbid after a heavy rainstorm, it's almost a sure sign that runoff water is getting into the spring.

Disinfecting the Spring

A contaminated spring should be disinfected—much like a well or cistern. A solution of water and chlorine bleach may be poured into the spring box. This disinfectant should be allowed to run through the spring line to the house until its chlorine odor can be smelled at all fixtures. Disinfectant should sit in the system for as long as twenty-four hours, if that's possible. Then it can be flushed out.

Spring water has been known to be contaminated between the spring itself and the storage tank or pressure tank within the house. Pollutants were traced to faulty tubing connections. Ends of polyethylene tubing that are to be joined should be heated with a propane torch first. This softens the plastic, allows the nylon connector fitting to slide in more easily, and lets the sharp ridges of the connector bite better. The result should be a sanitary seal. Pay special attention to clamping both sides of the connector. Once the joint is completed, the spring line should be buried well below frost line.

With good planning, two people can lay about 100 feet of plastic tubing in an hour—if one sits at the controls of a backhoe, while the other stays in the trench with coils of tubing, clamps, a screwdriver, couplings, and a torch. Short sections of ditch can be dug, pipe laid, and the ditch backfilled as the machine moves along.

52. WELL DEVELOPMENT AND REDEVELOPMENT

You'll hear people talk about "developing" a well once it's drilled. And sometimes wells are developed *again,* after they've been in use for years. In many places development is nothing more than the natural completion of the drilling process. Silt and fine sand, created and stirred up during drilling, must be completely removed from the well screen before groundwater stored in an aquifer can be tapped.

Developing is done by reversing the normal upward flow in a well, causing a surge of water to be forced backward out of the screen. This might be done with a high-velocity water jet, compressed air, a combination of the two, plunger-like tools, in some cases dry ice, and even dynamite—all parts of a well driller's bag of tricks. After enough surging has been done to clear both the intake screen and the subterranean area around the well base, the well has been developed and is ready to be used.

Wells drilled in New England bedrock may need no development at all. In many parts of the Midwest, though, wherever an aquifer lies in unconsolidated geological strata, development is usually standard practice. Here, in simple bored, jetted, or dug wells, a piston or plunger is used to surge water in and out of the screen. Larger particles are pushed away, while the finest are sucked into the well and pumped out.

A well that produces less and less over time may not be draining its aquifer. It may just need redevelopment, to remove not only dirt particles but slime from its well screen or casing slots. It may only be that sediment has built up in the well bottom. Surging should remove all the grainy deposits, but chemical treatment may be needed to kill the slime-producing bacteria.

When Well Fails

If all goes well, a well will see decades of use without needing any attention. Sooner or later, like any machine, it will fail, though probably not irreparably. When it does stop producing, almost surely it's for one of four reasons: 1. The pump will quit. 2. The water level in the well and the cone of influence will get too low. 3. The screen will get plugged up. 4. So much sand and silt will accumulate in the well hole that water *can't*.

Any of these problems can be solved as long as there's good access through the top of the casing—a provision in almost any modern drilled well. When a wellhead is opened for surging, or *any* work is to be done in a well, the water supply will be contaminated, and the well should be disinfected again, just as it was when it was sealed the first time.

Calcium hypochlorite is perhaps the most common well disinfectant. It comes in capsules or tablets like the ones I saw Bill Gabaree throw into the well casing next to Lake Champlain. (47) When mixed with water, these tablets make a solution very much like household laundry bleach and water (also used sometimes). Either way, for the well to be disinfected completely, chlorine solution should remain in the well for as long as twenty-four hours before it is pumped out and any water is used.

An abandoned well, by the way, can be a hazard and a route for contamination to get into neighboring wells. State regulations may prescribe acceptable ways a well can be closed. Usually they require that the hole be filled, perhaps with concrete, to keep surface water out. Artesian wells, particularly, need to be plugged to keep groundwater from flowing to the surface.

Unless you live in a place where soil drainage is practically nil, it's probably a mistake to try to store water in a well that's already dry, or going dry. Many who have tried to retain water in a "dry well" have watched the supply slowly disappear into the subsoil or thirsty aquifer.

53. HYDRO-PNEUMATIC STORAGE

Where the source holds plenty of water, and large-capacity intermediate storage tanks or cisterns are not needed, a pressure tank may be the only point of artificial storage in an individual water system. Whenever this is so, the pressure tank performs three main roles:

1. It keeps the pump from running constantly, or from turning on and off—cycling—too frequently. The more it cycles, obviously, the faster the pump wears out. Thirty starts per hour is the absolute maximum cycle rate for most pumps. A new way of defining *drawdown* might be to say it's the quantity of water the *tank* must deliver between the time the pump shuts off and its next start-up. (It's too bad plumbers don't dream up a new term. It's too easy to confuse well drawdown and tank drawdown.)

2. The storage tank also provides water, under pressure, to the rest of the system, as has been mentioned already. The most pressure it can deliver is equal to the maximum capacity of the pump. In other words, the tank doesn't generate any pressure, it can only receive it and pass it on.

3. Finally, the hydropneumatic tank stores enough water to supply the household with all it needs during times of peak demand—even if the well

can't provide enough at that point. The total storage capacity of a pressure tank (forty-two gallons is standard) will be far below the total daily, or even hourly, needs of the family. In fact, if every valve in the house were turned on at the same time, the pressure tank might hold enough water to supply every outlet for only about one minute. If it's correctly sized, a pressure tank should hold about ten times the gallons-per-minute capacity of the pump.

Here are some things you should know before launching into further discussion of pressure tanks. All the water a pressure tank can supply between the time the pump stops, then starts again, is called *usable water*. The tank's *supplemental supply* is a fraction of the total usable water. In a sense, it's the system's reserve supply, because it can exist in *addition* to the tank's drawdown. Understand, too, that the total volume of usable water (drawdown plus supplemental supply) is less than the total volume of the tank. Air takes up the remaining space.

Just before the pump starts, a system will be at *minimum operating pressure*. Minimum operating pressure is just enough to move an adequate supply of water through the plumbing. We already know that standard minimum operating pressure is twenty psi.

Pump-start pressure is self-explanatory. It's the amount preset in the pressure switch—sometimes twenty psi, more often thirty psi—which, when reached, activates the pump. Minimum operating pressure may or may not be equal to pump-start pressure. If pump-start pressure is set higher (thirty psi, for instance) than the minimum operating pressure (twenty psi), the ten pounds of difference creates the supplemental supply within the tank. If pump-start pressure and minimum operating pressure are equal, there *is* no supplemental supply.

A hydropneumatic pressure tank is supercharged when it holds more than one atmosphere of air pressure, and that extra pressure has been blown into the tank right on the job site. (Normal atmospheric pressure, remember, is 14.7 psi at sea level. *That's* one atmosphere. Anything above that means the tank is supercharged.) If the tank was charged earlier, at the factory, it's said to be *precharged*. Whenever a tank loses its charge and returns to normal atmospheric pressure, it's waterlogged and can't do its job. Waterlogging can develop even if the tank has no leak, since water has the ability to absorb a certain amount of air. Clearly a waterlogged condition must be corrected right away.

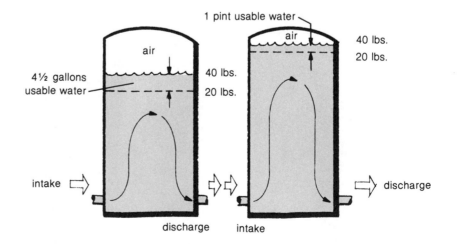

Pressure tank at left is partially waterlogged, meaning that the tank's air has been gradually absorbed by the water passing through it. Only 4½ gallons of water can be delivered as pressure drops from 40 psi to 20. Pressure tank at right is badly waterlogged. There's almost no air, and only about a pint of water can be used each time the pump cycles. Both these tanks need to be recharged.

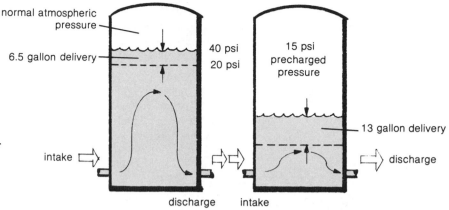

At sea level, a 42-gallon pressure tank (at left) will deliver about 6½ gallons when the air inside is at normal atmospheric pressure. But if the tank is "precharged" with an additional 15 psi (right), the tank will deliver twice as much water every time the pump cycles.

54. PLAIN STEEL PRESSURE TANKS

As you'd expect, *plain steel pressure tanks*, as they're called, come in various sizes. "Extra small" one-gallon tanks are mounted on pumps that supply water as needed—in systems where there's little or no need for storage. A "small" tank usually has a twelve-gallon capacity, and may have a pump mounted on its top. A "standard" size tank holds forty-two gallons. An eighty-two-gallon tank is "oversize," and is used with pumps that have high capacity. There are, of course, pressure tanks that hold 1,000 gallons or more. Some plain steel pressure tanks are mounted horizontally, some vertically.

Compressed air is the storable energy that builds pressure in a plain steel tank, just as it does in a *bladder* or *diaphragm tank*, described in the next section. As water is pumped into the tank, the volume of air there is decreased. Decreased air volume means increased pressure. Pressure is allowed to build to forty or fifty pounds per square inch before the pump shuts off. When a valve in the system is opened, the compressed air *uncoils*, pushing water out of the tank into the water lines. Water will continue to flow until there's no more pressure, at which point more water must be forced into the tank.

Air Space

No pressure tank stores vast quantities of water. In a standard forty-two-gallon tank, air might take up as much as a third of the space, even when it's most compressed. If the tank held one atmosphere of air, compressed to forty psi, and a valve were opened to let water out, 6.5 gallons would be delivered by the time the pressure was reduced to twenty psi. Take that same tank, and supercharge it with fifteen psi of additional air pressure, and the tank will deliver exactly *twice* as much water—thirteen gallons between forty psi and twenty psi. But there will be less water in the tank, and a larger percentage of air. In other words, the usable water might be only 20 percent of the tank's total volume.

Plain steel tanks have both intake and discharge lines near the bottom of the tank. These two connections allow the tank to be mounted *in line*, meaning that the system's water comes in one side, stays for a while, and passes out the other. Because water will absorb and rob some of the tank's air on its way through, carrying it away to the rest of the system, many plain steel tanks have floats installed, which are designed to keep the air and water separated from each other. These are called *air seals* or *absorption barriers*, and they're no more than large rubber or plastic discs. The round

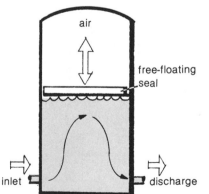

If a free-floating air seal is installed in the tank, water and air are isolated from each other, and absorption is reduced.

wafer floats on the water, moving up and down with fluctuations in air pressure. Because of the disc, this type tank must be mounted vertically.

Unfortunately the wafer can't totally prevent contact between water and air. And for this reason periodic supercharging of the tank is needed to prevent waterlogging. Air can be injected through an air charging valve. (Supercharged pressure is often set about five psi lower than pump-start pressure to provide maximum tank drawdown.) The air-volume control is mounted on the outside of the tank, approximately even with the inside water level when it's at pump-start pressure.

55. DIAPHRAGM/ BLADDER TANKS

Diaphragm or *bladder tanks* have watertight membranes stretched across that tank's interior. The membrane totally separates water and air. With this arrangement, no air is lost, and the need for supercharging is eliminated. In bladder tanks there is a single water connection which serves as both inlet and outlet for the tank. This fact places it in the *floated tank* category, since it's located outside the main in-line flow of the system. A check valve located near the intake keeps water *leaving* the tank from returning into the pump discharge line.

Because air within them is secure, diaphragm/bladder tanks are precharged long before they're installed. If the precharge is set below the pump-start pressure, the tank can provide a large drawdown and the system

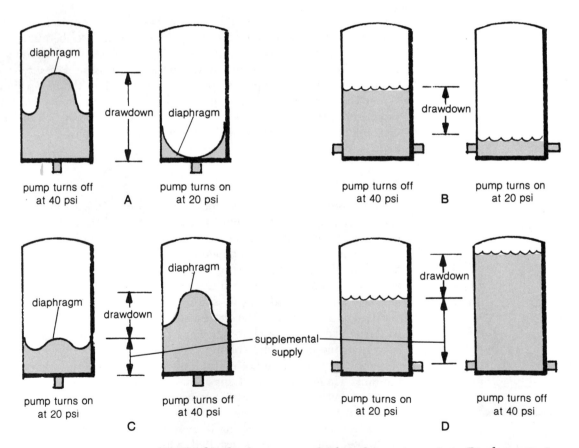

(A) Flexible diaphragms completely isolate water and air. Diaphragm tanks can be precharged or supercharged. (B) So can plain-steel or wafer-type pressure tanks. (C) Precharged diaphragm tanks can provide supplemental supply, as can supercharged plain steel tanks (D).

has excellent cycle control. But when the pump starts, the tank is empty of usable water, and there is no supplemental supply to help out during peak demand periods. *The Water Systems Handbook* describes how plumbers make adjustments for supplemental supply:

> In cases where the pump cannot meet peak demand, a supplemental supply is required. This can be accomplished in two ways: (1) with a difference in pressure setting, and (2) with additional tank capacity. For supercharged tanks, the pump cut-in pressure should be set somewhere above the supercharge pressure. For example, if the tank is supercharged to 20 PSIG (pounds per square inch gauge), the pump cut-in pressure is set at 30 PSIG. The water between 20 and 30 PSIG pressure range is called supplemental supply. For precharged tanks, again the pump cut-in pressure is set somewhere above the precharge pressure and the same example above applies.

> If the pump cannot keep up with the demand, the pressure will drop, and the tank will continue to deliver additional water to meet peak demands. When the minimum operating pressure is reached, the tank is empty of usable water.

> If the demand is greater than what is available from the tank by the difference in pressure method, extra tank capacity is required. . . .

As we know by now, any pressure tank is controlled by its pressure switch, which tells the pump to start whenever in-take pressure falls below the prescribed setting. The pressure switch operates with the help of a flexible diaphragm working against an adjustable spring and lever mechanism, set at the factory to start the motor at twenty or thirty psi and stop it at forty or fifty.

A *pressure relief valve,* usually installed in the tank intake, is the tank's fail-safe device. It's spring controlled and set to blow if the pressure switch somehow malfunctions. Most pressure relief valves release when pressure builds beyond sixty psi. More on both of these controls in sections 89 and 92. . . .

56. ELASTIC PRESSURE CELLS AND TANKLESS PRESSURE CONTROLS

Elastic pressure cells, like extra-small tanks, are used in cases where a wealth of water at the source means there's little need for storage. Pressure cells are metal cylinders with a stretchy rubber liner inside. They might hold three gallons at the most—just enough to take care of leaky faucets and very small water uses. As the flexible liner expands, pressure is exerted on the water line, and the pump is kept from short-cycling.

Keep in mind that it's the expansive quality of the rubber liner that provides pressure, and that the cell itself is not charged with air. They are pre-

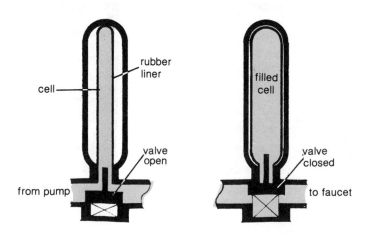

Elastic pressure cells can be used to store small quantities of water under pressure. Several cells might be used together.

Pressure Tank Selection Chart

Pump Capacity (gallons per min.)	Pressure-switch Range Settings (pounds per square inch)					
	20 to 40	30 to 50	40 to 60	50 to 70	60 to 80	70 to 100
	Pressure-tank Sizes (gallons)					
4	42	82	82	120	120	120
8	82	120	180	220	315	315
12	120	180	220	315	315	315
15	144	220	315	525	525	525
18	180	315	315	525	525	525
24	220	315	525	525	1000	1000
32	315	525	525	1000	1000	1000

set by the manufacturer, and unlike hydropneumatic tanks the pressure they supply can't be adjusted up or down.

Several pressure cells may be used in a series. One unit is needed for every ten gallons per minute of pump capacity. There *are* larger cells available too. The AAVIM explains further:

> If your pump will be operating under higher pressures than 50 pounds per square inch, figure on only 2 gallons of storage per cell. If you have a larger capacity pump, rather than installing several small cells, you can install a larger size one that has about 12 gallons capacity.
>
> One type of pressure cell is designed for mounting down in a well casing. If you use this kind, check the manufacturer's recommendations for the proper size unit. There are various sizes to fit well casings of 5 to 8 inches in diameter.

Elastic pressure cells have the advantage of taking up less space than a pressure tank. But *tankless pressure system controls* will fit in even smaller spaces. There are several models on the market. Each is designed to accumulate a small amount of water, maintain a constant discharge pressure, and eliminate the need for a larger pressure tank.

In systems where the source and pump capacity are greater than the household demands, mechanical tankless control valves simply allow the pump to start each time a normal amount of water is called for. Because

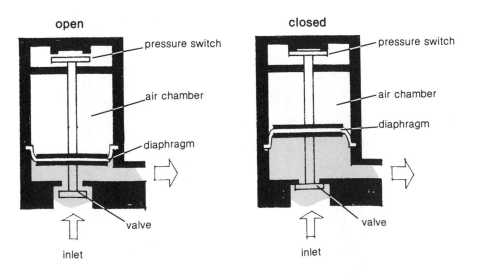

A mechanical tankless control valve.

they have such a small accumulator capacity, however, they're easily affected by any leak in the system. With so little margin for error, if there *is* a leak, the pump may be forced to cycle too frequently.

57. FREEZE PROTECTION

Depths at Which to Lay Small Water Pipes

State	Depth (feet)
Alabama	1½ to 2
Arizona	2 to 3
Arkansas	1½ to 3
California	2 to 4
Colorado	3 to 5
Connecticut	4 to 5
Delaware	2 to 3
Florida	1 to 2
Georgia	1½ to 2
Idaho	4 to 6
Illinois	3½ to 6
Indiana	3½ to 5½
Iowa	5 to 6
Kansas	2½ to 4½
Kentucky	2 to 3½
Louisiana	1½ to 2
Maine	4½ to 6
Maryland	2 to 3
Massachusetts	4 to 6
Michigan	4 to 7
Minnesota	5 to 9
Mississippi	1½ to 2½
Missouri	3 to 5
Montana	5 to 7
Nebraska	4 to 5½
Nevada	3 to 5
New Hampshire	4 to 6
New Jersey	3½ to 4½
New Mexico	2 to 3
New York	4 to 6
North Carolina	2 to 3
North Dakota	5 to 9
Ohio	3½ to 5½
Oklahoma	2 to 3
Oregon	4 to 6
Pennsylvania	3½ to 5½
Rhode Island	4 to 6
South Carolina	2 to 3
South Dakota	5 to 9
Tennessee	2 to 3
Texas	1½ to 3
Utah	3 to 5
Vermont	4 to 6
Virginia	2 to 3½
Washington	4 to 6
West Virginia	3 to 5
Wisconsin	5 to 7
Wyoming	5 to 6
District of Columbia	4

One of the most striking properties of water is that when it's transformed from its liquid state to a solid, through the process we all know as freezing, its volume increases by 11 percent. This expansion is more than enough to shatter any pipe, container, or machine in which water is allowed to freeze. Water, of course, freezes more quickly when it's not moving. So it's particularly vulnerable when it's being stored. Freeze protection, then, is an important part of all storage considerations.

It goes without saying that any storage tank, pressure tank, or pump located above the frost line must be kept in a place where it can't possibly become frozen during the winter. A buried cistern might have its top above the frost line, so long as its outlet is below the freezing level. In very cold places along the northern tier of the United States in-ground reservoirs are sometimes insulated along their tops.

Heat tapes wrapped around pipes, together with insulation, may prevent pipes from freezing wherever they're exposed to freezing temperatures. When pipes do freeze, but don't burst, they can be thawed with a portable heat source such as a propane torch.

Milo Moore, Extension Service housing and utilities specialist at the University of Vermont, located in a state where frost is often five feet deep, says,

> Freezing normally occurs where (water) lines must be shallow because of bedrock or where lines pass under roads, driveways, paved areas, or barnyards where soils have been compacted. If possible, route water lines to avoid these areas. If shallow bedrock areas cannot be avoided, mound the soil over the pipe.
>
> Where it is necessary to run a line under a paved area or barnyard, sleeve the pipe with a larger diameter pipe and place extruded polystyrene at least two feet in width and two inches thick on all sides of the pipe before the soil is replaced. Extruded polystyrene is superior to other insulation materials because it exhibits a low thermal conductivity and is virtually impervious to moisture.
>
> Sand and fine gravel should be placed on all sides of the pipe to a thickness of several inches. Soils should never be intentionally compacted as compaction reduces the resistance to heat flow. Soils should be kept as dry as possible because the thermal conductivity of moist compact soil is significantly greater than that of dry uncompacted soil.
>
> The thermal conductivity of frozen soil is four times greater than that of unfrozen soil. During years with little snowfall, bales of straw or woodchips, piled over the pipeline route, can be a cost-effective method of preventing or delaying freezing.

TREATING WATER

58. SOURCES OF CONTAMINATION

Water quality is every bit as important as the quantity of supply. The physical, chemical, bacteriological, and radiological characteristics of water are all things worth worrying about. Water quality fluctuates a great deal (hardness of Mississippi water, for instance, doubles from summer to winter), and it can deteriorate rapidly. Water picks things up wherever it goes. Gases can be held between its molecules. Sediments can be held in suspension. Raindrops absorb carbon dioxide as they fall, along with dust, smoke, and acids.

As we learn more about water quality, we learn we have more to worry about. Water problems might include iron, sulfur, alkalinity, hardness, pathogenic organisms, too much organic matter, heavy metals, and a host of other things. The list is growing. The more crowded we get the more we contaminate each other's water. And we're beginning to recognize that more developed communities have more developed water problems.

Lately we've been blaming ourselves. In a fine new book called *Domestic Water Treatment*, authors Jay H. Lehr, Ph.D., Tyler E. Gass, Wayne A. Pettyjohn, Ph.D., and Jack DeMarre remind us, "There is no such thing as 'pure' water; all of it contains gases or minerals. Although these substances can be removed by treatment, the water may still retain some impurities and, in fact, the amount of dissolved minerals may be greater after the treatment than before."

Domestic Water Treatment goes on to suggest we shouldn't flog ourselves so guiltily. They make a distinction between "natural pollution" and "human-induced" pollution:

'Pure as the driven snow' is a phrase that has been used with little question for decades. Only recently has the chemical quality of rain and snow been questioned, largely because of public awareness of the effects of air pollution. Examination of the data, however, reveals that the quality of precipitation, even before the evolution of human beings, was neither pure nor clean. Air pollution was not a phenomenon that developed in the twentieth century.

Acid rain *is* introduced by industrial wastes—smog-producing things like carbon monoxide, sulfur dioxide, and nitrous oxide we have released into the atmosphere. But droplets of polluted water can form around natural nuclei too, like dust, ice, volcanic ash, salt from sea spray, plant spores, and pollens. Forest fires, started by man only part of the time, create vast quantities of common but polluting atmospheric gases. Even the everyday decomposition of organic matter generates carbon dioxide which can fall out of the air as acid rain.

108

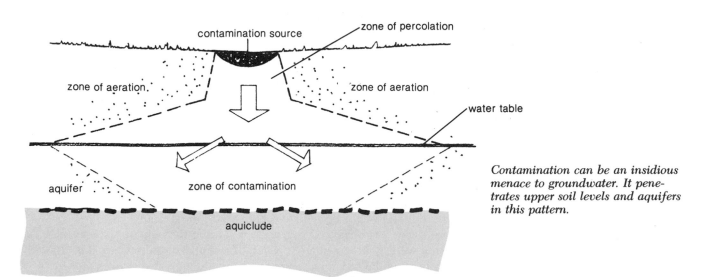

Contamination can be an insidious menace to groundwater. It penetrates upper soil levels and aquifers in this pattern.

Natural Contamination

Mother Nature is not all that sanitary herself. She constantly pollutes her own surface water with silt, algae, decaying leaves, a multitude of salts, chemicals, bacteria, and protozoans. Because groundwater is always in contact with soil and rock, it's riddled with impure elements like calcium, magnesium, sodium, potassium, gypsum, anhydrite, unhealthy amounts of fluoride, even arsenic!

The experts comfort us somewhat, telling us we've managed to pollute only a very small percentage of the earth's gigantic stores of groundwater. Nonetheless, throughout the world 10 million people die of waterborne diseases each year. So there must be something wrong in our efforts to bring the most accessible groundwater to us.

Any well, in fact, penetrates the protective seal of a groundwater source, and may offer a route for surface water to seep, unfiltered, into the earth. Too little effort is made to keep casings and spring boxes impervious to contaminating water from outside. Six hundred previously good wells around New York City have been closed in recent years because they've become hopelessly polluted. Where we tend to cluster, we tend to foul our water supply.

Salt-water Problems

Heavily populated coastal areas in New Jersey, Texas, Florida, and California are pumping salt water into their fresh-water aquifers. Cape Cod, in Massachusetts, has so many wells its fresh groundwater supply is starting to self-destruct. Houston is sinking a bit each year, for the same reason, as briny water encroaches from Galveston Bay.

A famous inn, on more famous Martha's Vineyard, is also having a brine problem. Its fresh-water well got salty. So crews dug another one farther inland, and it too has started to get salty. They discovered the problem when the chlorinated swimming pool water turned brown.

Asked if it was possible to maintain a fresh groundwater supply on a small island in the sea, an official of the company that owns the hotel in question said, "Sure it's possible. Fresh water is heavier than salt water. It pushes the salt water out . . . *until* it's really depleted. We've been telling people on the island for years: stop developing. We've been telling them, 'Look, we're going to run out of fresh water.' But they keep building and they keep digging wells."

Unfortunately, clean, pleasant-tasting water isn't necessarily safe. Sometimes we have salty wells and can't taste the salt. Magnesium sulfate (Epsom salts) and sodium sulfate (Glauber's salt) and plain old sodium chloride (table salt) are generally conceded to give water a disagreeable taste. But it depends on whom you're talking to. Humans, adaptable as we are, grow to like what we're used to. Those of us with "bad" water visit elsewhere and complain that their "good" water tastes terrible.

Contamination from sewers, cesspools, and septic tanks (if not yours maybe your neighbor's) should always be considered. Human and livestock wastes contain multitudes of bacteria and viruses, most of which are not harmful. But a few, like typhoid and hepatitis, can be deadly.

Consult your local health department regarding the *minimum* distance between a water source and any portion of a septic system. As a guide, 100 feet can be used. Pollution has a knack of traveling great distances underground—often in limestone or in crevices between solid rock formations. Chemicals, salts, and detergents that dissolve in water, go along too, and sometimes are not filtered out before reaching an underground receptacle. Chlorides and nitrates found in a water source are indicators of sewage pollution.

Widespread Contamination

Whole aquifers can be contaminated by cleaning solvents, pesticides, road salt, and many industrial chemicals. *Sanitary landfill* dumps, in many cases, may not be so sanitary after all. Recent studies show they too are points of origin for toxic wastes that end up in our drinking water. The government has identified at least 250 "hazardous" dump sites in thirty-five states, each within a mile of a drinking water source. It's hard to speculate about how many other poisonous feeder stations we've established.

Accidental spills, chemical and radioactive, happen. Some realists claim they're unavoidable, no matter how much we police ourselves. Gasoline is spilled regularly, and seems to find its way into a nearby water source quickly. Because it floats on water, it presents a fire and explosion hazard. Water that's mingled with highly corrosive mining wastes is particularly harmful to us. So are fertilizers, leached from fields into wells.

Lehr and his colleagues say in *Domestic Water Treatment,*

> In Colorado automatic fertilizer feeders attached to irrigation sprinkler systems are becoming increasingly popular. However, their operation may create a partial vacuum in the lines, causing fertilizer to flow from the feeder into the well. Even more serious is the suspicion that some individuals are dumping fertilizers directly into the well to be picked up by the pump and distributed to the sprinkler system. Such practices lead to direct and dangerous groundwater pollution. . . .

They go on,

> For decades, human beings have disposed of liquid wastes by pumping them into wells . . . (And) literally hundreds of thousands of abandoned exploratory wells dot the countryside. Many of these holes are drilled to determine the presence of underground mineral resources. (Seismic shot holes, coal, salt, oil, gas, etc.) The open holes permit water to migrate freely from one aquifer to another. A fresh water aquifer could thus be joined with a polluted aquifer, or polluted water could drain into fresh water zones. . . .

Distance from Wells

Source of Contamination	Minimum Distance (feet)
Waste disposal lagoons	300
Cesspools	150
Livestock and poultry yards	100
Privies, manure piles	100
Silo pits, seepage pits	150
Milkhouse drain outlets	100
Septic tanks and disposal fields	100
Gravity sewer or drain not pressure tight	50
Pressure-tight gravity sewer or drain	25

THE HOME WATER SUPPLY

Impurities, whether natural or humanly induced, are of four basic types: gases, suspended matter, soluble material, and living organisms. Water quality is also judged, officially, on the basis of four characteristics designated by the EPA:

1. The *physical characteristics* of water are its taste, its color, its level of turbidity, its temperature, and its odor.
2. Its *chemical content* is primarily its "hardness" or "softness."
3. *Biological ingredients* in water, primarily microorganisms, have a direct bearing on our health.
4. *Radiological substances* must of course be avoided, as must any water that has in any way contacted radioactive materials.

Data from the U.S. Geological Survey might provide a partial analysis of your own, or an adjacent water supply. Make use of government information and people. They're sympathetic and their services are often free.

It might be helpful to know where, and in what direction, groundwater flows through your property. But this might not be possible to learn without considerable expense. Finding out what's *in* your water, before you treat it, will be easier—and cheaper. Then keep in mind that treating water for only one purpose is simple. The EPA reassures us, "There are seldom more than one or two conditioning problems with any one water source." *Real* problems only appear when there are several things wrong.

When more than one piece of water treatment equipment is needed, it must be correctly installed—*in the correct sequence* with other treatment components—and properly serviced. Conditioners billed as cure-alls probably are not very good at curing anything.

59. SAMPLING AND TESTING

Taking a water sample is a tricky process, and testing it is an exact science. Most of us are qualified to do only the first. The success of an analysis depends on how the sample is taken, and on who interprets the results. Because exact analysis can be muddied by a number of inexact human factors, and because water quality may fluctuate, careful testing by an authorized laboratory should be done on a regular basis—even *after* water conditioning equipment has been selected and installed, and favorable results have been achieved.

A bacterial analysis, the most common water test, is meant to insure the biological safety of those in the household. And nobody should drink any water from a source until this has been done. The laboratory, either state-run or private, will determine whether the water contains pathogenic bacteria, protozoans, or viruses. Accuracy in sampling and speed in delivering the sample to the lab are essential. If possible, a technician from the laboratory should be called to draw the sample.

Three Types Sought

A bacterial analysis is primarily a search for three types of bacteria, found only in warm-blooded animals. These are fecal coliforms, fecal streptococcus, and total coliforms. Although these microscopic life forms may be inherently harmless themselves, they *indicate* the possible presence of disease-causing microbes. Remember that the test only indicates what's in the water *at the time of sampling*.

A chemical analysis of an individual water source is done less often, usually when an unhealthy amount of chemical substance is suspected. Copper, iron, tin, manganese, zinc, sodium, magnesium, calcium, molybdenum, cobalt, chromium, arsenic, and selenium, found in most water, are necessities for human life. *But in very small amounts.* Lead, mercury, and cadmium, on the other hand, are heavy metals that accumulate in the body over time, and may gradually poison us.

Taking a water sample for either chemical or bacterial analysis is essentially the same, though the lab should be contacted for special information or instructions before a sample for chemical analysis is taken. Often the lab will want you to include a description of the water's physical properties at the time of sampling (color, odor, taste, and turbidity).

How to Take Sample

These are some general rules and procedures for taking a water sample, as recommended by the EPA and others:

1. It's best to check with the laboratory ahead of time, alerting it a sample is to follow. Give it all the information requested. Use the sterile bottle it provides, and don't rinse it first. (If you're to provide your own sample container, a glass jar with a screw-on lid should work fine. The jar and lid should be boiled in water for one minute or more to sterilize them.)

2. Allow nothing except the water to be sampled to get into the container.

3. If sample water is to be taken from a faucet, make sure the faucet doesn't leak. Also remove the aerator. (If there *is* a leak, it's a potential route for contaminates, and a different sampling point should be found—as near the storage location as possible.) Sterilize the inside of the faucet with the flame from a torch. Then don't wipe it or touch it at all.

4. Allow water to run for five minutes or more, long enough to clean the line. Don't change the flow rate before collecting the sample. Fill the bottle about 5/6 full.

5. Don't let any of the water contact your hands during sampling or as you close the container. Don't leave the bottle standing, or gases will have a chance to escape. Cap it immediately.

6. Take or send the sample to the lab right away. It's best if it can be there within an hour. For the test to be at all accurate, the sample must be in the laboratory before twenty-four hours have passed.

Domestic Water Treatment suggests that any sample be sent with a letter describing excavation, land filling, irrigation, waste disposal, road salting, oil drilling, or accidental spills that might have taken place anywhere near your water source. The letter should also include:

1. The name and address of the owner.
2. The type of water source (well, spring, cistern, pond, etc.).
3. Exactly where the sample was taken.
4. When the sample was taken.
5. The name of the sampler, if different from the owner.
6. The sampling procedure that was followed.

The results should give you a good idea of what water conditioning unit(s) will be needed. Local suppliers of water-treatment equipment can be found in the Yellow Pages, or by contacting the Water Quality Association, Lombard, IL 60148. The question of who's to *service* water treatment equipment is as important as who's to install it. Maybe you'll have to do some of the servicing yourself. (Changing a filter is simple enough.) Maybe you'll sign a service contract with the dealer who sells or rents you the units.

Water Quality Problems

Problem	Description	Concentration Levels of Impurities at Which Treatment is Usually Recommended
Dissolved Calcium and Magnesium	Produces hardness, white scale in pipes and water heaters; causes insoluble soap curd on dishes and fabrics.	Above 85 mg/l
Iron Oxide	Discolors water; stains clothing and plumbing fixtures reddish brown. In excess gives water bad taste and color; can interfere with water conditioning equipment.	Above 0.3 mg/l
Iron Bacteria	Bacterial growth in pipes, screens, and strainers.	If present
Acid Water (low pH)	Causes corrosion: attacks piping and tanks; red stains from galvanized pipes, bluish green stains from copper pipes.	Below a pH of 7.0
Sulphur (hydrogen sulfide)	Produces bad taste and the odor of rotten eggs; tarnishes silverware, causes corrosion.	Trace
Nitrates	Can cause serious illness and occasional fatal poisoning of infants.	Above 45 mg/l (10 mg/l as nitrogen)
Chlorides	Bad taste; corrosive.	Above 250 mg/l
Manganese Oxide	Produces black stains on plumbing fixtures, dishes, and fabrics. In excess gives metallic taste to water.	Above 0.05 mg/l
Manganese Bacteria	Bacterial growth in pipes; discoloration or staining; oily scum on water surface when heated.	If present

60. IRON AND MANGANESE

Mr. Roe's voice was soft and sympathetic as he answered the phone. He's used to hearing people's water problems. I gave him my sob story: clogged faucets; red stains in sinks, in the dishwasher, in the toilets, in the bathtub; unclean silverware and glasses. I told him about the brown tint in our white clothes, a discoloration Clorox seemed to make *worse*. He laughed when I described the polite questions from guests who washed their hair here.

Like any good doctor, he offered no immediate diagnosis—or prognosis. Instead, he calmly explained how to take a water sample, and suggested I bring one to the office right away. Thirty minutes later I walked into the Manosh Company headquarters with a Mason jar of water from our kitchen tap. Mr. Roe was waiting behind the counter.

I said hello, handed him the sample, and started to leave.

"Do you want this right now?" he said.

"Don't you have to send it to a lab?" I said.

"I can do some of it right here," he said. "But I've got some other calls to make first. Are you going to be home in about an hour?"

It was less than an hour. The phone was ringing as I walked through the door.

"Ready for a report?" asked Mr. Roe. I was ready.

"When we talk about 'hardness'," he said, "we talk about grains per gallon. Your water has six grains per gallon—not bad, but not real soft either . . . Acidity and alkalinity is measured on a 1-to-14 pH scale. Your pH is 7.4, just above neutral. So that's all right. Now the iron: here we talk about parts per million. Yours is 1.2 parts per million. That's high, even though it doesn't sound like a lot. The state of Vermont recommends that water be treated if it shows more than .05 ppm of iron. I can't check your water for manganese here in the office, but I'd like it checked. I'll have to send your sample to the State Lab. It looks like you'll need an iron filter, but let's wait a few days for the lab results. . . ."

Appears Red

Overall, iron makes up about 5 percent of the earth's crust. So it's not surprising that groundwater in many places contains small quantities of this troublesome mineral. Sometimes iron water will appear red. "Red water" contains ferric iron. Other water with iron content may *look* clear when it's pumped, but once it's in contact with oxygen for any length of time, it produces rusty red-brown particles. This *clear water* has ferrous iron which will fall out of suspension when oxidized.

Iron not only turns laundry brown and tastes bad in coffee and tea, it turns downright black when mixed with whiskey. It stains fixtures and utensils. If there's enough of it, potatoes will turn black when cooked in iron water.

"Iron bacteria" present further problems. Colonies of these microorganisms feast on dissolved iron and create a gelatinous red slime sometimes found near the top of a well casing or in a toilet tank. Chlorine bleach inhibits their growth, but that's only a temporary solution.

If there's a *lot* of bacterial iron, chlorination or *superchlorination* may be necessary. (71) A *chlorine feeder*, installed in the suction line between the well and the pressure tank, pumps chlorine into incoming water. The feeder is normally wired to the pressure switch, so it injects disinfectant only when the pump is running. A carbon filter (70) can later remove both the iron residual *and* the chlorine.

Manganese often accompanies iron in water, particularly in surface water that's acidic. (65) On its own, manganese may produce a gray or black stain on fixtures. Ion-exchanging *water softeners* (61) can remove low concentrations (less than two ppm) of both iron and manganese, which, if left unchecked, can collect within steel pipes and otherwise plug up water equipment—much like hardening of the arteries in humans.

Polyphosphate feeders are also used to control iron in water, so long as the iron has not yet oxidized and settled out as rust particles. A phosphate feeder then, like a chlorinator, is installed *before* the pressure tank. Phosphate feeders are often used in combination with a water softener. More phosphate material must be added to the feeder about once a month.

In water with more than two ppm of iron, an oxidizing filter containing

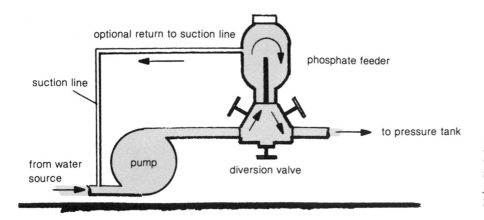

Phosphate feeder intercepts some water on its way from the pump to the pressure tank. Some phosphate feeders return a portion of phosphate water to the suction line.

manganese dioxide might be used. The manganese dioxide (*green sand*) precipitates iron particles out of solution and removes them. In fact, green-sand oxidizing filters can clean up water containing up to ten ppm of iron, but these filters need to be backwashed as often as once a week.

Oxidizing filters that are also charged with *potassium permanganate* (KMnO4), on the other hand, are effective in removing both iron and manganese, and they need to be charged with that chemical very infrequently. This is considered to be a fail-safe system by many plumbers, since "potassium permanganate renews the oxidizing properties released from the manganese greensand bed," as the sales literature in one filter brochure puts it.

Others agree that potassium permanganate works well, but argue that, although it presents no health hazard in a properly functioning filter, it *is* a poisonous chemical. Get some on your hands and it will leave a purple stain that won't wash off for days. One plumber showed me where potassium permanganate had eaten a hole in the sleeve of his nylon jacket.

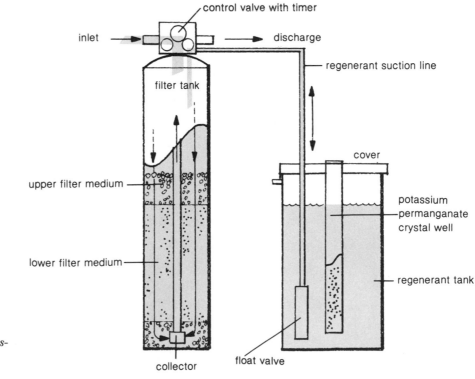

A potassium permanganate filter may be the best way to remove both iron and manganese from water. As long as the filter functions properly the poisonous potassium permanganate presents no health hazard.

In cases where water contains both dissolved iron and iron bacteria, a combination chlorinator-and-filter unit may be the best solution. Chlorine kills the bacteria and the filter strains them out, along with the iron. The newest iron filters are equipped with automatic backwashing. They need practically no attention, although the filtering chemicals may need to be replenished every few months.

61. HARDNESS

Water-softening pellets come in eighty-pound bags, and in smaller packages which are easier to manage.

We know about acid rain. As raindrops fall through the atmosphere they combine with carbon dioxide to form *carbonic acid.* As this weak acid lands and is filtered through the soil, it helps water dissolve minerals like calcium and magnesium (as well as iron), and carries them, in solution, deeper still. The presence of these minerals explains why well water is frequently harder than surface water.

Groundwater in areas of very high rainfall, ironically, is likely to be *softer* than water in arid places such as those many dry regions west of the Mississippi. This is because heavy rains percolate through the soil more rapidly, and have long since leached away much of the mineral content there. The character of water in any aquifer, of course, depends on what minerals it has seeped through en route to the underground basin. For the most part, deeper aquifers have a higher degree of hardness, since there is more opportunity for minerals to pass into solution during the infiltration process.

The best explanation of why hard water is so named is that it's *hard* to use. Calcium and magnesium inconveniently tie up the natural cleaning action of soaps and detergents. A bathtub filled with soapy hard water will inevitably have a dirty ring when it's emptied. Hardness also leaves *scale* in pipes and in some metal cooking pots. Hard water often contains what the EPA terms "other harmful and disagreeable substances" in addition to calcium and magnesium, and these can corrode parts of a water system. Copper, for example, may not be unhealthy or corrosive, but it will taste bad if its quantity is greater than one ppm.

Soft water has less than one grain per gallon (Abbreviated: gpg. If you're interested in conversions: 1 gpg = 17.12 mg/L). Over 85 percent of the water in the United States contains more than one gpg, say the authors of *Domestic Water Treatment,* and is thus labled slightly hard, moderately hard, or very hard. *Very hard* water has about 10.5 gpg. That's roughly equivalent to the volume of two aspirin tablets in a gallon of liquid.

Hardness is broken down into two basic types: temporary hardness and permanent hardness. *Temporary hardness* can be removed by boiling the water. *Permanent hardness* cannot. In some homes *post-faucet* water-conditioning methods are used. A water-softening powder is added to water that's drawn from a tap. The powder dissolves and reacts with calcium and magnesium, quickly removing them. In some cases the water remains cloudy, in others it clears up. This type of softened water is generally used for dishwashing and laundry.

Pre-faucet softening eliminates hard minerals in water before it ever reaches the household plumbing, and involves a relatively costly water-conditioning appliance. A water softener is a tank, usually filled to just over half its volume with a bed of resin beads. Water enters the top of the tank, flows through these beads, and exits, often through the bottom of the tank. This is called an "ion-exchange" unit because it contains an exchange medium—the resin, often known as Zeolite.

Zeolite never dissolves, is never consumed, and seems to respond indefinitely to regeneration. It contains electrically charged particles of sodium—

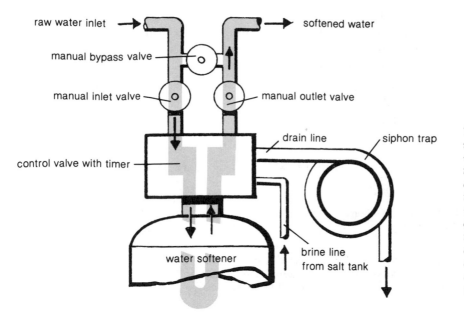

raw water inlet →

softened water

manual bypass valve

manual inlet valve →

manual outlet valve

drain line

siphon trap

control valve with timer

water softener

brine line
from salt tank

The resin beads in a water softener need to be backwashed, or recharged with salt solution, from time to time. The salt solution comes from a brine tank located next to the softener. During the rinsing phase, when calcium, magnesium, and other impurities are flushed from the tank, they exit through the drain line. A siphon trap prevents any of the drained fluid from accidentally running back into the tank.

sodium *ions*—which replace calcium and magnesium ions as water passes through it. After a while Zeolite runs out of sodium, and gets overloaded with the hardness ions it has been collecting. At this point it needs to be recharged with salt solution (sodium in this case). Plumbers call this solution *brine*. These days recharging is usually automatic, controlled by a preset timer mounted on the tank.

The recharging process has three steps:

1. During *backflushing*, the water flow in the tank is reversed and pushed up through the resin bed. This loosens and removes particles of dirt, calcium, magnesium, and other minerals from the Zeolite.

2. The resin is then soaked in a salty brine consisting of sodium and chloride ions. This concentrated solution is made by mixing water with salt tablets, grains, or pellets which must be periodically fed into a separate container. This second step is called *brining*.

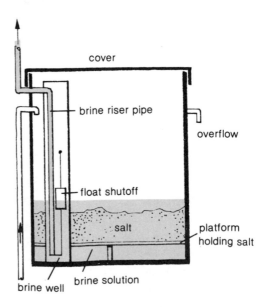

cover

brine riser pipe

overflow

float shutoff

salt

platform
holding salt

brine solution

brine well

Cutaway of a brine tank, showing brine valve and salt platform.

3. Last, calcium, magnesium, and other impurities are flushed from the tank with clean water. This is the *rinsing* step. In many parts of the country water softeners can be rented, and serviced—for a fee. Check to see if this is more economical than owning your own unit.

Obviously water softening adds salt (sodium chloride) to drinking water—a condition that's unsuitable for people with heart, kidney, or certain respiratory complaints who are on salt-restricted diets. In such instances plumb-

Methods of Softening Hard Water

Method	Advantages	Disadvantages
Post-Faucet Methods Precipitating	Can be added when wanted to water.	Must be added each time soft water is needed. (Time and money.)
Inactivates hardness ions in a visible solid form.	Avoids capital outlay for water softening unit or monthly service charge.	Water which is left un-soft-ened can still do damage.
		Visible solids can cause washing film.
		If any of the washing film is left in rinse water, it can irritate the skin and weaken fibers.
Non-Precipitating	Can be added when wanted to water.	Must be added each time soft water is needed. (Time and money.)
Inactivates water hardness ions in an invisible soluble form.	Avoids capital outlay for water softening unit or monthly service charge.	Must be carefully measured to be effective.
	Surrounds and imprisons hardness minerals and does not form washing film.	Water that is left unsoftened can still do damage.
Pre-Faucet Method Water Conditioning Appliances	Most economical way to soften entire home water supply.	Requires initial capital outlay for purchasing unit, or monthly rental charge.
Exchanges hard water ions for soft water ions.	Can be adjusted to effectively soften all kinds of water supply.	Salt for recharging the appliance must be added periodically.
	Can be effective in the removal of iron.	
	Recharging can be done automatically.	
	Avoids time and nuisance of adding powdered water conditioners and cleaning filters.	
	Family can always enjoy benefits of soft water.	
	Can screen out sediment in addition to water hardness minerals.	

ing may be reconstructed so the water softener serves only the hot water lines (making washing and bathing more pleasant), but allowing unconditioned cold water to come directly to the tap for cooking and drinking.

62. MICROORGANISMS AND OTHER ORGANISMS

Most microorganisms in water are harmless—even beneficial to the water in which they live. The few that are pathogenic (disease-causing), potentially dangerous, or just annoying include iron bacteria, of course, deadly microbes like *salmonella*, cholera-producing bacteria, viruses, *actinomycetes* which manufacture distasteful odors and tastes, microscopic creatures that transform sulfur-containing matter into hydrogen sulfide (with its "rotten egg" smell), and *E. coli*, the most common coliform bacteria.

There are also algae, discussed previously, molds, protozoa, and parasitic worms. As we know, disinfection using chlorine (71) removes all or most of these problems. But turbidity (63) protects some organisms from disinfection, and it must be removed beforehand.

Coliform bacteria (specifically E. coli) live in the intestines of man, and other warm-blooded animals, including birds. They also survive in water, if conditions are right. Unfortunately, bacterial exams for coliforms tend to be somewhat misleading since they only indicate the number of microorganisms present in a particular sample at the time the sample was taken. (59) Test results, then, are often described in terms of *the most probable number* (mpn) of microbes per unit of volume.

Groundwater in unconsolidated formations—sand, coarse silt, clay, or gravel—is apt to be safer, microbiologically, than water in fractured rock, limestone, or crushed lava. Geologic material that's broken up fine filters out most bacteria before they ever reach an aquifer.

What's even better news is that cold and dark storage conditions in an aquifer (or elsewhere) do not favor bacterial growth. To put it another way, groundwater doesn't usually have all the conditions necessary for bacterial survival—harmful or otherwise—but it's probably not totally antiseptic either.

Disinfection for individual systems using groundwater is often ignored in many parts of the country, even though chlorination is an integral part of almost all communal systems. (95) Decisions about installing microbe-killing water-treatment equipment should be based on the results of numerous water samples taken over an extended period. Farm water that's going to come in contact with milk, and any surfaces that will contact milk, must of course be free of all bacteria, as well as any yeasts or molds that can break down fats and proteins in raw milk. Dairy farms in particular need adequate disinfection equipment.

63. TURBIDITY

Turbidity is no more than soil particles carried in water. But even a speck of soil is bound to contain millions of microorganisms, and a certain amount of organic matter. So turbidity can present a complexity of problems—both physical and chemical. Turbidity is measured in a laboratory by comparing the amount of light scattered by particles in the turbid water to the amount of light diffused by very clear distilled water. Its extent is described in parts per million. Water with turbidity greater than ten ppm is thought to be objectionable, and probably does not conform to public health standards.

Surface water that's continually agitated will hold grains of silt and other matter in suspension as long as the water is moving. A *settling basin* is a

Symptoms	Probable Cause
Hardness Sticky curd forms when soap is added to water. Causes well-recognized ring in bathtub. The harder the water, the more soap required to form suds. Glassware appears streaked and murky. Hard, scaly deposits form inside of metal pipes. Your skin roughens from washing.	Calcium and magnesium in the water (may be in the form of bicarbonates, sulfates, or chlorides). Iron also contributes to hardness. (See next group of symptoms—Red Water.)
Red Water Dissolved Iron Red stains appear on clothes and porcelain plumbing fixtures, even if as little as 0.3 ppm is present. Causes corrosion of steel pipes. Water has metallic taste. Freshly-drawn water sometimes appears clear at first. After exposure to air, rust particles form and settle to bottom of container. Iron Bacteria Red slime develops in toilet tanks.	Iron (sometimes including manganese). Caused by dissolving action of water as it passes through underground iron deposits, or contacts iron and steel surfaces. Caused by living organisms (bacteria) that act on iron already in the water. Often associated with acid or other corrosive conditions.
Brownish-Black Water Fixtures stain brownish-black. Fabrics stain black. Coffee and tea have bitter taste.	Manganese is present usually along with iron. Manganese bacteria.
Acidity "Eats away" copper and steel parts on pump, piping, tank, and fixtures. If copper or brass are being "eaten," water may leave green stains on plumbing fixtures under a dripping faucet. If water contains iron, iron-removal methods are less effective.	Water contains carbon dioxide picked up from air, or from decaying vegetable matter, which combines with water to form a weak acid. In rare instances, water may contain mineral acid such as sulfuric, nitric, or hydrochloric acids.
"Rotten Egg" Odor and Flavor "Eats away" iron, steel, and copper parts of pumps, piping, and fixtures. If sulfur and iron are both present in water, finely-divided black particles may develop, which is commonly called "black water." Silverware turns black. Not satisfactory for cooking.	Hydrogen-sulfide gas. Sulfate-reducing bacteria. Sulfur bacteria.
Other Off Flavors Water may taste bitter, brackish, oily, salty, or have a chlorine odor or taste.	Extremely high mineral content. Presence of organic matter. Excess chlorine. Water passage through areas containing salty or oily waste, etc.
Turbidity Water with a dirty or muddy appearance.	Silt. Sediment. Small organisms. Organic matter.

pool of quiet water where larger suspended particles are allowed to settle out—possibly with the aid of alum. This kind of open water treatment, including the use of alum, dates back to the ancient Egyptians. (48)

A *sediment trap* is a more sophisticated version of the settling trap. It may be a tank with two separate compartments, where water can be held for twenty-four hours or more. In the first compartment, gravity does the job of pulling particles out of suspension. In a good sediment trap, the intake distributes water uniformly over the surface of the settling area. There may even be a series of baffles to slow water as it comes into this chamber.

Adding hydrated aluminum sulfate (alum) to the water once it's passed to the second compartment, furthers the process. This chemical encourages the particles to combine, forming *flocs*. Larger coagulated pieces, produced by *flocculation*, settle to the bottom of the tank where they can be removed. The AAVIM says, "Now there are polymer compounds available which are more effective than alum and less costly." Ferric chloride and ferric sulfate are also used as coagulants.

A *diatom filter* is another efficient way to remove turbidity. Diatoms are the remains of marine algae whose tiny shells don't decompose after the plants die. An accumulation of these white, snowflake-like shells (as many as 50 million per cubic inch) is known as *diatomaceous earth*, a superfine filtering medium which strains out miniscule particles of turbidity.

A cylindrical diatomite filter may be installed on either the suction side or the discharge side of a pump. The AAVIM explains how it works:

> The filtering element usually consists of a porous surface called a "septum." It may consist of wire cloth, plastic fiber cloth, or any of several materials that will let water pass readily. A coating of diatomite filter material is then applied to the septum to form a "precoat." It is this material that provides the filtering action when the filter is first put into operation. . . .
>
> Maintenance of a diatomite filter consists of adding diatomite-filter-aid material as the filtering action starts to slow. This increases the flow rate through the filter. The point is finally reached where further addition of filter aid has little effect. At this stage the entire filter cake must be removed and a new diatomite material added to the septum to form a new cake. If your filter is properly sized to your water use, the filter cake should not require replacing more than about every two months.

Another possibility: *rapid-sand filters* or *pressure filters*, as they're called in some parts of the country, are floated tanks, partially filled with fine sand and quartz gravel to a depth of twenty-four to thirty-six inches. The tank is placed on the delivery side of the pump. Pumped water enters the tank near the top, passes downward through the filter material at a rate of approximately two to three gpm per square foot of filter surface area, then back up and out of the filter unit through the treated-water line. *Multi-media* rapid-sand filters might also contain filtering matter such as anthracite or bituminous coal, limestone chips, plastic pellets, and even pieces of garnet, a semi-precious stone.

Be forewarned that rapid-sand filters remove only the largest particles of turbidity. In severe cases, a jelly-like substance called *filter-aid* is also fed into the tank. Filter-aid rests on top of the sand bed and removes smaller particles which would otherwise make it through the filter. The *disadvantage* of a rapid-sand filter is that if it's not backwashed every seven to ten days, the water pressure supplied by the pump can force built-up dirt particles through the filter and into the plumbing lines.

Domestic Water Treatment adds,

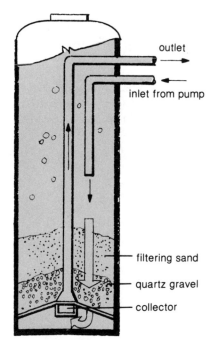

outlet

inlet from pump

— filtering sand

— quartz gravel

— collector

A rapid-sand filter removes suspended particles in water. Water is pushed through the tank by the system's pump.

Effectiveness Under Normal Conditions:	Disinfection Methods			
	Simple Chlorination	Superchlorination-Dechlorination	Electric Pasteurization	Ultraviolet Radiation
For Killing Bacteria	Effective.	Effective.	Effective.	Effective for clear water.
For Killing Viruses	Effective with some viruses. Complete effectiveness has not been determined.	Effective with many viruses. Complete effectiveness has not been determined.	Effective with many viruses. Complete effectiveness has not been determined.	Effective with many viruses. Complete effectiveness has not been determined.
Speed of Kill (Bacteria)	Requires at least 20 minutes contact time with minimum chlorine residual of 0.2 to 0.5 ppm.	Requires about 10 seconds contact time with minimum chlorine residual of 5 ppm. (Longer contact times—5 to 7 min.—effective with many viruses.)	15 seconds.	Fast acting at proper light intensity level in water that is free of suspended particles and ultra-violet absorbing matter in solution.

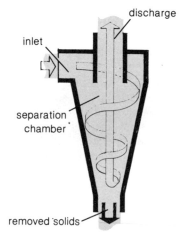

inlet

discharge

separation chamber

removed solids

Turbid water is spun at great speeds in a hydrocyclonic separator. Solids are thrown outward against the sides of the separation chamber, while clear water stays near the center.

Pads, ceramic cylinders, paper, porous stone, and slow-sand filters are not recommended for filtering turbid water. They are not satisfactory because of their low filtering capacity, the ease with which water can channel, their tendency to crack, their inability to filter out fine material, or the ease with which they may clog.

In-line cartridge filters containing activated charcoal are sometimes placed in water lines to remove turbidity. (64) Some are located right at a tap. *Hydrocyclone devices* or *separators* designed to spin turbid water a great speeds, offer another in-line alternative. These work like a small centrifuge. Within the separation chamber solids are thrown outward against the chamber walls by centrifugal force, then removed. Clarified water stays near the center of the chamber, where it can pass through and into the water line. Manufacturers of hydrocyclones claim they're 98 percent effective in removing turbidity.

In some situations where persistent sand or silt continues to be a problem at the screened intake near the bottom of a well casing, hydrocyclones are installed in conjunction with the submersible pump—right in the base of the well.

64. TASTES AND ODORS

Organic matter found in water may or may not be visible to the naked eye. Usually it consists of algae or plankton in some form. Algae growth, triggered by light, heat, and the presence of carbon dioxide, is increased by nutrients like nitrogen, phosphorus, and potassium (the chemicals in common fertilizers), which can easily find their way into surface water. Eliminating one or more of these conditions—keeping the temperature of stored water too cold to support life, and keeping it in darkness, for example—usually reduces the problem.

Dead algae are often a source of disagreeable odors and tastes in water. But actinomycetes, nematodes, all kinds of decaying organic matter, and chemical pollutants can be contributors too. Sometimes chlorine relieves the problem, but in some cases it makes it worse. Copper sulfate is frequently

Effectiveness Under Normal Conditions:	Disinfection Methods			
	Simple Chlorination	*Superchlorination-Dechlorination*	*Electric Pasteurization*	*Ultraviolet Radiation*
Effect of Minerals in Water	Some chlorine is "used up" if iron or sulfur is present in water. If mineral content varies from time to time, dosage will need to be adjusted with simple chlorination to maintain proper chlorine residual. With super-chlorination, dosage is not readily affected.	Heating may cause mineral deposits to form thus slowing heat movement.	Minerals gradually coat lamp sleeve surfaces and reduce efficiency.	
Effect of High Water Alkalinity	Purifying action slowed.	Purifying action slowed.	Not affected.	May tend to coat lamp sleeve(s).
Effect of Suspended Particles in Water (Such as contained in pond water)	Water should be filtered to remove particles. Otherwise, it is difficult to maintain proper amount of chlorine residual, and the particles may protect some bacteria from the killing action of the chlorine.		Slows heat movement. May foul heat exchanger.	Greatly reduces effectiveness. Particles may protect some bacteria from killing action of light. Water must be effectively filtered first to remove all particles.
Effect of Incoming Water Temperature	Increase in temperature speeds disinfecting action. Lower temperatures slow action.		Purification is not affected.	Most efficient at 100° F. water temperature. Less effective as temperature lowers.
Residual Effect (Ability after treatment to keep water disinfected)	With chlorine residual of 0.2 ppm or more, protection continues for several hours after treatment.	3 ppm or more residual provides excellent protection for many hours after treatment.	No protection after leaving pasteurizer.	No protection after leaving ultraviolet unit.
Effect on Water Taste	May have some chlorine taste but is still palatable.	Not palatable for some humans until dechlorinated. Activated carbon filter is used at kitchen faucet to remove all chlorine taste for drinking-water purposes. Water is palatable to livestock and poultry.	Taste not affected.	Taste not affected.
Protective Means Used to Assure Proper Operation	Color check with test kit enables user to determine amount of residual chlorine present. Water should be checked weekly.	Odor of chlorine is noticeable in super-chlorinated water before dechlorination.	Solenoid (electric) valve shuts off water supply when heating element burns out. It also returns water to heater if inadequately heated.	Equipped with solenoid (electric) valve to shut off water supply when lamp(s) dims or burns out, or electric service is interrupted.
Capacity	Available for any capacity water system.	Available for any capacity water system.	20 gal. per hour (size presently available).	Various size units available for any capacity water system.
Advantages in Addition to Disinfection	Can be used to remove iron, sulfur, and certain tastes and odors. Kills iron and sulfur bacteria.		None.	None.

Odd Tastes or Odors in Water

Chemical	Taste or Odor Characteristics in Water
Iron	Bitter taste
Manganese	Bitter taste
Sulfate	Bitter taste
Hydrogen sulfide	Rotten-egg odor
Sodium chloride	Salty taste
Bicarbonates	Flat, soda taste
High TDS content	Salty taste

SOURCE: *Domestic Water Conditioning*, Lehr et al, copyright 1979, used by permission of publisher, McGraw-Hill Book Co.

used as a substitute for chlorine in the treatment of waterborne organic matter, but it too is far from a perfect solution. An activated carbon filter may be the best way to remove odors and foul tastes—particularly if chlorine is injected into the system as well.

Activated-carbon filters come in two types: cartridge filters and carbon-bed filters. The carbon itself, found in both types of filters, is made from selected coal, hardwood, and burned pecan shells. The charcoal is pulverized to maximize the surface area of the carbon filtering medium, which will absorb odors and tastes until it's totally saturated with organic matter.

Corrugated filtering elements in a cartridge filter are coated with activated carbon. In large units, the filter itself can be removed for cleaning, although the number of times this can be done before the filter needs to be replaced is limited. The entire cartridge is replaced in smaller in-line units—whenever odors reappear, or whenever water pressure in the system drops, indicating the filter is full of organic matter that's slowing the passage of water.

From the outside, a bed-type, activated-carbon filter looks much like a rapid-sand filter. Any carbon-bed tank must be backwashed regularly, the frequency depending on the diameter of the filter and the amount of or-

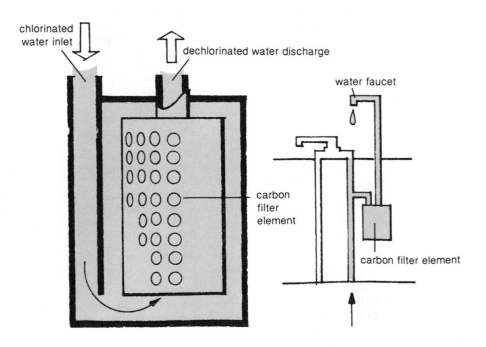

Activated carbon filters remove chlorine from drinking water. Units are often mounted beneath a sink. The multi-channeled filtering element can be removed and replaced periodically. Drawing at left shows detail of small box in installation at right.

124

ganic matter in the water being treated. The carbon filtering material might last one to three years before it needs to be replaced.

"Aeration" is still another way to remove tastes and smells. The idea is to expose as much water to as much oxygen as possible. The process eliminates even the sulfur-water odor caused by the presence of hydrogen sulfide. Surface water is treated quite practically with aeration. Fast-running streams and pond spillways are points of natural aeration.

In public waterworks jets of water are sprayed in the air to aerate water artificially. There are also small aerators for use in the private home. These are simple devices where streams of water are passed through a series of perforated plates to mix oxygen with the liquid. A byproduct of aeration, beyond taste and odor removal, is the oxidation of minerals like iron and manganese. (60)

65. pH

It's worth knowing the level of acidity or alkalinity in your water supply, so any serious corrosion or scale problems can be avoided. On the pH scale—which ranges from one to fourteen—seven is neutral. Each pH number variance to either side of seven indicates ten times greater strengths of acidity or alkalinity.

Water with a pH below seven is acidic. Corrosion can develop in pipes if water passing through has a pH lower than 6.5. Needless to say, when you reduce the corrosion possibilities, you extend the life of your system. The action of water passing through pipes actually sets up a small electrical current there. Acidity, in combination with dissolved minerals that increase the water's electrical conductivity, the presence of oxygen, carbon dioxide, and increased temperatures, all tend to enhance corrosion. Too low a pH also inhibits the functioning of iron-removal systems. (60)

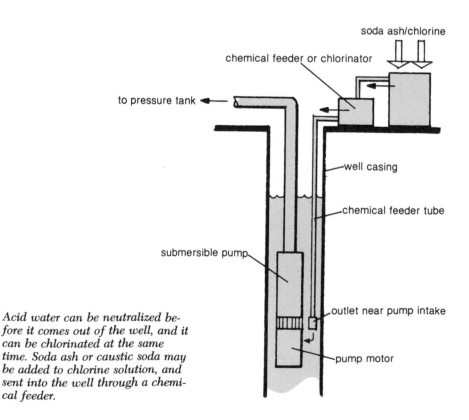

Acid water can be neutralized before it comes out of the well, and it can be chlorinated at the same time. Soda ash or caustic soda may be added to chlorine solution, and sent into the well through a chemical feeder.

If a water's pH is above seven, it's *basic,* or alkaline. Above 8.5 it will have a strong caustic taste, will cause scale buildup in plumbing, and will reduce the effectiveness of chlorination. The pH of water can vary dramatically with seasonal, even daily temperature fluctuations, biological activities such as photosynthesis, and most important, exposure to air. For these reasons a pH test should be done as soon as possible after a sample has been taken.

Acid water with a pH below five can be treated with an alkaline *soda-ash* (sodium carbonate) solution that's fed into the system via a feeder pump. This feeder pump may also supply chlorine at the same time. The neutralizing solution should contain three pounds of soda ash for every four gallons of water. Less acidic water—with a pH between four and seven—might be passed through a simple neutralizing filter containing *calcite. Any* neutralizing filter should be installed ahead of a water softener.

Directly into Well

In systems where there is no chlorinator, both soda ash and chlorine may be fed directly into the well through a *"chemical feeder."* This has the added benefit of protecting the well casing as well as the rest of the system

The Approximate pH Values of Some Common Substances

Reaction	pH Scale	Substance
	14.0	
		◁ Household Lye
Extremely Alkaline	**13.0**	
		◁ Bleach
Extremely Alkaline	**12.0**	
		◁ Ammonia
Extremely Alkaline	**11.0**	
		◁ Milk of Magnesia
Strongly Alkaline	**10.0**	
Moderately Alkaline		
	9.0	◁ Borax
		◁ Baking Soda
Slightly Alkaline	**8.0**	◁ Sea Water
		◁ Blood
Neutral	**7.0**	◁ Distilled Water
		◁ Milk
		◁ Corn
Slightly Acid	**6.0**	
Moderately Acid	**5.0**	◁ Boric Acid
		◁ Orange Juice
Strongly Acid	**4.0**	
Extremely Acid	**3.0**	
		◁ Vinegar
		◁ Lemon Juice
Extremely Acid	**2.0**	
Extremely Acid	**1.0**	
		◁ Battery Acid
	0.0	

Common Range For Most Natural Waters

from corrosion. Soda ash, available from chemical supply houses in 100-pound bags, adds no hardness to water, as some believe. For *severely* low water pH (below four), caustic soda (sodium hydroxide) must be added. This strong base, like equally dangerous acid, must be handled with great care.

Any water with a pH above eleven is highly polluted as well, and should be examined closely by a qualified chemist. Diluted sulfuric acid may be added to lower the pH in extreme situations like this. Whenever acid *or* caustic soda is being used, rubber gloves and goggles should be worn. A standard warning about acid solutions: *"Always add acid to water slowly, not water to acid!"*

In any system with a moderate-to-low pH problem, a *neutralizing tank* might be an adequate countermeasure. The neutralizing unit, installed *after* the pressure tank, has a bed of limestone and marble chips which offset the water's acidity. Unfortunately these materials—as well as calcium carbonate, which is also used sometimes—*will* increase hardness.

The flow rate through a neutralizing tank must be slow enough to give the limestone and marble chips an opportunity to do their job. To keep this process from endangering the pressure level in the whole system, more than one neutralizing tank might be installed to keep up with the water demand. If the pH is to be raised in this way, before water reaches an ion-exchanging water softener, any hardness added in the neutralizing tanks will be corrected in the softener.

Marble chips and limestone in the tank will eventually be consumed by acidity, and must be replaced. An annual check and resupply is usually all that's necessary. Backwashing, however, may be needed as often as every other day, depending on the pH of the water. Installing an automatic timer will make the backwashing and rinsing procedure a lot more convenient.

66. GASES

Besides dissolved oxygen and carbon dioxide, which are normally found in water, other waterborne gases can bring explosion hazard, further corrosion danger, and obnoxious odor problems to your water supply. Methane and hydrogen sulfide are two gases that often lurk in water.

Methane is usually produced naturally by anaerobic (nonoxygen-using) bacteria during the decomposition of organic matter. It may be particularly abundant in groundwater near industrial waste dumps, and around oil and natural gas refineries. Methane is colorless, odorless, and tasteless, yet it's explosive and can cause asphyxiation. "Water supplies that contain methane should be carefully vented so that it cannot accumulate in distribution lines, water heaters, pressure tanks, water treatment equipment, or well houses." So warns *Domestic Water Treatment.*

Hydrogen sulfide, most famous for its rotten-egg smell, can cause black stains on silverware. Worse, it's a flammable, highly toxic gas—a fact that's not widely understood or recognized. It too is a byproduct of natural decomposition. The EPA recommends that this gas, in concentrations higher than .05 mg/L, be removed from drinking water.

Fortunately, activated carbon has an affinity for many dissolved gases, including hydrogen sulfide. And activated charcoal filters (64) will remove relatively low levels of this smelly gas. How long the filter will last before saturation is reached, can't be accurately predicted, however.

If dissolved hydrogen sulfide is present in amounts greater than .05 ppm, an oxidizing filter, which uses potassium permanganate (60) may be the answer. The process of oxydizing hydrogen sulfide to elemental sulfur, though, takes about three times as much oxygen as does treating the same amount of iron water. So the filter needs *frequent* treatment with potassium permanganate—as often as once a day. This fact alone discourages many homeowners from installing such a filter.

Continuous chlorination through a chemical feed pump is the most foolproof solution to this particular gas problem. Chlorine also oxidizes hydrogen sulfide, but bear in mind that the sulfur precipitate that's formed as a result also needs to be filtered out.

67. HEAVY METALS AND OTHER CHEMICAL POLLUTANTS

In this country, as we gradually convert to the metric system, the amount of pollutant in water will be described more and more frequently in terms of milligrams per liter (mg/L) instead of parts per million (ppm). Yet the two are essentially equivalent; one part per million being about the same as a milligram in a liter.

We'll become closer observers of what would have seemed infinitesimally small differences in our water's chemical content just a few years ago. The discovery of pollutants like *heavy metals* and other trace elements in groundwater is relatively new—*so* new, health officials admit, they're still struggling to learn how to deal with it. If you live in the state of New York, for example, and take your water from a well, chances are two in five your water contains some sort of chemical contaminant. That's the official word from the state Department of Health.

Love Canal

The by-now famous Love Canal tragedy was a widely publicized national disaster. Pregnant women in that community near Niagara Falls, New York, had an abnormally high incidence of miscarriage, and too many of their children developed inexplicable diseases. The deadly problem was traced to a variety of chemicals in a long-abandoned industrial dump. What frightens officials most is the likelihood that Love Canal is not an isolated case. There is "enormous potential" for contamination from other dumps, spills, pipeline and storage-tank leaks, they say.

Gasoline, found in almost any home, is a very toxic and persistent sub-

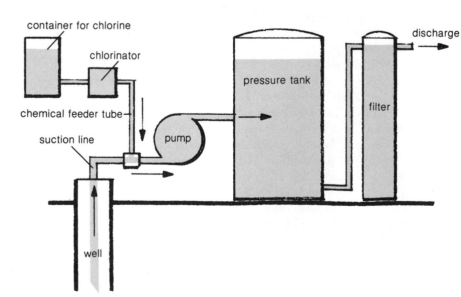

A fail-safe system for removing all types of quantities of iron in drinking water. Adding chlorine caused iron particles to form, and these are removed in the filtering unit. The chlorine also kills iron bacteria, which might otherwise stain fixtures in the home.

stance containing, among other things, benzene, a cancer-causing chemical. Petroleum products are spilled more often than any other toxins, and are considered by the New York Department of Environmental Conservation to be the single most common chemical pollutant.

Water is considered "unfit for human consumption" when it contains just three ppm of gasoline—about three drops in a bathtub of water. After a spill, gasoline in the ground may form an attachment to soil particles for a long period of time, and is very slow to break down into simpler, less harmful ingredients. Later, when there's enough moisture, this fickle but insidious substance divorces itself from the soil, takes up with passing groundwater, and eventually makes its way into somebody's water supply.

A complete chemical analysis can be expensive—between $400 and $500 (in 1988) to test for just ten possible contaminants—says Jack Hill, public health administrator for the Dutchess County, New York, Department of Health. And the chemical analysis may not bring peace of mind. Test results may take three months or more to return because laboratories have such heavy backlogs.

These are some of the things the busy chemists are looking for:

COBALT, like many trace elements, is essential to human health—but only in minute amounts. Too much in our water causes liver damage. Arsenic, lead, cadmium, mercury, and selenium, in excessive doses, are other substances that have adverse effects on human health. Industry, mining, agriculture, even the use of everyday household items like detergents, all contribute to the poisoning of groundwater.

ARSENIC, for example, is found naturally in many rocks and soil, where it dissolves too slowly to present a threat. But it's used in unnatural amounts during some manufacturing processes, including tanning, metal preparation, and the making of both ceramics and pesticides. The federal limit on arsenic in drinking water is .05 mg/L. BARIUM, another pollutant, is limited to 1 mg/L. CADMIUM is a heavy metal that accumulates in the liver, kidneys, and thyroid. A drinking water supply should contain no more than .01 mg/L of cadmium, the government tells us.

CHROMIUM and COPPER are often common contaminants, each limited to .05 mg/L. Lead is a cumulative poison that remains in the human system indefinitely. Prolonged accumulation causes illness and death. It's also believed to contribute to mental retardation in children. LEAD usually comes to us indirectly through automotive exhaust, paints, lead roofs, lead pipes, and the solder used to connect copper tubing. There are historians who believe the fall of the Roman Empire can be partially attributed to the fact that Romans moved much of their water through primitive lead pipes. MERCURY is another dangerous heavy metal, found in astonishing quantities recently in fish in Lake Erie and in Japan.

SELENIUM causes disease in land animals, particularly livestock. SILVER, used in electroplating, and food, beverage, and photographic processing, causes "argyria" in humans—a permanent bluish skin color. Selenium concentrations should be limited to .01 mg/L, silver to .05. ZINC is used in galvanizing, paint, and some insecticides. It's not deadly unless consumed in very large quantities, but it produces objectionable tastes and can make water appear milky or scummy. Water samples in some parts of the nation now show "hazardous" amounts of radioactive materials like Radium 226 and Strontium 90.

CHLOROFORM, BENZENE, and PCBs cause other serious problems. PCBs, known less often as *polychlorinated biphenals*, form a toxic oil that accumulates in our body fat and can eventually become carcinogenic. Sulfates have a laxative effect if more than 250 ppm are borne in drinking water. What's more, various pesticides have been found with frightening frequency in homes that have been treated for termites.

Alarming as the presence of these toxins may be, it's reassuring to learn that some of them, particularly strontium, copper, and barium, are greatly reduced, along with iron calcium and magnesium, when water is treated in an ordinary home water softener. Zinc, cadmium, arsenic, molybdenum, aluminum, silver, nickle, cobalt, lead, chromium, and vanadium are not.

68. NITRATE

In *Drinking Water Standards*, the U.S. Public Health Service says,

> Serious and occasionally fatal poisonings in infants have occurred following ingestion of well waters shown to contain nitrate (NO3). This has occurred with sufficient frequency and widespread geographic distribution to compel recognition of the hazard by assigning a limit to the concentration of nitrate in drinking water.
>
> Nitrate poisoning appears to be confined to infants during their first few months of life; adults drinking the same water are not affected, but breast-fed infants of mothers drinking such water may be poisoned. Cows drinking water containing nitrate may produce milk sufficiently high in nitrate to result in infant poisoning. Both man and animals can be poisoned by nitrate if the concentration is sufficiently great.

Nitrate originates, to a certain extent, in the atmosphere, in legume plants and in decomposing plant material, but it comes to us in dangerous quantities primarily through sewage and nitrogenous fertilizers. *Domestic Water Treatment* says, "In several of the heavily fertilized and irrigated regions west of the Mississippi River, the concentration of nitrate in both surface and groundwater has increased to alarming amounts." It affects very young pigs, calves, and brood animals as well as human babies.

Nitrate diminishes the oxygen-carrying capacity of the blood, and blueness of the skin is one of the most obvious symptoms of nitrate poisoning. Nitrate concentration in water can vary a great deal from one season to the next. During the growing season it's used by plants, but during wet times, when plants are dormant, large amounts of nitrate can infiltrate the water table.

A strong coloring agent called *fluorescein* is sometimes used to solve the riddle of underground contamination by nitrates as well as bacteria. Poured in a toilet or manure pile as far as a mile away, it traces subterranean water movement from the barn or septic system to a well, spring, or pond. It shows up as bright red coloring in water where pollution is strong, and light green if the solution is weak.

The outlook for water supplies seriously filled with nitrates is not optimistic at this point. Authorities agree that the best solution is either removal of the contaminating source, or relocation of the well. Nitrate *can* be removed by several types of ion-exchange demineralization, reverse osmosis (69), or distillation—any one of which could prove a very expensive process.

The chief problem with trying to remove nitrate in water through complete deionization is that the resin in such a softener must be regenerated with hydrochloric acid and sodium hydroxide, two materials that are both corrosive and very hazardous. To make matters worse, the effluent coming from such a deionizer that has *failed* to be regenerated will have a stronger concentration of nitrate than water going in.

69. REVERSE OSMOSIS

Plants contain relatively high concentrations of dissolved salts, and it's for that reason they're able to feed themselves, through their roots, with the help of osmosis. The root wall, separating the saltiness within from the fresh water outside, is little more than a thin membrane. During osmosis, fresh water moves through the membrane to mix with the salt water on the opposite side. It's a natural process long recognized by science. In fact, osmosis experiments may be performed by any junior high school science class.

Water science has taken it a step further, realizing that if pressure is applied to water on the *salty* side of a membrane, osmosis can be reversed. As salt water is pushed to the fresh-water side, in this case, salty minerals, hardness minerals like calcium and magnesium, dirt particles, bacteria, and viruses will all be strained out by the membrane.

Reverse osmosis, although it's slower than normal ion-exchange water softening, is now used more and more to remove salt and brackishness from drinking water. It's particularly beneficial to those on sodium-restricted diets. Regular water softeners, remember, subtract calcium and magnesium ions, but *add* sodium to the treated water in exchange. (61)

Reverse osmosis (RO) units are sometimes advertised as water *purifiers.* And they purify well. One of two types of membranes may be used in such a purifier: a *cellulose acetate (CA) membrane,* or a *nylon membrane.* The cellulose acetate membrane is considered the more versatile of the two. A high-pressure pump pushes water through the membrane at a force between 200 and 400 psi—many times the normal 20 to 60 psi in-line household pressure. One pressure gauge should be installed immediately before, and a second gauge right after this pump.

Within the membrane module, solids caught by the membrane are continually cleaned away by incoming water, then sent out of the module in reject water. Typically about one gallon of reject water is produced for every three gallons of purified water. So there must be an abundant supply of untreated water to begin with, if reverse osmosis is to be used.

If the water is also pretreated with chlorine, the membrane will be constantly disinfected as well. In other words, the module is self-cleaning, and should rarely need servicing. An activated carbon filter, also installed before the membrane module, can remove large particles before they ever reach the membrane. In most cases the membrane itself needs to be replaced every one to three years. And during its active life it can be expected to reject 98 to 99 percent of the sodium chloride, sodium carbonate, sodium sulfate, calcium chloride, and calcium carbonate from incoming water.

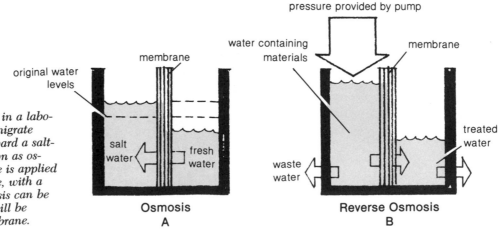

(A) *In nature, as well as in a laboratory, fresh water will migrate through a membrane toward a saltier solution. This is known as osmosis. (B) But if pressure is applied to water on the salty side, with a pump for example, osmosis can be reversed, and minerals will be strained out by the membrane.*

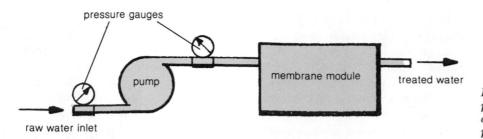

Basic reverse-osmosis unit. Because pressure is critical, it must be closely monitored, so gauges are placed before and after the pump.

Very *cold* water, however, cannot be treated as effectively as warmer water. *Domestic Water Treatment* says, "A typical RO system will produce water much more efficiently at higher temperatures. In fact, it will produce only half the quality of 40° F. that it would produce at 80° F."

Because reverse osmosis is slow, the unit may need to work full time. The actual module should present few problems. But extra storage and a repressuration pump will be needed, making the complete organization of an RO system fairly complex. It should be monitored closely, and will undoubtedly need maintenance from time to time.

70. FILTERS

There have been several detailed discussions of filters in earlier sections, but it might be appropriate at this point to make some general cautioning remarks about filtration:

Most hydrologists agree that water in the natural environment must pass through at least ten feet of earth before it can be considered "completely filtered." Many man-made filters are direct imitations of natural filtration. A simple bed of sand or gravel, for example, might be expected to remove impurities in a space far less than ten feet.

The effectiveness and speed of *any* filter, of course, depends on the size and consistency of the filter media. In nature, clay and hardpan filter best because the media is the finest. But it's also known that the finer the filter material, the slower water passes through it—*unless* there's pressure exerted on it artificially, as in the case of reverse osmosis. When there's pressure, though, there's the added possibility of exceeding the filter's capacity to remove unwanted substances from the water. Hurrying water through a filter to maintain pressure or fulfill demand may be to sacrifice purity.

A *slow-sand* filter, for instance, where water is permitted to soak through a bed of very fine sand, may have a capacity between 60 and 180 gallons a day per square foot of filter. *Pressure sand* filters, where water is pumped through the media (63), work a good deal faster. But are they as effective? Of course the answer has a great deal to do with the nature of the untreated water. All filters that are left un-backwashed become ineffective at best. At worst, they're totally unable to transmit water at all.

Clarifier filters are just what the name suggests. They're meant to free water of suspended matter. Unfortunately, as we've learned, clarity is not a sure sign of safe water, and the clarifying efforts may be little more than cosmetic. Small faucet units, used in many households, made of porous stone, ceramic or unglazed porcelain, are often called *Pasteur filters*, but some don't pasteurize. (72) Activated charcoal filters, as we've also learned, absorb dissolved gases, fine particles of turbidity, and dissolved organic matter.

New Technology

Carbon filter technology has only been around since 1956, and it's proving *not* to be the wonder cure we'd hoped. Carbon filters are not completely effective in removing chemical pollution from water—though many health authorities, at both the state and local levels, insist they're one of the best solutions available.

Activated carbon *does* filter out water pollutants by causing poorly dissolved chemicals to cling to its surface. One ounce of porous activated carbon, incredibly, has about a square mile of surface area—enough to collect a lot of waterborne chemicals. The problem develops when carbon can't accept any more pollutants, and poisonous substances are no longer removed. At this point the filter must be replaced before it actually contributes *more* contamination. But the only way to tell if the filter is working properly is to test the filtered water. So frequent testing is necessary—but often forgotten.

A carbon filter may continue to remove turbidity, taste, and odor from water, even after it's no longer removing chemical pollutants. In 1979 and 1980 the EPA spent more than a year testing a wide variety of carbon filters on the market, and found that their effectiveness ranged from 0 to 100 percent. Frank Bell is an EPA official who became deeply involved in the 1981 controversy surrounding IBM's Fishkill, New York, plant. The huge business-machine manufacturer was accused of massive groundwater contamination, and the situation threatened to become another Love Canal. As locals scrambled for every activated carbon filter in sight, Bell cautioned them not to believe all they read on a filter manufacturer's claim.

Quoted in the *Poughkeepsie Journal*, he said, "You can say just about anything you want until the Federal Trade Commission stops you, but they aren't doing anything now in the way of stopping false claims (about filters)." In other words, let the buyer beware.

Some home water filters, he added, have silver mixed with the carbon. (75) The silver is meant to prevent harmful bacterial buildup in the activated charcoal. But silver itself is often used as an ingredient in insecticide, and may possibly make the filter more dangerous still. Be skeptical as you select filters for your home.

Effectiveness of Slow-Sand Filter Media

Material Passing Sieve (percent)	U.S. Sieve No.	Material Passing Sieve (percent)	U.S. Sieve No.
99	4	33–55	30
90–97	12	17–35	40
75–90	16	4–10	60
60–80	20	1	100

71. CHLORINATION AND SUPERCHLORINATION

Just so there's no confusion: when water is freed of living things—bacterial and viral contamination—it's "disinfected." When it's treated to remove inert substances, minerals, and chemicals, it's being "conditioned."

During emergencies (and during a pinch when your chlorinator breaks down), water can be disinfected by boiling it, vigorously, for a full minute. Five to ten drops of tincture of iodine in one quart of drinking water will kill all disease-causing bacteria, and just about everything else living in the container. Chlorine bleach can be used just as well, at the same rate of ten drops per quart.

Automatic disinfection is accomplished by chlorination, pasteurization (72), ultraviolet light (73), ozonization (74), silver (75), or iodization. (76)

Those with any knowledge of water will agree that disinfection, where needed, is *the* most important water-treatment process, and that chlorination is by far the most popular method of disinfection. They'll also be quick to point out that high turbidity (63), "locks up" bacteria and other organisms, making chlorination less effective. The clearer the water to be treated, the more effective the treatment.

What's more, disinfection works better in water with a higher temperature, but a *lower* pH. (65) The higher the concentration of chlorine, the faster, and more complete the disinfection—exactly as you'd expect. Chlorine should contact water being treated for twenty to thirty minutes. There are pump-type chlorinators, injector chlorinators ("jets"), and tablet-type chlorinators.

Chlorine is available in three forms: solid, liquid, and gas. Chlorine gas is often used as a disinfectant in municipal water systems, but rarely in smaller home systems. Liquid chlorine is *sodium hypochlorite,* better known to most

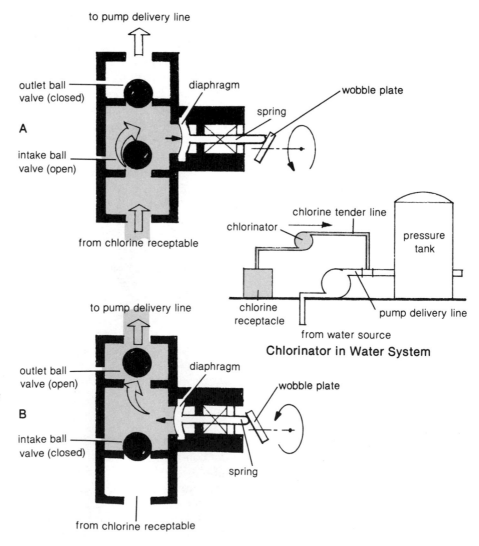

A diaphragm-type chlorinator operates whenever the pump is running. (A) In the suction stroke, the motor-driven wobble plate allows the spring to pull the diaphragm back. The partial vacuum opens the intake valve, and chlorine enters the chamber. (B) As the wobble plate rotates 180 degrees, the diaphragm is pushed in, forcing the chlorine out to the pump delivery line. This is the delivery stroke. A fixed amount of chlorine solution is pumped out with each stroke. In other illustration, the chlorinator is shown fitted into the water system.

134

of us as *laundry bleach*. Clorox. Purex. Dry or solid chlorine is *calcium hypochlorite*, which comes in powder or tablet form.

A *pump-type chlorinator* is a positive displacement chemical feeder in that it delivers a definite amount of chlorine solution with each stroke. It's much like a positive-acting piston pump. (38) A piston and diaphragm are used to move chlorine solution into the pump delivery line. It's installed before the pressure tank to be sure chlorine mixes thoroughly in the water.

Injector-type chlorinators, also called aspirators or jets, work more like ejector pumps. (41) A small amount of water is diverted from the pressure tank to the injector unit. Here it passes through a nozzle at high velocity, creating a partial vacuum in the chlorine suction line. The amount of chlorine flowing from its container can be regulated by a convenient feed-adjusting screw.

Tablet hypochlorinators use a small amount of water from the pump delivery line. (This extra bit of water is put off to the side with the help of a *restricting valve*.) It's circulated through a tank containing calcium hypochlorite tablets, and the resulting solution is then sent to the pressure tank.

The language of chlorination is complex but not that difficult to understand. *Dosage* is the amount of chlorine fed into the system. As it mixes with organic matter, minerals, and chemicals in the water, a certain amount of this dosage is used up before any disinfection takes place. The amount that's used, then, is the *chlorine demand*. What's *left over* is called the *chlorine residual*, and it's the chlorine residual that disinfects. There's just one catch. . . .

If the water contains ammonia nitrogen (as pond or surface water might),

Well Water Disinfection

Depth of Water in Well (feet)		Well Diameter (inches)															
		2	3	4	5	6	8	10	12	16	20	24	28	32	36	42	48
5	A	1T	1T	1T	1T	1T	1T	2T	3T	5T	6T	3 oz.	4 oz.	5 oz.	7 oz.	9 oz.	12 oz.
	B	1C	1C	1C	1C	1C	1C	1C	1C	2C	4C	1Q	2Q	3Q	3Q	4Q	5Q
10	A	1T	1T	1T	1T	1T	2T	3T	5T	8T	4 oz.	6 oz.	8 oz.	10 oz.	13 oz.	1½ lb.	1½ lb.
	B	1C	1C	1C	1C	1C	1C	2C	2C	1Q	2Q	3Q	4Q	4Q	6Q	8Q	2½G
15	A	1T	1T	1T	1T	2T	3T	5T	8T	4 oz.	6 oz.	9 oz.	12 oz.	1 lb.	1½ lb.	1½ lb.	2 lb.
	B	1C	1C	1C	1C	1C	2C	3C	4C	2Q	2½Q	4Q	5Q	6Q	2G	3G	4G
20	A	1T	1T	1T	2T	3T	4T	6T	3 oz.	5 oz.	8 oz.						
	B	1C	1C	1C	1C	1C	2C	4C	1Q	2½Q	3½Q						
30	A	1T	1T	3T	3T	4T	6T	3 oz.	4 oz.	8 oz.	12 oz.						
	B	1C	1C	1C	1C	2C	4C	1½Q	2Q	4Q	5Q						
40	A	1T	1T	2T	4T	6T	8T	4 oz.	6 oz.	10 oz.	1 lb.						
	B	1C	1C	1C	2C	2C	1Q	2Q	2½Q	4½Q	7Q						
60	A	1T	2T	3T	5T	8T	4 oz.	6 oz.	9 oz.								
	B	1C	1C	2C	3C	4C	2Q	3Q	4Q								
80	A	1T	3T	4T	7T	9T	5 oz.	8 oz.	12 oz.								
	B	1C	1C	2C	4C	1Q	2Q	3½Q	5Q								
100	A	2T	3T	5T	8T	4 oz.	7 oz.	10 oz.	1 lb.								
	B	1C	2C	3C	1Q	1½Q	2½Q	4Q	6Q								
150	A	3T	5T	8T	4 oz.	6 oz.	10 oz.	1 lb.	1½ lb.								
	B	2C	2C	4C	2Q	2½Q	4Q	6Q	2½G								

NOTE: Quantities of calcium hypochlorite, 70 percent (rows A) and liquid household bleach, 5.25 percent (rows B) required for water well disinfection. Quantities are indicated as: T = tablespoons; oz. = ounces (by weight); C = cups; lb. = pounds; Q = quarts; G = gallons.

Figures corresponding to rows A are amounts of solid calcium hypochlorite required; those corresponding to rows B are amounts of liquid household bleach.

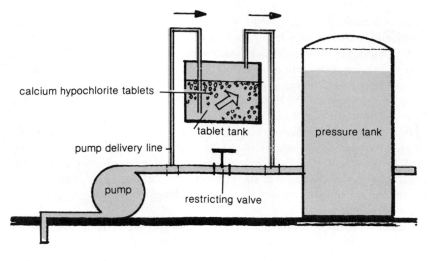

calcium hypochlorite tablets

tablet tank

pressure tank

pump delivery line

pump

restricting valve

water source

A tablet hypochlorinator. The restricting valve is used to divert a small amount of water through the tablet tank. Here it mixes with calcium hypochlorite tablets, and the resulting solution is sent to the pressure tank.

chlorine will combine with it to form *combined chlorine residual.* Unfortunately this marriage isn't very potent as a disinfectant. Any chlorine that *doesn't* combine with ammonia is known as *free chlorine residual. It's* twenty-five times more effective as a bacteria-killer than combined chlorine residual.

Contact time is the period between the injection of chlorine and when the water is used. Health authorities recommend twenty to thirty minutes of contact time, with a free chlorine residual of .2 to .5 parts per million chlorine. If the pressure tank fails to provide enough contact time for chlorine to do its work, a coiled pipe can be installed on the supply side of the pump, or by adding a mixing tank. The idea is just to stall the water before it gets to the faucet. Sometimes chlorine is fed directly into the well below the pump, as has already been mentioned.

Superchlorination is a way to *reduce* contact time by adding a higher concentration of chlorine. Here the idea is to maintain a free chlorine residual of three to five ppm—about ten times the amount used in simple chlorination. All bacteria will be killed in five to seven minutes, although nobody seems to agree on the exact time. As you might expect, superchlorination will leave water with a strong chlorine taste. Drinking water can be *dechlorinated* with an activated carbon filter at or near the faucet.

The beauty of chlorine is that it continues to provide antibacterial protection, it's reasonably priced, and the amount of chlorine residual can easily be measured if you own an inexpensive test kit. Like all good things, however, chlorination is not without its drawbacks—real and suspected.

Chlorine doesn't help a bit in correcting water contaminated with chemicals. In fact, its effect is just the opposite. In some cases it's been proven to *enhance* rather than decrease the harmful effects of chemical pollution.

Does it cause cancer? It's been suspected for some time. When combined with organic matter it forms substances called trialomethanes, which, sure enough, cause cancer in laboratory mice. More recently, an EPA study released in December 1980, links heavy chlorination to bladder, colon, and intestinal cancer. Yet, aside from ozonization, which leaves no helpful residue in treated water, there seems to be no vastly superior alternative to chlorination. At least for the time being.

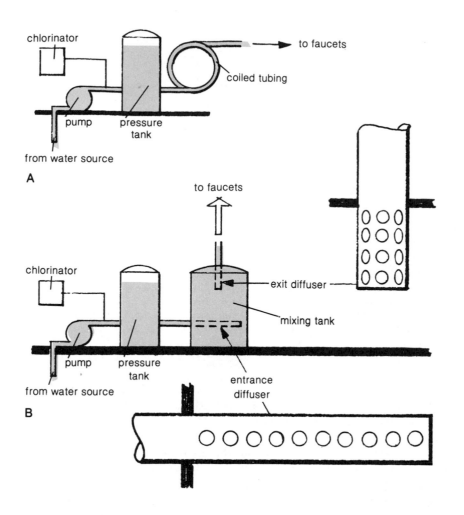

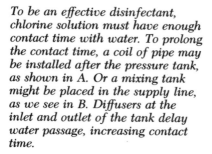

To be an effective disinfectant, chlorine solution must have enough contact time with water. To prolong the contact time, a coil of pipe may be installed after the pressure tank, as shown in A. Or a mixing tank might be placed in the supply line, as we see in B. Diffusers at the inlet and outlet of the tank delay water passage, increasing contact time.

72. PASTEURIZATION

The concept of pasteurization has been around for some time, but the idea of disinfecting drinking water with heat has been applied to domestic water systems only recently. It works the same as milk pasteurization. If water temperature is raised above 140° F. and held at that temperature, all pathogenic organisms will be destroyed.

A pasteurizing unit consists of an extra water loop installed before the pressure tank. Within the loop are a small circulating pump, an electric heating element, a retention tube, a solenoid valve, a heat exchanger, and a storage tank. Water enters the system through the heat exchanger. Here its temperature is raised to around 150° F. by water *already* pasteurized at 161° F.

This preheated water moves out of the heat exchanger, through the circulating pump, and into the heating element, where its temperature is boosted to 161°F. From the heating element it moves into the coiled retention tube. This tube, about thirty feet long, retains the water for at least fifteen seconds, long enough for pasteurization to take place. It's then passed on to the solenoid valve.

The solenoid valve may be the most critical element in the system. A sensor in its thermostat switch lets the solenoid know the temperature of water about to enter the valve. If it's 161° or higher, the solenoid passes the pasteurized water to the heat exchanger, where it gives up about ten degrees of its heat to incoming water, before moving on to the treated-water storage

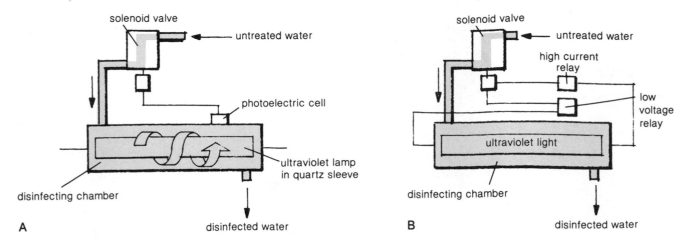

solenoid valve

untreated water

photoelectric cell

ultraviolet lamp
in quartz sleeve

disinfecting chamber

A

disinfected water

solenoid valve

untreated water

high current
relay

low
voltage
relay

ultraviolet light

disinfecting chamber

B

disinfected water

Water that's exposed to ultraviolet light (UV) will be disinfected. A thin layer of water must pass close to the UV lamp. (A) Water flow might be controlled by a solenoid valve directed by a photoelectric cell located right at the disinfecting chamber. (B) Other units use two electrical relays, one for high current, one for low. As the UV lamp gets older, its intensity diminishes, and more electrical current must be supplied.

tank. It will arrive in storage at about 150°. Any water passing through the solenoid valve that's *colder* than 161° is directed back through the heating element via a bypass line to the pump.

Because only a small amount of water can be pasteurized at one time, the capacity of the treated-water storage must be great enough to meet peak demands. From storage, it is moved by the regular water system's pressure pump into the pressure tank, then toward the various outlets in the house.

Unfortunately, water pasteurization is not cheap. It uses a lot of electricity. To be at all efficient the unit must operate about half the time—at least twelve hours a day, producing twenty to twenty-four gallons of treated

In a pasteurizing unit, water is disinfected through heating. Unprocessed water enters the heat exchanger where it is warmed by water that has already been treated. Then it passes to the electric heating element where its temperature is raised to 161° F. It's held at that temperature in the retention tube, before moving to the thermostatic switch. A sensor in the switch lets the solenoid know the temperature of the water about to enter that valve. If it is 161° or higher, the solenoid sends the water to the heat exchanger. Any water passing through the solenoid that is colder than 161° is sent back to the heating element.

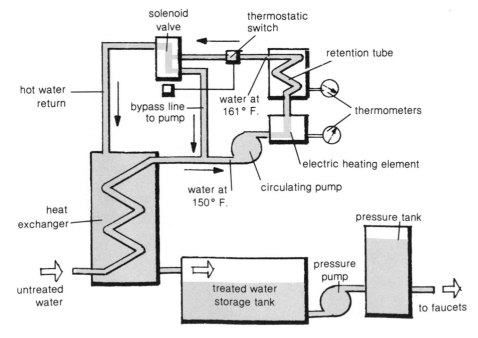

solenoid
valve

thermostatic
switch

retention tube

hot water
return

bypass line
to pump

water at
161° F.

thermometers

water at
150° F.

electric heating element

circulating pump

heat
exchanger

pressure tank

pressure
pump

untreated
water

treated water
storage tank

to faucets

water per hour. If it works less often, the heating-up and cool-down periods create an even higher and more costly demand. Also, unlike chlorine disinfection which provides ongoing germicidal protection in the chlorine residue, there's no guarantee pasteurized water won't become reinfected in storage, or at some point later in the system.

73. ULTRAVIOLET LIGHT

Ultraviolet light ("UV" for short) is deadly to bacteria, and there are units available which circulate untreated water around a central ultraviolet lamp. It's another successful effort on man's part to imitate nature—in this case the killing action of sunlight in open streams and other bodies of surface water.

An ultraviolet lamp is not unlike an ordinary fluorescent light, except that

Care and Maintenance of Disinfection Units

Service and Inspection Jobs	Methods of Disinfection			
	Simple Chlorination	*Superchlorination-Dechlorination*	*Electric Pasteurization*	*Ultraviolet*
Mixing of Chemical Solution	Laundry bleach is diluted with soft water. Proportions vary, 1 part laundry bleach diluted with 4 to 10 parts water. Mix every 2 months in cool weather, monthly in hot weather.	Can use laundry bleach (sodium hypochlorite) without dilution. Calcium hypochlorite requires dilution.	No chemicals used.	No chemical used.
	Amount of chlorine needed—approx. 1 gal. of laundry bleach (5.25% solution) will treat 50,000 gal. of water at rate of 1 ppm.	Amount of chlorine needed—one gallon of laundry bleach treats about 10,000 gallons of water at rate of 5 ppm.		
Mechanical or Electrical Servicing	Footvalve on chlorinator may stick from accumulation of deposits if hard water or calcium hypochlorite is used. Valve sticking may develop on pump-type units for same reason. Orifice clogs on jet-type units. (The orifice is the small opening in the jet which develops pumping action.)		Heating element(s) may need to be changed about every 3 to 5 years. (Field experience is too limited to know whether other troubles may be encountered.)	Units with automatic safety controls require lamp tube replacement about every 1 to 3 years. If operated without automatic safety controls, change lamps about every 6 months. Tubes may break in plumbing systems that develop water hammer.
Recommended Frequency of Inspection	Weekly.	Weekly.	Weekly.	Weekly.
Recommended Frequency of Cleaning	Twice yearly to check and remove any accumulated deposits (and clean strainers on some units).		No definite period; however, accumulating tank may have to be cleaned or disinfected with chlorine occasionally. May have to flush deposits from pasteurizer yearly with calgon or similar cleaner.	Tubes should be removed and cleaned about every 4 to 6 months. Filter, used to remove small particles, should be serviced monthly.

the inside of the UV tube has no phosphorescent coating meant to transform ultraviolet radiation into visible light. The UV tube is surrounded by a quartz sleeve to protect the lamp from the chilling effect of cold water entering the unit. The lamp itself must be kept hot enough to have a germicidal impact on waterborne microorganisms.

Each UV disinfecting unit is designed to allow a very thin layer of water to pass by the lamp, so each drop is exposed to light. UV's killing action is instantaneous, but tiny particles of mud (turbidity) can shield bacteria from the light, making the disinfection less effective. Iron in water can also interfere with light transmission. For these reasons incoming water should be filtered *before* it enters the disinfecting chamber. Flow through the unit can be increased or slowed at the regulator valve.

As any UV lamp gets older it gives off less light. An electric eye, or *photoelectric cell,* installed next to the disinfecting chamber, measures the amount of light passing through the water at all times and instructs the solenoid valve to close whenever the light intensity gets too low. Obviously, any water allowed to pass through an ultraviolet purifier during an interruption in electrical service would receive no treatment. So such safety devices are needed.

Some units use a *time delay* device. This allows the lamp to reach its full output of ultraviolet light before any water is permitted to enter the chamber. Others use two electrical relays, one for high current, one for low. If there's no current at all, or very low voltage, the low-current relay shuts off the water supply. As the lamp gets older and UV intensity decreases, more current must be gradually supplied to the tube. When the current becomes *too* high, the high-current relay shuts off the water.

In time, the quartz sleeve will become coated with dirt particles that screen light from the lamp. Most manufacturers of UV disinfectant units provide a wider mechanism for cleaning the quartz surface. Some of these wipers are hand-operated; others work automatically using a small water turbine within the chamber.

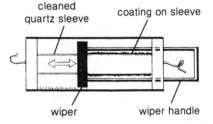

cleaned quartz sleeve

coating on sleeve

wiper

wiper handle

A hand-operated wiper cleans the quartz sleeve.

Ultraviolet irradiators operate continually more or less, and are usually installed downsteam from the pressure tank. They require little maintenance and add no materials to the drinking water, thereby producing no tastes or odors. On the negative side, they're far less effective if water is not thoroughly filtered beforehand to remove turbidity and bacterial slime. UV also leaves no germicidal residual. Because ultraviolet lamps lose their strength in time, they need to be replaced two or three times a year. A final disadvantage may be that there's no easy way to measure how effectively the unit is working at any given time, without taking a water sample.

74. OZONIZATION

In *Domestic Water Treatment*, the first paragraph of the section on ozonization reads like a sales pitch:

> Ozone is a form of oxygen having three atoms per molecule, rather than the two atoms typical of atmospheric oxygen. Ozone has greater germicidal effectiveness against bacteria and viruses than chlorine. It also reduces iron, manganese, lead, and sulfur concentrations in water and eliminates most tastes and odors. Furthermore its potency is not affected by pH, temperature, and ammonia content.

Then why isn't ozone regarded as a universal panacea for all water ills? Part of the answer may be economic, part mechanical, and part habitual. The book goes on to say that ozonization is used for water disinfection in more than 1,000 cities throughout the world. Yet, because it leaves no germicidal residual that can be carried into the rest of a system's distribution lines, it has not been widely accepted in the United States. In short, we're used to chlorine.

Ozonization equipment requires a higher initial investment than a chlorination system, and is more expensive to operate. The EPA found, for instance, that a system in Grand Isle, Iowa, needed extensive maintenance, adjustment, and constant attention even during its first year of operation. Still, the experts predict we're likely to see a boom in individual ozonization systems before the 21st century.

The chemical symbol for ozone is O_3. Normal oxygen is O_2. O_3 is an unstable molecule. It will happily give up one of its atoms and revert back to O_2. So ozonization must take place near the point of water use. To make ozone, O_2 is passed through an electronic discharge gap between two electrodes and a single insulating *dielectric*. Within this arc, O_2 is broken down in individual oxygen atoms, some of which regroup as O_3. A byproduct of this electrical process is heat, and the electrodes need to be cooled, either by air or water.

Water to be treated by this ozone is passed through a nearby venturi, and the partial vacuum that results pulls the newly created ozone into the water. There is no need to regulate O_3 dosage. As long as there's an excess of O_3, which will soon dissolve out of the water, changes in ozone demand will be taken care of automatically. The dramatic results of ozonization can be measured right after the point of treatment.

75. SILVER TREATMENT

Silver, in very small doses, is a strong yet safe disinfectant—even though the substance is generally considered poisonous. When applied to water, it destroys the proteins in the cell protoplasm of bacteria.

In a silver-treatment unit, a diatomaceous-earth filter or an activated-carbon filter is impregnated with silver nitrate or silver in some other form. Thus silver is slowly imparted to water making its way through the filter. These units are simple, and small enough to be placed in almost any water line. Once drinking water has been disinfected, no taste or odor is left in it.

Silver-treatment filters increase the silver concentration of water to about .03 ppm, well below the EPA's strict limits of .05 ppm. This .03 ppm is more than enough to destroy almost all microorganisms, including pathogenic viruses.

The problem with silver filters is that they are easily fouled by turbid water. Prefiltering may be needed, as well as frequent backwashing and replacement. Silver also reacts with organic matter, iron, sulfur, and other chemicals in a way that decreases its germicidal efficiency. Necessary contact time for silver is also much longer than for chlorine.

Eventually silver treatment may prove to be very economical—in spite of silver's status as a precious metal—because it's used in such miniscule quantities. For now, the federal government is dragging its feet on approval of silver treatment for home systems. They're still concerned about interfering chemicals and the long contact time needed for disinfection.

76. IODINATION

Iodine behaves much like chlorine as a disinfectant, though it costs much more. Its special advantage is that it doesn't react negatively to ammonia in water, as does chlorine. NASA uses iodination to protect drinking water for our astronauts in space, the U.S. Forest Service has used the process for years in many of its remote facilities, and our armed forces have long used

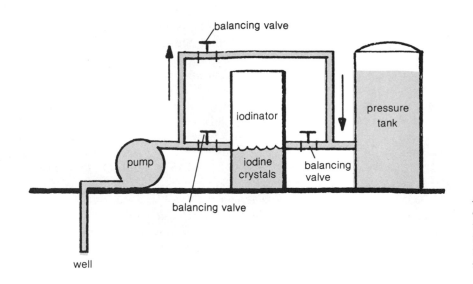

balancing valve

iodinator

pressure
tank

pump

iodine
crystals

balancing
valve

well

balancing valve

*An iodinator is relatively simple
and easy to maintain. Iodine is fed
into the water supply line between
the pump and pressure tank. Contact time must be 15 minutes or
more.*

iodine to disinfect drinking water in the field. Iodine's main advantage, according to *Domestic Water Treatment,* is that while chlorine loses its effectiveness when water reaches a pH of eight or more, iodine will disinfect
until a water's pH gets as high as ten.

In a home iodinator, elemental iodine (I_2) or hypoiodous acid (HOI) is
continuously fed into the water supply line between the pump and the
pressure tank. This is accomplished when water is diverted through an iodination tank filled with iodine crystals. Contact time must be fifteen minutes or more. If water is not likely to be held in the pressure tank that long,
a special detention tank may have to be installed. For the most part, iodination equipment is simple and easy to maintain because it has no moving
parts.

To its discredit, iodine costs about twenty times as much as chlorine. And
some people are allergic to it. It may also leave a slight taste and iodine
smell in drinking water. These are harmless, but some people find it objectionable.

My Water Softener

In the end, after exhaustive research on all kinds of water-treatment
equipment, I bought a standard ion-exchanging water softener. I'm not entirely sure why. An iron filter, suggested by Mr. Roe, might have been
enough. I guess it was the potassium permanganate that scared me.

Mr. Roe's colleague, Emmett Morton, recommended a Marlo Series 155
water conditioner, known to be "especially effective on iron-bearing water."
The unit would eliminate iron, soften, and cost about the same as an iron
filter. It was also readily available, had a fine warranty, and Emmett's
plumbers knew it well. That meant it could be easily installed, and repaired
whenever necessary. Like anybody else, I was as much influenced by cost,
convenience, salesmanship, and ease of service as by the character of the
water to be treated. But it seems to have been a good choice. . . .

The plan of attack also seemed a sound one. We'd kill three birds with
one stone. On a Tuesday Bill Gabaree would install the conditioner, and explain its operation to me in detail. At the same time the Manosh Company
would supply a backhoe. Since my well had an annoying propensity to turn
artesian each spring and fall, spewing rusty-looking water out the top of its

casing and into my driveway, Bill would also put in an overflow line below frost level. (Emmett said, "You should have done that to begin with.") Third, we'd correct the eroding embankment next to the house—the one that miraculously turned into a spring each November, only to dry up again in May. But that Tuesday Murphy's Law prevailed.

The day was a disaster. I was frustrated, furious, and fascinated all at once. The backhoe bucket ate into the bank under a rock outcropping. Four feet below, water suddenly gushed out of the ground, and soon there was a pool of water that grew wider and deeper by the minute. It was a beautiful lesson in spring development. In summer the water simply retreated to a lower level. The hole was enlarged and several yards of one- to two-inch stone were dropped into it.

Trouble Ahead

Bill stepped in and laid two eight-foot lengths of four-inch perforated drain tile in a V formation atop the stone. The near ends of both pipes were connected with a "Y" fitting, while the far ends spread to either side of the huge rock, now unearthed. This tile would intercept water as it rose in the bank and draw it away. Sixteen yards of stone were then added, over the pipe, to fill up the hole. At that point it started to rain—lightly. And what could possibly go wrong, was about to. . . .

The trench from the spring was to pass next to the well casing, about twenty feet nearer the house. Digging hurriedly, the operator forgot the buried coaxial cable for the TV, pointed out to him earlier, and severed it— neatly.

It started to rain harder. My mind flashed back to the previous year, when excavation on the pond had to be halted because of too much rain. The pond could have been finished, the dam seeded and mulched. Except it poured for two weeks. And it was *months* before the job was done. That Tuesday I should have said, "Stop! Wait for drier weather."

But I shut up. The ditching continued, and the pipe from the Y was extended. At the well, Bill burned a hole in the casing with a cutting torch, four feet below grade, attached a fitting, and ran a one-inch overflow line directly into the four-inch spring line. This main line was run to the footing drain beside the house, where it was connected with a "T." Now water from the unwanted spring, and the well overflow could run past the house foundation to an outlet just above the pond, where it would empty.

By the time he had it hooked up it was *pouring* (as it seems to only in Vermont, western Washington, and Oregon), and Bill was working in several inches of water—in the bottom of a 40-foot open trench! In the next two hours it rained over two inches. The young backhoe operator worked frantically to refill the ditch, replace the bank, and move out the excess dirt. But the dirt was turning to soup. I wondered if the driveway would ever be right again.

Softener Connected

Bill went inside to install the softener. Both the thin, resin-filled exchanger and the shorter, fatter brine tank fit between the pressure tank and the water heater. He cut the cold-water line from the pressure tank, ran copper tubing to the softening unit, then back to the cold-water main.

Then he ran a drain line to connect with a trap near the outlet from the clothes washer, leaving an air gap at its end to prevent any possibility of sewage being siphoned back into the softener. The brine-line connection was made, and the unit was plugged into an electrical wall outlet. Bill adjusted the timer so the softener would automatically backwash every other day at 3:30 A.M., and put the brine control at the lowest setting on the dial. The conditioner was ready to go.

Outdoors the rain got heavier. The mud got worse, but the determined operator struggled harder with his backhoe, doing more harm than good. I couldn't look at the mess, and I couldn't sit inside as one should on such a day. In full raingear and rubber boots I wandered the property—depressed. Water was precipitating faster than the ground could accept it, and for the first time ever I saw how surface water moved across my land during a storm.

Pond Rising

The pond level was rising visibly. I began to see why French aristocrats and their groundskeepers of the 18th and 19th centuries became obsessed with the intricacies of drainage. I studied existing drains and planned new ones. Soon I had a shovel and was digging little ditches, directing water here toward the pond, and there away from the house. That afternoon I was a child playing in water, an adult watching springs come to life, a well overflow, experiencing the hydrological cycle firsthand.

When the backhoe broke down the second time, Manosh's men knew it was time to quit. They left me standing in my mud-hole driveway, vowing they'd return as soon as the weather dried. (They ultimately did so, and cleaned up nicely. But the operator forgot again, and cut the by-now spliced TV cable—irreparably this time.) When I drove out of the garage to pick up the kids for supper, I sank to the hubcaps in mud, and nearly got stuck.

But the rain was letting up. Lower in Stowe Hollow, where the Gold Brook parallels the road, I saw that stream-turned-torrent raging full of turbid water, carrying some of my muddy land away with it. . . .

In the middle of the night an unfamiliar chugging and gurgling woke me. My watch said 3:45. The new water softener was in its rinse cycle, right on time. At 7 the shower water felt more slippery than before, and it took longer to rinse shampoo out of my hair with soft water. Coffee tasted differ-

There were headaches the day it was installed, but the water softener works flawlessly now. From left, gas hot water heater, softener, pump control box, pressure tank, and brine tank. The softener unit plugs into the outlet beside the circuit-breaker box.

ent. I *guess* I like softer water better. I'm not sure. I'm still getting used to it.

Emmett Morton dropped by the next day, to check the settings and commiserate about the mess. He was bearing gifts. He handed me two boxes of "Super Iron Out," a commercial mixture of sodium hydrosulfite and sodium bisulfite. (Iron Out, Inc., Fort Wayne, IN 46805)

Three tablespoons of Iron Out in each of the toilet bowls, and half a pound in each toilet tank cleared up the orange water there and removed all stains in less than twenty-four hours. The stain in the dishwasher persists. The fiberglass bathtub/shower had to be scrubbed with Iron Out, and it worked fine. Except it took two days. And breathing the fumes from that cleaning chemical made us cough and choke. All in all, the water's better. But I wonder: if I'd known that spring was right there, and had tapped it sooner, I might not have needed a well at all, and. . . .

7 *DISTRIBUTING WATER*

77. PLANS AND DIAGRAMS

Wilbur and Orville Wright, who made the first flying machines, always insisted, "If you get it right on paper, it will turn out right when it's built." Water distribution systems turn out best when they're thoughtfully planned, diagrammed, and tailored to circumstances rather than bound by tradition.

Long-term considerations for any plumbing machine (it *is* just that) must see beyond initial costs. Convenience and adequate supply to all corners of the system are not the least of your worries. Nor is energy use. Maintenance costs are another large factor. And noise in your system can become a big annoyance.

Plumbing within the house itself may be part of your home's building plan. Plumbing "schematics" normally constitute one page of drawings in a full set of working house plans. Outside sillcocks and hydrants are another story, and here you'll need to do your most careful thinking. For instance: both the USDA and the National Fire Protection Association recommend that hydrants or hose connections be located no farther apart than 100 feet, so a fifty-foot hose can reach just about anywhere there's fire danger. *Your* decision is: how convenient are these fire locations going to be in day-to-day life? Maybe some sort of compromise is in order.

Make a sketch of your property, including all buildings and outbuildings. If you draw it to scale, using graph paper, the whole project will become that much easier to understand and estimate. Include in the drawing any driveways, ledge, underground electrical service, buried wires and pipes, plus any other known obstacles that would make a straight trench (between house and chicken coop, for instance) difficult.

Figure Demand

Now you need to figure the demand at each outlet. This is calculated much the same way as planning for peak demands before selecting a pump. (32) Not only will you need to estimate a *peak demand allowance* for each building, you should also determine which outlet will have the greatest *fixture flow rate*. In the house this will be either the shower/tub, or the clothes washer. Each may have a peak demand of eight gpm. Then try to visualize which other uses compete most directly with these biggest demands. Lawn sprinkling might be next, taking five gpm. Then figure each fixture on an individual basis.

What about garden watering? Where will it be easiest to wash off machinery, cars, tools? Is there a swimming pool? Is there a dressing room at the swimming pool? With a shower? Toilet? How much water will each of these require?

If you're on a farm, there's almost certainly a barn. If it's a dairy barn,

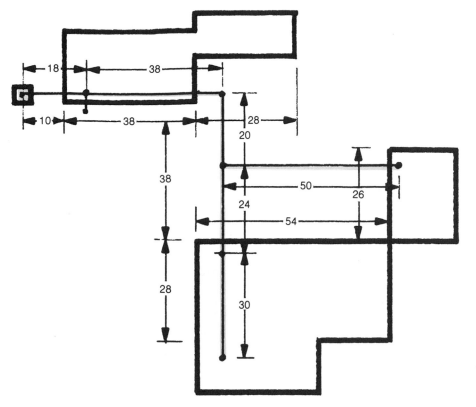
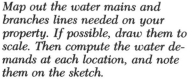

Map out the water mains and branches lines needed on your property. If possible, draw them to scale. Then compute the water demands at each location, and note them on the sketch.

there should probably be one automatic drinking cup for every two stanchioned cows. Other general-use outlets should be installed every 100 feet. In the milking parlor there must be at least one hose connection for washing down the floor. If milking machines are used, it's best to have an outlet for every two cows—in *addition* to the waterers. In the milk room, there should be a minimum of one hot-water outlet for utensil washing, and a separate one for cleaning the floor. A hog house needs one or more automatic waterers, plus connections for floor cleaning and other movable waterers. A hog wallow requires still another outlet. Poultry facilities will have similar needs.

Now go back to the drawing. First draw a line from the source, such as the well, to the point of largest demand—probably the house. Draw a second line to the next closest major demand, and others to all other locations. Pipe should be laid as straight as possible in trenches dug below frost line, but there may be situations where a straight line is the shortest, but not necessarily the easiest distance between two points. It may be better to route a line around a paved patio or an exposed area where there's freeze danger. (57) Also plan for cutoff valves throughout the system. Locate them so that when one part of the system needs to be shut down for repair, service everywhere else isn't interrupted.

The route water takes from the source to the pressure tank is called the *house-service line.* (If you're connecting to a city or community water system, the house-service line hooks up to a gate valve installed by the water company. Connections made to the town system may need to be approved by a municipal official.)

All pipes leading *from* the pressure tank are *internal supply lines.* These lead to smaller *branch supply lines,* ending eventually at fixtures. (83) Along the way, water will almost certainly pass through *fittings* (84), which will contribute to friction and head loss. (80) Pipe sizing (81) depends not only on how much water you need where, but on the length of tubing used to connect source to outlet. In time, certain types of piping will corrode or collect deposits which interfere with water flow. Tubing selection, then, is an important consideration. (79)

All internal piping, fittings, their accessories and their configuration must conform to local plumbing codes. A copy of your town's plumbing ordinances can usually be obtained either at your city hall or county courthouse. You can get a copy of the *National Plumbing Codes* by writing the American Society of Mechanical Engineers, United Engineering Center, 345 East 47th St., New York, NY 10017.

There are a few fundamentals you should keep in mind if you plan to draw your own internal plumbing schematic. First, all horizontal water lines should slope backward slightly—toward the house-service line. A *stop-and-waste valve* should be placed here, in the lowest point of the piping, so the system can be drained when necessary. The pipe size for any line should obviously be big enough to supply all the fixtures on it with sufficient pressure.

Generally ¾- to 1-inch piping is used to deliver water to a water heater, exterior hose connections, and washers. Three-quarter-inch pipe is also used for both hot- and cold-water mains serving two or more fixtures. And *generally* branch lines distribute water to fixtures through ½-inch tubing.

A shutoff valve, usually a *gate valve*, should go into every main and branch line where water may need to be cut off, for any reason. Each branch line should also have an *air chamber*. An air chamber is nothing more than a foot or more of dead-ended pipe, sticking up from the line. The top of this pipe is capped, so air is trapped within it. The air is compressed by water moving through the line. As water is turned on, or shut off suddenly, the air absorbs some of the shock created by quick starting or stopping of water. With air chambers, the clunking noise (plumbers have named it *air hammer*) is eliminated.

Main supply lines are normally run beneath floor joists and fastened in place by special hangers. Hot- and cold-water lines generally run parallel— at least six inches apart. Both may be wrapped in pipe insulation: the hot-water line to save energy, the cold-water line to prevent sweating. At the end of a hot-water supply line the tubing should be adapted and connected to the fixture so it's on the *left*, as you face the fixture.

The EPA offers some more general advice:

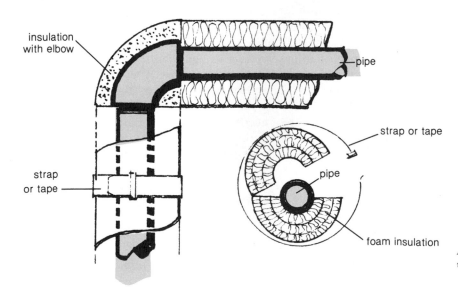

insulation
with elbow

pipe

strap
or tape

strap or tape

pipe

foam insulation

Pipe insulation on hot water lines will save dollars on utility bills.

Recommended Pipe Sizes

Type Fixture	Lavatory	Tub or Shower	Toilet	Sink	Garbage Disposal	Dish-washer	Clothes Washer
Fixture Drains Branch Drains Re-Vent Lines	1½″	1½″ or 2″	3″–4″	1½″–2″	1½″–2″	1½″–2″	1½″
Fixture Supply Lines Branch Lines	⅜″ or ½″	½″	⅜″ or ½″	½″	—	½″	½″
Trap	1¼″	2″	—	1½″	1½″	1½″	1½″

SOURCE: *The Plumbing Handbook*, Sears Roebuck.

The water supply inlet to water tanks used for livestock, laundry tubs and similar installations should be placed with an air gap (twice pipe diameter) above the flooding level of the fixtures to prevent danger of back siphonage. There should be no cross-connection, auxiliary intake, by-pass, or other piping arrangement whereby polluted water or water of questionable quality can be discharged or drawn into the domestic water supply system.

They go on to point out that before any distribution system is put into service, it should be flushed out thoroughly and disinfected. A mixture of liquid laundry bleach (two gallons of bleach for every 1,000 gallons of water) should be run through the entire distributing system, including the pressure tank, and be allowed to sit there for at least twenty-four hours. When it's finally turned on, the smell of chlorine residual should reach each faucet.

Although it's not within the scope of this book to discuss it in great detail, the drainage system comprises almost half of any water-use scheme. Drainage and sewage disposal almost everywhere is strictly controlled by codes. The *Plumbing Handbook*, published by Sears, Roebuck and Company, does a fine job of outlining *both* plumbing and drainage procedures. About home drainage they say,

Four requirements must be met to make sure the drainage system is safe:
1. Pipes must be sloped so water will flow downhill all the way to final disposal.
2. Pipes must be fitted so sewer gases cannot leak out.
3. System must be vented to carry off sewer gases safely.
4. Each fixture with a drain should be equipped with a water trap. Water standing in the trap seals the drain pipe and prevents gases from backing up.
In addition, re-vents, or by-passes, for air between a branch drain and the vent portion of the stack should be provided in any situation where there is danger of water from a trap being siphoned off. Re-vents and by-passes should also be provided in other situations as specified by local codes.

You'll notice that many of the illustrations in this chapter include the beginnings of a drainage schematic.

Again, in the case of plumbing, I advise leaving the job to licensed professionals. It goes without saying: when your water system quits, it causes serious inconvenience, maybe hardship. It's worth investigating which plumbing contractor can do the best installation at the best price, as well as which will provide the best service.

Take your time figuring out what you want and need. Once you have your schematic drawn, take it to a good plumber, lay it out on the table, and ask, "Think it'll fly, Orville?"

78. PROTECTING OUTDOOR PLUMBING

The two biggest threats to outdoor plumbing are frost and mechanical damage caused by vehicles, machinery, and livestock. When I was fourteen, and just learning to drive, I worked a summer at a nearby orchard. Driving the farm truck one day, in marginal control, I turned the corner of a workroad and nicked a riser pipe from a buried water tank with my left rear wheel. I hardly felt it, but the damage was great, and my boss was not the least bit pleased. The tank had to be dug up and replaced. And I worked several weeks thereafter for free—until the new tank was paid for.

Water outlets should be located where large animals and adolescent drivers can't get at them. Mark them clearly. Fluorescent surveyors' tape attracts attention to a pipe sticking out of the ground. Keep hydrants on the opposite side of a fence from cattle, and mount them against rigid posts that can't be knocked over. A totally exposed hydrant in an open space might be surrounded by a concrete well tile and enclosed on top with a manhole cover. A short length of threaded steel pipe, like well casing, surrounding the smaller water pipe and capped on top, provides even better protection.

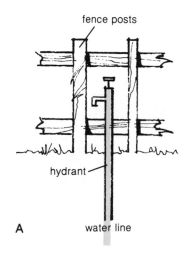

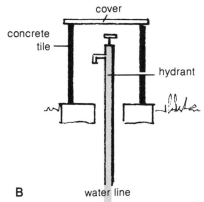

Outdoor hydrants of water outlets may need protection from animals or farm machinery. (A) Placing a hydrant in a wooden fence line might be safe enough. (B) But in an open area the outlet might need to be surrounded by concrete well tile.

Protect Tubing

Where plastic pipe must be run in a shallow trench beneath a road, driveway, or other area of heavy traffic, there's always danger of puncturing the tubing with a sharp stone or metal fragment as weight is exerted from above. Here it's best to run polyethylene tubing through a steel pipe, just as electrical wire is run through conduit. If the protective outer pipe is of large enough diameter to allow the plastic pipe to be insulated as well, you'll be giving it double protection. (57)

We know that all exterior water lines should be buried well below frost level, even though continuous water movement through a pipe supplies a little heat to the soil. Any pipeline that's *not* used in winter should be drained. A stop-and-waste valve can be installed at the lowest point in the line. When this valve is opened, its waste-water outlet automatically opens too, and all water in the sloping line escapes. The area immediately surrounding the valve—the *sump*—should be filled with one- to two-inch stone, and possibly drain tile to draw waste water away from the pipe. Whenever a line is drained, all faucets served by it should be opened. This lets air into the pipe, assuring complete drainage.

Because the stop-and-waste valve is underground, it's operated through a long valve handle that extends above grade. This handle must be marked so it's easily found (it will disappear in weeds), and it should be protected. One of the best ways to keep it from being snapped off is to encase it in metal pipe or tile.

Danger Point

Freeze problems are worst wherever exterior water pipes must surface. Two situations immediately come to mind. One involves automatic livestock

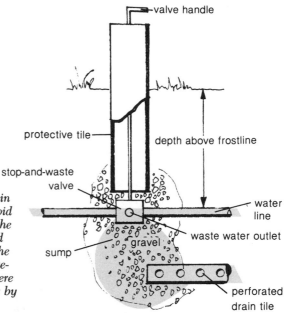

Water lines that are used only in summer must be drained to avoid winter freezing. A handle lets the stop-and-waste valve be opened from above ground. Water in the sloped line seeps from the waste-water outlet into the sump, where it's picked up and moved away by the perforated drain tile.

waterers. The other happens where a water supply line extends above the ground on its way through the floor of a building with no foundation. In either of these cases, insulation should wrap the riser pipe, and the pipe should be shielded on the outside with larger tubing of some kind. An electric, thermostatically controlled heat tape that spirals up the pipe should provide enough low voltage current to prevent freezing—as long as there's no power failure.

Use frost-proof sillcocks and hydrants. Frost-proof hydrants automatically drain off any water remaining in the riser as soon as they're turned off. As it leaves the hydrant's drain port, waste water is carried away through drain tile run to the underground sump.

Health authorities have expressed some concern about some frost-proof hydrants. When the drain port is open there *is* some opportunity for waste water to reenter the supply line, causing contamination. If the sump is properly drained, however, this shouldn't be a problem.

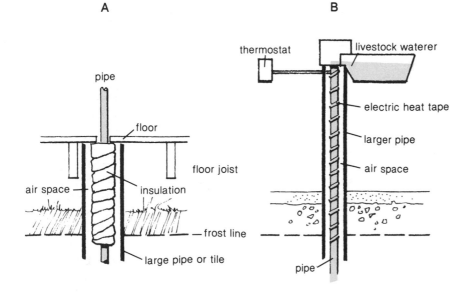

(A) *In cold climates, wherever an underground water line must pass between the ground and the floor of a shed or other outbuilding, the pipe should be insulated. (B) Cattle waterers that extend above grade should be protected with thermostatically controlled heat tapes.*

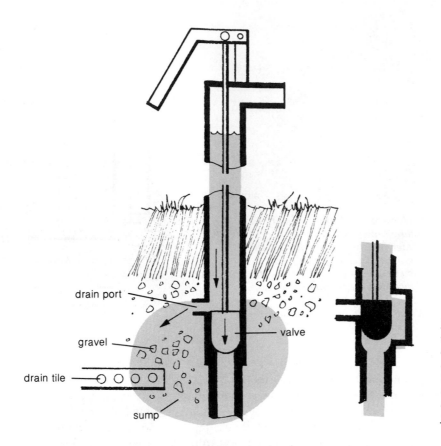

drain port

gravel

drain tile

valve

sump

Frost-proof hydrants drain automatically (left) when they're shut off. Remaining water runs back down the riser and exits through the drain port. When the hydrant is on, the double-duty valve closes the drain port (right). This is built-in freeze protection.

Pipes May Burst

Any pipe that freezes hard enough may burst, and a section will have to be replaced. Sometimes water flow within a line will be blocked by ice, though no damage is done to the pipe. When this happens the pipe can be thawed with either hot water or a propane torch. The worst hassle is locating the frozen section.

When you find it, open a faucet or valve in the line, so any expansion is relieved and water can flow out of the pipe once the ice has melted. If you use hot water, first wrap the frozen length with cloth that's been soaked in warm water. Pour more hot water over the cloth from one end to the other, until the line is clear.

If you use a torch, open a valve and work the flame along the pipe, starting at the end closest to the outlet. Gradually heat the pipe a foot or two at a time until water flows freely. Be careful not to hold the flame in one place too long. Steam could build between two sections of ice and cause the pipe to explode. If you're working near a wooden building, don't get so absorbed in thawing that you set the place on fire. It's happened. *I've* scorched or blistered paint on more than one wall.

79. TUBING SELECTION

There are many choices. Select concrete, cast-iron, galvanized steel, copper, or plastic tubing on the basis of underground soil-corrosion potential, the possibility of corrosion and deposits within the pipe, safe working pressure, effect of freezing, local plumbing codes, and of course cost. Connections between different types of pipe can be made. Avoid asbestos or lead plumbing.

Cast-iron soil pipe, sometimes called *black pipe*, is still used for drainage and waste systems in many parts of the country. Lengths of black pipe are joined using molten lead or *oakum* (special rope impregnated with tar). I believe we'll continue to see a steady decline in the use of this type of pipe.

Galvanized steel has a protective coating of zinc. It's long been used for underground water supply lines in rural areas everywhere, though some experts now recommend *against* burying it. Standard 21-foot lengths come in ½-, ¾- and 1-inch sizes, along with a wide variety of malleable galvanized fittings. It's easy to assemble, since its threaded joints are simply screwed together and tightened with a wrench.

Copper tubing comes in two basic forms. Interior plumbing is often made of *rigid copper tubing. Soft copper tubing,* which comes in fifteen-, thirty-, or sixty-foot rolls, is also common in household plumbing. Both types are found in nominal sizes, described by either their inside diameter (I.D.) or the outside diameter (O.D.) of the pipe. I.D. is used most frequently, and is less misleading because it explains the exact amount of space in the water passageway.

Rigid copper tubing is hard-tempered, and comes in standard ten-foot lengths, with an I.D. of ⅜, ½, or ¾ inches, sizes typical for indoor use. Outside and underground, rigid copper tubing may be ¾, 1 inch, or larger. It's neatest looking because it's straight, and it's connected with solder-type fittings, so it's used most often in portions of a plumbing installation that are exposed to view.

Soft copper tubing comes in the same sizes, but it's somewhat more expensive. Because it can bend around corners without fittings, soft-tempered tubing is often buried in trenches and snaked within already existing walls of older buildings. Either solder-type or "flare-type" fittings can be used with soft copper. Flare fittings screw together and are generally dependable, but they probably shouldn't be used inside walls where they're difficult to get at.

Type K, heavy-duty grade copper tubing (rigid or soft), has the thickest wall. Its price is exorbitant. Type K is used most often in lines that must withstand large outside pressures—in a pump suction line beneath a driveway with heavy traffic, for example. Type L tubing has medium thickness, and is the standard weight for all-around use. Type M has the thinnest tube wall, and is regarded as bargain grade copper pipe.

There's a strong tendency toward plastic plumbing today, despite the fact that building codes in some places specifically forbid it. (Arguments about the health aspects of plastic are starting to become political.) Like copper tubing, plastic pipe comes in rigid and flexible forms—in ten-foot lengths for the rigid, and 100-foot coils for the soft. White or grey PVC (polyvinyl chloride) plastic pipe is sometimes used for both hot and cold drinking-water lines. ABS (acrylonitrile butodrine styrene) is normally restricted to drains and waste and vent lines. PE (polyethylene) is flexible, usually black in color and should be used only for carrying cold water. "Poly" is adversely affected by long exposure to sunlight. PE and PVC have pressure ratings between 100 and 200 psi. Plastic produces little internal friction. It's easy to cut, connect, and install using clamps, fittings, and solvent cement.

In the early 1980s PVC pipe constitutes about 15 percent of the plumbing market. That's up 20 percent since 1970. Probably because PVC is deadly in its gaseous form, the Environmental Protection Agency suggests that PVC tubing may present a health risk. I understand, however, that they've found little evidence it's dangerous unless ignited. To be sure of good quality PVC, use the type certified by the National Sanitation Foundation, Inc. Note the "NSF" marking printed on the outside of the tubing, near the indication of pipe size and material.

Do plastic pipes that deliver drinking water cause cancer? What about birth defects? Marty O'Brien, an executive for Shell Oil, America's largest manufacturer of plastic pipe, insists that it's "as safe or safer than metal tubing." It is flammable, however, and may emit toxic chemicals as it burns.

In the spring of 1982 a bill was introduced to the California Legislature, designed to ban the further installation of plastic pipes in that state (though existing plumbing could remain in use). Lobbyists for the California building industry protested, claiming it is no more dangerous than any other plumbing material. Ultimately the California Supreme Court is expected to rule on whether plastic drinking water pipes constitute a "serious health hazard." Tests to determine if, in fact, PVC is a carcinogen have been ordered, but the study results are not expected for some time. Meanwhile it may be best *not* to install plastic for drinking water lines. But it's fine for drainage and waste lines.

80. HEAD LOSS

Head, as we learned in Section 35, is nothing more than pressure expressed in height of water. Exactly 2.31 feet of head equals one pound per square inch of pressure. Or, 1 foot of head equals .434 psi. Computing head helps in both pump and piping selection.

Water that's moving through a tube is naturally turbulent. And turbulence is made worse by fittings and tight corners in pipe. The more turbulence, the more friction between the water and the inside surface of the tubing. When flow increases so does friction loss. (You might recall from

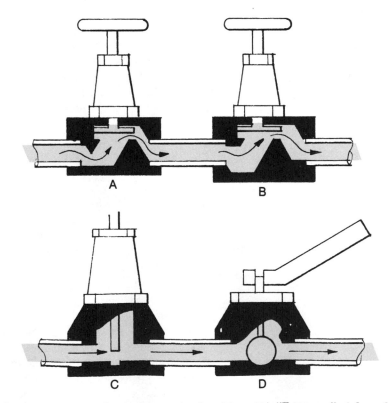

The valves you select might create massive head loss. (A) "Economy" globe valves, for instance, twist water through them, creating enough friction to equal 50 to 200 feet of pipe length. (B) Globe valves with larger passages are somewhat better. (C) A gate valve offers almost no friction resistance, nor does a ball valve (D).

previous discussions that when flow rate doubles, pressure drop increases four times.)

Head loss is the same as friction loss. It's a function of pipe length, its type, its size, its internal smoothness, the nature of its fittings, as well as the flow rate. Head loss is measured in loss of discharge pressure per 100 feet of pipe. Fittings, as just mentioned, often account for the greatest head loss. A standard 90° elbow in a ¾-inch copper pipe, just for example, generates as much friction loss as a three-foot length of straight pipe the same size. Valves, elbows, tees, and other fittings can combine to produce tremendous head loss.

In *New Concepts of Farmstead Water-System Design,* Elmer Jones points out,

> Within 5 feet of the hydropneumatic tank there will normally be found from three to six elbows or tees and two valves. For 1-inch line with four elbows, two tees side outlet, and two gate valves, the equivalent length (in pipe) is 36.2 feet. With two full size globe valves it is 96.4 feet. With two undersize globe valves it may exceed 658 feet. . . .

Globe valves are just one type of cut-off fitting, but they're particularly conducive to massive friction, hence head loss. The valve opening is much smaller than the diameter of pipe leading to and from it, and water must make two direction changes as it passes through a globe valve.

Depending on the type of globe valve, friction loss may equal anywhere from 50 to 200 feet of pipe length. A *gate valve,* on the other hand, offers much less friction. When the gate opens, there's a straight water passage through the fixture. An open *ball valve* is also more efficient than a globe valve when it comes to expediting water movement.

Water-treatment procedures outlined earlier protect the health of a water system as much as that of people drinking the water. Minerals, chemicals, and an imbalance in a water's pH can create corrosion and deposits within the arteries of a plumbing scheme. Healthy piping with a smooth inner surface offers little frictional resistance, while a rough, corroded interior restricts flow. Eventually corrosion and scale buildup by untreated water can strangle a water system. When head loss reaches an intolerable level, the only solution is to replace pipes—at considerable expense.

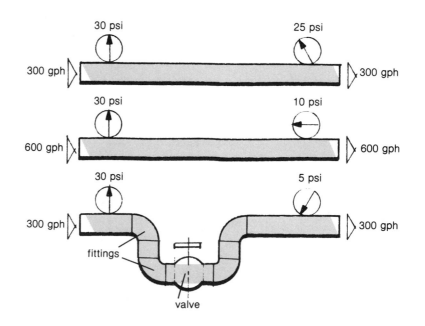

Water pressure decreases as friction within the lines increases. Friction is influenced by pipe length, flow rate, and fittings which make water turbulent.

Rates of Flow

Location	Flow Pressure* (pounds per square inch) (psi)	Flow Rate (gallons per minute) (gpm)
Ordinary basin faucet	8	2.0
Self-closing basin faucet	8	2.5
Sink faucet, ⅜ inch	8	4.5
Sink faucet, ½ inch	8	4.5
Bathtub faucet	8	6.0
Laundry tub faucet, ½ inch	8	5.0
Shower	8	5.0
Ball-cock for closet	8	3.0
Flush valve for closet	15	†15–40
Flushometer valve for urinal	15	15.0
Garden hose (50 ft., ¾-inch sillcock)	30	5.0
Garden hose (50 ft., ⅝-inch outlet)	15	3.33
Drinking fountains	15	.75
Fire hose 1½ inches, ½-inch nozzle	30	40.0

* Flow pressure is the pressure in the supply near the faucet or water outlet while the faucet or water outlet is wide open and flowing.
† Wide range due to variation in design and type of closet flush valves.
SOURCE: Environmental Protection Agency.

81. PIPE SIZING

Pipe sizing is critical. If it's too small, delaying flow, you neutralize the positive effects of a properly sized pump. (44) Furthermore, the operating cost of the pump will be greater each year, as increased friction eats away at the pump's ability to generate pressure. Advice from plumbing experts is always the same on this score. It goes something like this, as quoted from one Maryland Extension Service bulletin, *"A small increase in the size of pipe installed will cost a little more initially, but will mean much in increased system efficiency and in providing for future needs."*

Here's an example, taken from the AAVIM: At two psi of friction loss per 100 feet of pipe, four gallons per minute will flow through a ¾-inch tube. Under the same conditions, 7.5 gallons will pass through a one-inch tube. In other words, increase the pipe size by ¼ inch, and you increase the flow by 87 percent—almost double! Give the pipe another ¼ inch of diameter, and that 1¼-inch tube will transport sixteen gallons per minute—four times as much as ¾-inch pipe.

If you need to figure pipe sizing to serve just one location—a house for instance—the calculations are simple. Determine the demand allowance for the home (say twenty-five gpm), and the distance from the pump to the house (say there's a fifty-foot well drop, and the well head is 100 feet from the house, for a total of 150 feet). The accompanying charts, for copper pipe, plastic pipe, and galvanized steel pipe, can be used to find the correct pipe size. In the example just cited, a 1½-inch plastic or copper pipe will be needed to bring enough well water to the pressure tank. If galvanized steel pipe is used, two-inch tubing will be needed, since galvanized pipe has more internal friction.

From the pressure tank to the water heater, and for hot and cold water lines serving two or more faucets, ¾- to 1-inch tubing will be needed. Branch lines within the house will be smaller. A lavatory and toilet can each be served by ⅜- or ½-inch pipe. Showers, sinks, dishwashers, and clothes washers will require ½-inch tubing.

Dual Use

On a farm or homestead where pipes must serve two or more locations in barns or other outbuildings, the pipe sizing problem becomes a bit more complicated. The demand allowance for each location must be estimated, and the water-use location *farthest* from the pump must be identified. How much water from competing demand locations between the pump and the most remote outlet "steal" as water travels through the main feeder line? Determine the length and pipe sizing necessary to serve each of these branch locations. *Then* figure the main line sizing, using the charts.

Some branch lines may need 1½-inch pipe, others 1¼-, 1-inch, or even ¾. The main feeder may be two inches or larger. To be a little repetitious: installing oversized pipe, while more expensive to begin with, will be cheaper in the long run than eventually digging up and retrenching old tubing that's proven too small.

82. MEASURING, CUTTING, AND JOINING PIPE

The simplest, clearest, and most thoroughly illustrated plumbing instructions I know of are found in the *Do-It-Yourself Plumbing Handbook*, put out by Sears, Roebuck and Company. It's aimed at the amateur, includes very little hard sell for Sears products, and the directions are virtually idiot-proof. I recommend it as a valuable reference to anyone planning to install his own water-distribution system.

Copper and plastic tubing are so easy to work with, it's hard to imagine an inexperienced homeowner choosing to start out with galvanized steel pipe, especially since galvanized needs to be threaded. It *is* universally accepted, however, and billions of miles of galvanized water pipes are at work throughout the world. There may be need to repair or replace portions of an existing system at some time.

Measuring galvanized, or *any* type of pipe, should be done with great care. The "face-to-face" method may be the most accurate. Measure the exact distance between the faces of fittings to be used, then add enough length to let the threaded pipe ends screw into these fittings. For ½- or ¾-inch pipe, allow ½ inch for threads at either end. For 1-inch and 1¼-inch pipe, allow an extra ⅝ inch. Inch and ½-pipe requires ¾ inch of threads to engage a fitting properly. Use chalk to mark where the pipe is to be cut.

Galvanized may be cut with either a pipe cutter or a hacksaw. It's most important that the pipe be cut square, so a plumber's vise to hold it in place during sawing is all but mandatory. A pipe cutter may be the better choice, since it practically insures a square cut. While cutting, apply threading oil to both the cutter wheel and the pipe. Once it's cut, all burrs should be removed from the pipe end—inside and out. Use a reamer to remove the burrs inside.

A "stock and die" are used to thread pipe. Choose the die that's sized the same as the pipe to be threaded. I'll let the Sears people take it from here.

Insert the die, making certain the printing on the die faces up, toward the cover plate. Slide the cover plate back in place and tighten the thumb nut.

You may use either an individual guide or an adjustable guide to start the die. Individual guides are marked with the pipe sizes they fit. Select the correct size guide (or adjust the guide to the correct size), insert it in the opening of the stock and tighten it in place with the lock bolt.

Place the pipe in the vise and slide the stock over the end of the pipe with the stock on the inside. Push the stock into the pipe until the die catches the

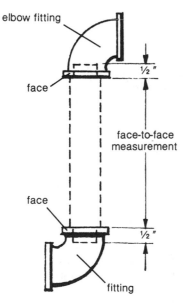

To measure tubing accurately, take the face-to-face measurement between fittings, then add ½″ at either end for ½- or ¾-inch pipe. You must add more for larger pipes.

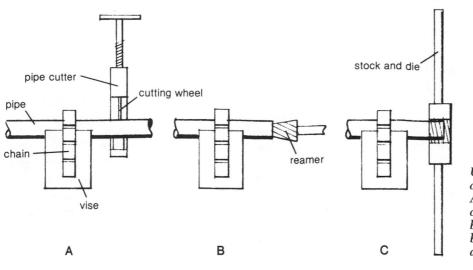

A   B   C

Using a vise and pipe cutter practically insures a square cut. (A) Apply oil to both the pipe and the cutting wheel. (B) Remove all burrs. Use a reamer for inside burrs. (C) Threads may be cut with a stock and die.

pipe. Slowly turn the stock *clockwise,* keeping the die pressed against the pipe. When you have cut just enough thread so the die is firmly on the pipe, apply plenty of cutting oil to the threads of the die and the pipe end.

Continue to turn the stock clockwise, backing off about a quarter turn after each half turn forward so you can clear away the chips. Continue threading, applying cutting oil frequently, until the pipe protrudes to the face of the die.

To remove the threading tool, turn it *counterclockwise.* Clean all chips from the threads and wipe off all surplus oil before using the pipe.

A pipe wrench is used to connect and tighten galvanized pipe to fittings. Tubing that's one inch or smaller requires at least a ten-inch pipe wrench. An eighteen-inch wrench is normally used for pipes up to two inches, and a twenty-four-inch pipe wrench is used to turn pipes up to 2½ inches.

Fittings

Connections between lengths of rigid copper tubing are made with copper fittings and solder. Plumbers and do-it-yourselfers call it *sweating* joints. When measuring, take the face-to-face dimension, then add the depth of the soldering hubs on either end. These are usually ½- or ¾-inch deep.

To sweat a joint you'll need four things: steel wool or emery paper; *flux,* which is a paste that looks like Vaseline; solder wire; and a heat source—usually a propane torch. These items are easy to find in a hardware store.

Use Hacksaw or Cutter

Copper tubing can be cut with a fine-toothed hacksaw (use a #24 blade), and you'll do a neater job if you set the tube in a jig. A small pipe cutter is an inexpensive tool and easy to use. It should make a perfect cut every time. After the tubing is cut, remove all burrs, inside with a reaming tool, outside with a file.

Before a connection is made, the outside of the tubing and the inside of the fitting have to be cleaned with steel wool or fine abrasive paper. Just get the surfaces shiny. Don't sand *too* much or you'll destroy the tight fit. This should be done immediately before you smear on the flux. (If you wait as little as an hour before soldering, the surfaces will have time to oxidize again, and you may not get a true bond.)

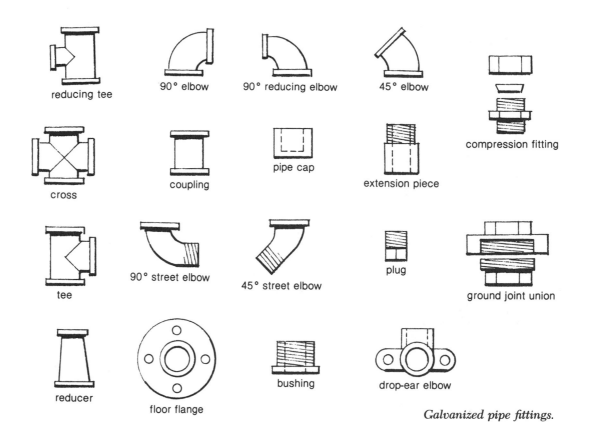

Galvanized pipe fittings.

Use a small, stiff brush to apply a generous film of flux to both surfaces, fit the joint together, and rotate it several times to spread the flux evenly. Now heat both the end of the tube and the fitting, applying flame from the propane torch to the fitting, while you touch the end of the solder wire to the joint. Be sure to heat the connection thoroughly on both sides. Don't try to heat the solder wire directly.

When the temperature of the copper is right, the solder will suddenly melt and flow evenly into and around all sides of the joint. If you're doing this for the first time it will seem magical, since the solder even flows uphill as a result of the strong capillary action created by the flux. If all goes well, you should have a perfectly watertight seal.

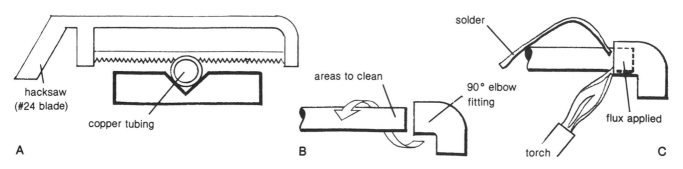

(A) Copper tubing may be cut with a hacksaw. Place the pipe in a jig to hold it steady, and make a square cut. (B) Both the end of the tubing and the inside of the fitting must be cleaned with steel wool or abrasive paper. (C) Apply flux to both surfaces, fit the joint together, rotating it several times to spread the flux. Heat the tubing end and the fitting, then touch the solder wire to the joint. Solder should flow smoothly into and around the joint.

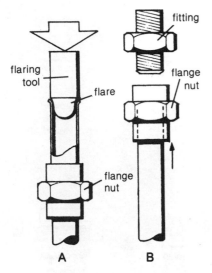

(A) In making a flare fitting, remove the flange nut from the fitting and slide it onto the end of the tube. Center the flaring tool in the tubing end, and tap it with a hammer to make the flare. (B) Now move the flange nut to the end and thread it to the fitting.

A drippy joint, where too much solder has been used, is better than one where there's too little—even though it may not look so professional and may reduce the inside diameter of the tubing. With practice you'll learn to wipe the joint quickly with a rag before the solder has solidified. But be careful not to burn yourself. Also be sure the tubing and fitting don't move while the solder is cooling.

Flare Fittings

Soft copper tubing can be soldered, but flare fittings are also used. Flare fittings have threaded flange nuts which hold the connecting tube ends in place. The flange nut must be removed from the fitting and slid onto the tube *before* the tube is flared.

Either a flaring tool or a flanging tool may be used. Once the flaring tool is centered in the end of the tube, and is straight, tap it with a hammer to widen (or "flare") the end of the tube. The flare should be wide enough to fill the recess in the flange nut. Now slide the nut up the tube end and thread it to the fitting. Use *two* wrenches to tighten the threads. This forces the "cupped" end of the tube against the fitting, making a tight seal.

Plastic Tubing

Before you buy and install any PVC plumbing for drinking-water distribution, check local plumbing ordinances to be certain it's legal. (79)

Both PVC and ABS plastic tubing are cemented together, each with its special solvent glue. It can be measured exactly like metal pipe, allowing enough length beyond the face-to-face measurement for insertion in the fitting. Plastic pipe can be easily cut with a saw. Use of a miter box, which guarantees squareness, is not a bad idea.

The end of the pipe and the fitting should be cleaned with emery paper to remove any roughness on those surfaces. Then brush on PVC or ABS cement to both surfaces. (Don't try to use PVC cement for ABS, and vice versa. And ABS, remember, is used only for drainage and waste systems—not for drinking-water lines.) Insert the pipe in the fitting, and rotate it into position. Wipe away the excess glue, but be sure to leave a continuous bead of cement around the outside shoulder of the fitting. Solvent cement starts to set up immediately, so position pipes and fittings right away. Then wait at least an hour before allowing any water pressure into PVC lines. Once the cement has hardened, open a faucet at the end of the line to remove all

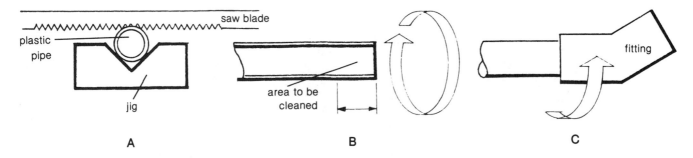

(A) Cut plastic pipe with a saw, and remove all burrs. (B) The pipe end and the inside of the fitting must then be cleaned with emery paper. Paint CPVC cement on pipe end and the inside of the fitting. (C) Insert pipe and rotate one-quarter turn to position. Wipe off excess cement, leaving a continuous bead around the fitting.

tee

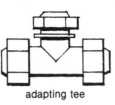
reducing tee

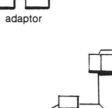
adaptor

adaptor

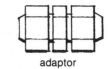
adaptor

drop-ear elbow

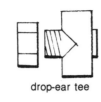
drop-ear tee

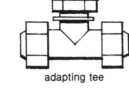
adapting tee

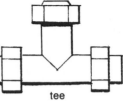
tee

union

end cap

90° adapting tee

90° elbow

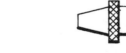
adapting tee

45° elbow

reducing adapter

90° adapting elbow

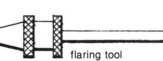
flaring tool

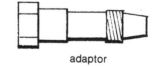
adaptor

adaptor

90° elbow

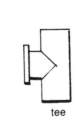
tee

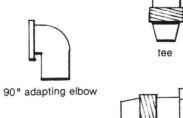
tee

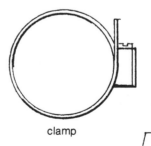
clamp

coupling

90° adapting elbow

coupling

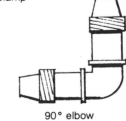
90° elbow

Plastic fittings.

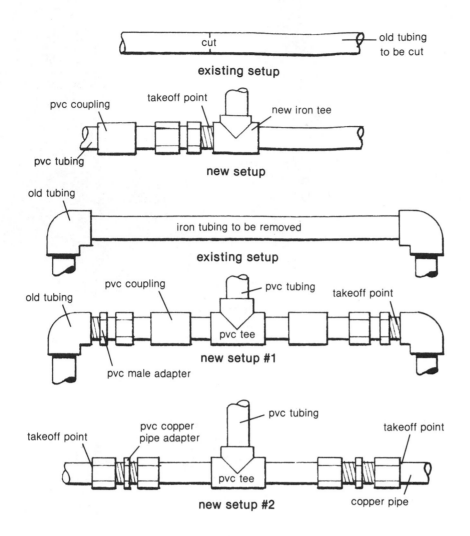

existing setup

cut — old tubing to be cut

pvc coupling   takeoff point   new iron tee

pvc tubing

new setup

old tubing

iron tubing to be removed

existing setup

old tubing   pvc coupling   pvc tubing   takeoff point

pvc tee

pvc male adapter

new setup #1

pvc tubing

takeoff point   pvc copper pipe adapter   takeoff point

pvc tee

copper pipe

new setup #2

Adding to plumbing, using PVC.

air within it, and turn it off when the pipe is full of water. Inspect all connections to be sure there are no leaks at any of the joints.

Here are some "don'ts" suggested by Sears: "DO NOT use PVC for hot water HEATING systems. DO NOT rely on PVC for electrical grounding—it is nonconductive. DO NOT use any cement other than the one specified for PVC pipe. DO NOT use damaged pipe or fittings for PVC installations."

83. FITTINGS, ADAPTERS, AND BOOSTER PUMPS

There's a wide range of fittings for galvanized pipe. Besides regular tees, elbows, couplings, and forty-five-degree elbows, there are reducing tees, reducing elbows, straight reducers, extension pieces, plugs, pipe caps, ground-joint unions, "street" elbows, crosses, bushings, drop-ear elbows, compression fittings, and floor flanges.

Solder-type fittings for copper include unions, tees, several types of elbows, drop-ear tees, reducing adapters, drop-ear elbows, couplings, flush bushings, reducing tees, and end caps. Typical flare-type fittings for flexible copper pipe are adapters of several types, unions, tees, and elbows, as well as the flaring tool itself. Several types of valves for metal piping have already been discussed. Gate valves permit a full flow of water whenever the gate is open, causing little internal friction. A globe valve, as we learned, restricts water flow somewhat. If it's fitted with a plug or cap, it can also function as a *stop-and-waste valve*, used to drain individual pipes or an entire system, depending on where it's placed. A gate valve can be used the same way. *Check valves* permit water to flow in only one direction.

The list of fittings for polyethylene pipe is fairly short. There are adapters, tees, and elbows. Each of these fittings is slid into the end of the plastic tube and secured with a clamp. There are PVC elbows, tees, reducing bushings, caps, adapters, slip couplings, forty-five-degree slip elbows, and even PVC valves. These are glued in place.

When retrofitting an older plumbing system or making additions to any water-distributing system, there's often need to connect plastic to galvanized steel, or plastic to copper. There are a number of adapters available for this kind of changeover, including male iron-pipe adapters for straight connections to female threads, female iron-pipe adapters for straight connections to male threads, male iron-pipe elbow adapters for tight-angle connections, female iron-pipe elbow adapters designed for spots where space is critical (such as connections for in-the-wall plumbing), and copper-tubing compression adapters for straight connections to plastic.

Plastic May Crack

It's important, whenever attaching metal to plastic, to be sure the rubber gasket in the PVC transition fitting is in place, and that everything is correctly aligned. Tighten the brass nut on the adapter with your fingers, then give it an extra quarter turn with a wrench to be sure the joint won't leak. Don't over-tighten or you'll risk cracking the plastic.

Inside buildings, pipes can be assembled in the open against walls and boxed in later, or they can be run *within* walls and floors.

Change in Studs

It's interesting to note the recent trend in new home construction in this country. For many years exterior walls were made of 2x4 studs. Now builders are using 2x6s to allow more space for insulation. But long before this,

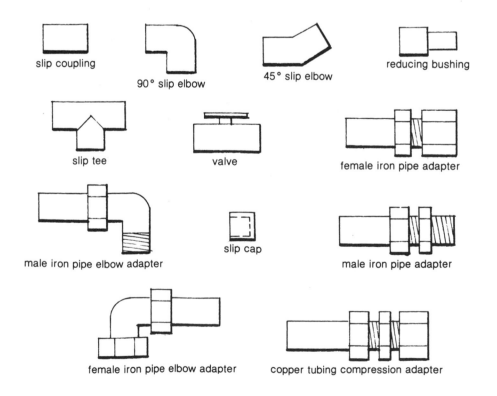

PVC pipe fittings, and PVC-to-metal adapters.

slip coupling

90° slip elbow

45° slip elbow

reducing bushing

slip tee

valve

female iron pipe adapter

male iron pipe elbow adapter

slip cap

male iron pipe adapter

female iron pipe elbow adapter

copper tubing compression adapter

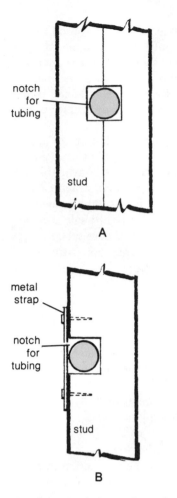

notch for tubing

stud

A

metal strap

notch for tubing

stud

B

Plumbing is often run through stud walls. (A) Holes may be notched through the centers of double 2x4 or 2x6 studs, or (B) single studs can be notched to accommodate tubing, which is held in place with metal strapping.

smart contractors were building 2x6 interior walls in bathrooms, to give themselves more clearance for piping there. A 2x4 partition allows just 3½ inches of clearance; a 2x6, 5½ inches. A 2-inch steel pipe won't fit inside a 2x4 wall because there's not enough turning space to assemble a fitting. Yet plastic and copper pipes, because they require no turning space, can be squeezed into limited areas. So a 3-inch copper or plastic tube *can* be run in a 2x4 partition.

Stud walls, whether they be 2x4s or 2x6s, as well as floors, must be drilled or notched to accommodate piping. This presents more problems for larger-diameter sewage and drainage pipes (particularly those from a toilet) than for thinner water-distributing tubes. Holes and notches can weaken structural framing members such as joists and studs. They should be strategically located and reinforced wherever it seems wise. Whenever possible, tubing should be run parallel to these members, rather than through them.

Cutting Studs

When a stud *must* be pierced, don't cut or drill any more than two-thirds of the 2x4, and reinforce it later with either a metal strap or a piece of wooden strapping. It's safer to cut away in the upper half of a stud than in the lower. It's also prudent to run plumbing through nonload-bearing partitions, rather than in critical structural walls. Always notch or drill as few studs as possible.

Where it's necessary to penetrate a joist, cut near its end instead of the middle where it's most vulnerable to weakening. Never notch deeper than one-fourth the height of the joist, and reinforce the notch with steel or wooden strapping. If a hole is to be drilled, run it through the center of the joist's height, and don't let its diameter exceed one-fourth of the joist height. The most efficient plumbing arrangement in a kitchen or bathroom, by the way, is to place all the fittings along one wall.

There's still one more possibility to consider in water-distribution lines. *Booster pumps* are used in sections of a system where additional pressure is needed beyond what can be provided by the regular pump. The *Water Systems Handbook* says, "Residences located on the outskirts of a city or high on a hill may experience very low water pressure during peak use periods.

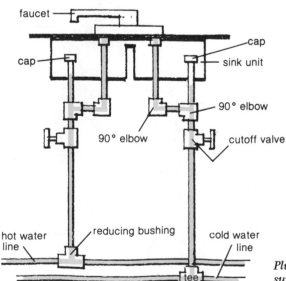

faucet

cap

cap

sink unit

90° elbow

90° elbow

cutoff valve

hot water line

reducing bushing

cold water line

tee

Plumbing layout for hot and cold supply to sink or lavatory.

Older residences, where water lines have become rusted or choked with scale, need booster pumps to overcome this added resistance to flow."

Using Booster Pumps

There are several options when it comes to booster pumps. In-line centrifugal pumps are used most frequently, but there are submersible boosters, end-suction centrifugal boosters, and positive-displacement booster pumps. (38 through 42) As you plan for a booster, take time to calculate what you wish to accomplish in terms of pressure and flow rate. You may find you need less boost than originally thought.

Booster pumps are controlled in three different ways, depending on how often the unit is expected to operate and how much water you need to move. A *manual switch* can be installed if the booster will only be used occasionally. Water will be boosted continually until you turn it off. A *flow-actuated switch* is activated by water movement within the line, and is used to prevent the booster pump from short cycling. Third, a booster pump can be controlled by a pressure switch (89) and hydropneumatic tank, exactly like a normal pump. (55–56)

Conversely, water pipes can have flow-*reducers* installed, as well as pressure-relief valves. (92)

84. FIXTURE HOOK-UP

I've said I was never a plumber. But I was a carpenter for several years, and plumbers and carpenters often work hand in hand. During that time I made the same mistake—*twice*. Don't do the same. In most cases a bathtub is too big to fit through the rough opening of a bathroom door. Plan ahead in a new house. Move the tub in *before* bathroom partitions are built, even though the tub or shower/tub will be in the way and you have to work around it. Forget this advice, and you'll end up having to tear out part of a wall. Embarrassing and time-consuming.

The tub, toilet bowl, toilet tank, lavatory, sink, laundry tub, and other fixtures will be bulky and heavy. "Handle with care," as they say, and have enough people on hand to jockey these items into position. Avoid scratching or chipping the finished surfaces. Rest them on pads, and don't stand on them when wearing work shoes. Once the tub has been muscled into its prepared space, put cardboard in its bottom, and try not to step into it, or onto any other fixture that's being hooked up. Once set, connections are relatively simple, as long as all the right plumbing components are on hand.

The bathtub should be placed first, followed by the toilet, then the lavatory. Blocking will run crosswise between wall studs as backing for the tub and sink—though blocking *won't* be necessary for vanity-type sinks. The tub and shower will be served by ½-inch hot- and cold-water supply lines, and connections are made with a slip-joint nut.

Toilet bowls and tanks have standard connections that make installation easy. There are two types of toilets: a one-piece tank and bowl combination, and separate tanks and bowls. The bowl is set into a floor flange at the discharge opening, and sealed with putty and/or a rubber gasket or wax ring. The tank may be supplied by a ⅜-inch line attached at a wall connection or run through the floor. A shut-off valve in this line is optional, but a very good idea.

Sinks

Lavatory height is normally thirty-one inches off the floor. These bathroom sinks are of three types: those that hang from a bracket fastened to

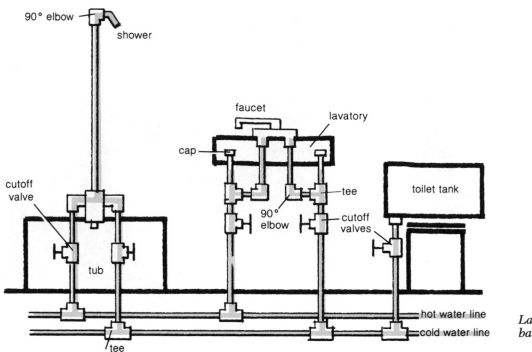

Layout for supply to full bath.

blocking in the wall, pedestal types that are supported by legs extending from the floor, and those that sit within a vanity cabinet. To each of these, ½-inch supply lines pass through either wall or floor flanges. Again, a shut-off valve is a recommended but optional convenience.

Drain-line and supply-line connections for sink, laundry tubs, and other fixtures are similar to those for the lavatory. It's important that traps be provided in drain and waste lines. A dishwasher and garbage disposer also require traps, as will laundry tubs and clothes washers. The supply lines, whether copper or PVC, will be ½ inch in diameter.

Bathtub and some sink or lavatory pipes are normally hidden in walls behind these fixtures. A removable service panel in an adjacent room or closet will be needed to permit access to the supply-line valve or drainage trap. Don't forget air chambers (77) in each branch line to a hot or cold water fixture.

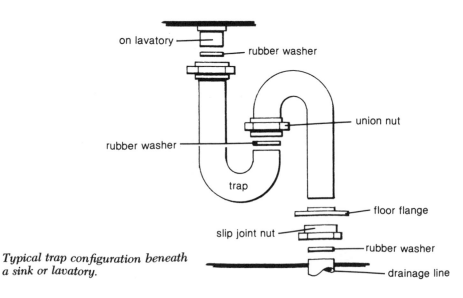

Typical trap configuration beneath a sink or lavatory.

THE HOME WATER SUPPLY

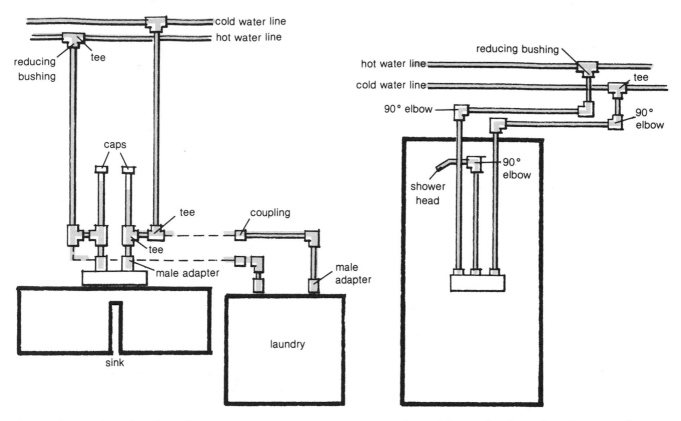

cold water line
hot water line
reducing bushing
tee
caps
tee
coupling
tee
male adapter
male adapter
sink
laundry

Layout for supply to laundry tubs.

reducing bushing
hot water line
cold water line
tee
90° elbow
90° elbow
shower head
90° elbow

Layout for overhead supply to basement shower.

Plan ¾-inch supply lines to water treatment equipment, hot-water heaters, and in booster-pump installations. (83) The water heater should have a pressure-relief valve in accordance with local codes. Water heaters may be fueled by oil, gas, or electricity. Gas or oil-burning water heaters should be placed within eight feet of a chimney large enough to provide venting through a flue. The cold-water supply line to the heater will be located on the right, as you face the fixture, the exiting hot-water line on the left.

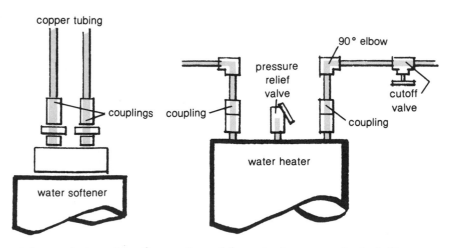

copper tubing
couplings
water softener

Layout for supply to water softener.

90° elbow
pressure relief valve
coupling
cutoff valve
coupling
water heater

Layout for water heater supply, including pressure relief valve.

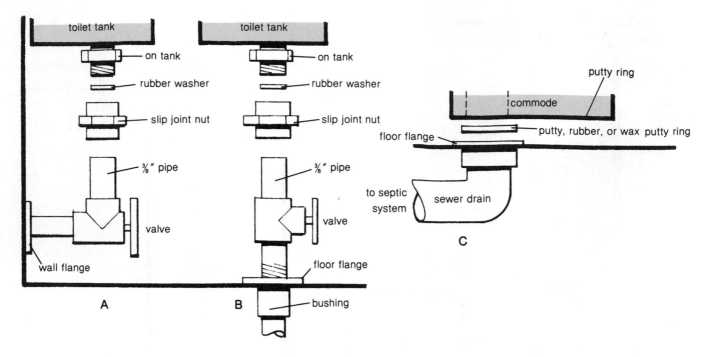

Toilet tank connection (A) from a wall; (B) from the floor. C shows toilet connection to floor flange of sewage line.

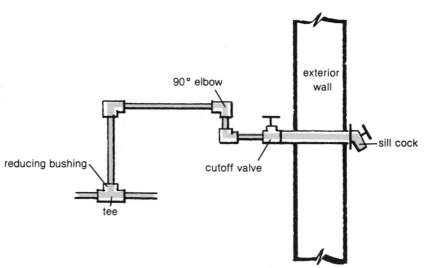

Layout for supply to outdoor sillcock.

8 CONTROLLING WATER

85. WIRING

The controlling energy in a modern water system is electrical current. Electrical impulses respond to pressures sensed at various locations in the total water-delivery mechanism. And it's the pump that receives the largest portion of electricity. If the wiring in the pump's feeder circuit is too small, the pump motor is starved, its life is shortened, and much energy is wasted—given off as excess heat from the motor. So correct wire sizing is necessary. Since the motor uses the most current when it's *starting,* wiring must be heavy enough to supply the motor adequately at this point.

The amount of electricity needed to feed the pump's motor is not the only factor to be considered in decisions about wiring size. Sizing also depends on the distance current must travel, and on the voltage you intend to use. The choice is between 120 volts and 240 volts. In most cases, unless there's a very low-capacity pump, 240 volts is the safer bet.

A 240-volt circuit has three advantages: The current (amps) is only half as great with 240 as with 120, meaning lower heat loss and higher motor efficiency. When the motor starts up there's no chance of lights dimming in the rest of the house. A smaller sized wire can be used.

Actual conductor wires may be copper or aluminum. Copper is the more conductive of the two metals, but aluminum is lighter in weight and cheaper. Again, size will be determined by the distance from the electric meter to the pump motor. Coatings that protect the copper or aluminum wire strands vary, dictated by whether the wire will be strung inside an existing building, will be run overhead from poles, or buried underground.

Two types of cable are used inside buildings, to connect to existing wire.

Type NM is a nonmetallic sheathed cable that is moisture-resistant and flame-retardant. It is usually used in either exposed or concealed locations that are normally dry.

Type NMC is similar, but can be used in damp locations.

Either single-wire conductors or cable are used for overhead wiring.

Type TW has a thermoplastic covering which is flame-resistant and moisture-resistant, while Type THW is flame-retardant. Both can be used in wet and dry locations.

The cable used for overhead wiring is Type SE, which is flame-retardant and moisture-resistant, and is made up of two or more conductors.

For underground wiring from the meter to the pump, two types of cable are available.

Type UF has a plastic covering which is flame-retardant and moisture-resistant, but shouldn't be exposed to the sun.

Type USE has a moisture-resistant covering and is used for service entrances as well as underground.

Wiring for the submersible pump is connected at the well head.

The pump's feeder circuit should be wired separately from all other electrical service lines to the house or other outbuildings, so it's isolated in case of fire. The pump motor itself will also need to be protected against overloading and from lightning surges. (93 and 94) Grounding will be necessary.

Copper Circuit-Wire Sizes for Individual Single-Phase Motors
(Based on 3 percent voltage drop on full-load current)

Motor Size (h.p.)	Distance from Meter to Motor (feet)								
	50	75	100	200	300	400	500	600	700
120 Volts				*Wire Gauge Number*					
¼	12	12	12	12	10	8	6	6	6
⅓	12	12	12	10	8	6	6	6	4
240 Volts									
¼	12	12	12	12	10	8	8	6	6
⅓	12	12	12	12	10	8	8	6	6
½	12	12	12	12	10	8	8	6	6
¾	12	12	12	10	8	6	6	6	4
1	12	12	12	8	6	6	4	4	3
1½	12	12	12	8	6	6	4	4	3
2	12	10	10	6	4	4	3	2	2
3	12	10	8	6	4	3	2	1	0
5	10	8	6	4	2	1	0	00	00

(If overhead wiring is used and span is more than 50 feet—use 8-gauge wire for strength; or larger if needed for motor. Spans under 50 feet can use 10-gauge wire unless larger size is needed for motor.)

Aluminum Circuit-Wire Sizes for Individual Single-Phase Motors
(Based on 3 percent voltage drop on full-load current)

Motor Size (h.p.)	Distance from Meter to Motor (feet)								
	50	75	100	200	300	400	500	600	700
120 Volts				*Wire Gauge Number*					
¼	12	12	10	8	6	4	4	4	3
⅓	12	10	10	6	4	4	3	2	1
240 Volts									
¼	12	12	12	10	8	6	6	4	4
⅓	12	12	12	10	8	6	6	4	4
½	12	12	12	10	8	6	6	4	4
¾	12	12	10	8	6	4	4	4	3
1	12	10	10	6	4	4	3	2	1
1½	12	10	10	6	4	4	3	2	1
2	10	8	8	4	3	2	1	0	0
3	10	8	6	4	2	1	0	00	000
5	8	6	4	2	0	00	000	4/0	4/0

NOTE: (If overhead wiring is used and span is more than 50 feet—use 8-gauge wire for strength; or larger if needed for motor. Spans under 50 feet can use 10-gauge wire unless larger size is needed for motor.)

86. ROUTINE REPAIRS AND MAINTENANCE

No water system, no matter how carefully it's designed and built, will be totally automatic and maintenance-free. Small leaks, minor repairs, adjustments, and little annoyances can be controlled by even the most unhandy homeowner without calling in an expensive plumbing expert. Most of the time no specialized tools or materials are called for.

Fixing Faucets

Fixing a leaky faucet, for instance, is usually only a matter of replacing a rubber washer. When you turn a faucet handle, a threaded *valve stem* turns as well. Turn the faucet off, and the valve stem forces the washer into the *valve seat*. Turn it on, and the washer is lifted out of the seat, allowing water to pass through. But when the washer gets worn, the faucet leaks in the off position. New washers can be purchased at any hardware store. They come in an assortment of sizes, and in flat or cone shapes. Use either shape.

To replace the washer, first shut the water off in the line. Remove the packing nut with a wrench, and lift out the long valve stem. Take the old washer off the bottom of the stem, being careful not to damage the rim, and put on a new one. If the valve seat looks scratched or worn (because the washer was neglected for so long the valve seat has been worn by the stem rubbing against it), you should replace the seat too. Then reinstall the stem, the packing nut, and the handle.

Running Toilet

Noise from a leaky, overflowing toilet can drive *anyone* to an insane asylum. But it's easily fixed. The ball-like float that rises and falls with the water level in the tank is attached to an intake valve through the float arm. When the tank is filled, the intake valve is supposed to shut off. If the water level is getting too high in the tank, you're wasting water, and the float arm should be bent downward. This will close the valve sooner, when the water is at the proper height within the tank.

When a toilet is flushed, the handle is turned, lifting the stopper from the discharge pipe opening through a chain or stopper wire. Water now rushes from the tank into the bowl. As the water in the tank drops, the discharge-pipe stopper falls back into its seat, ending the flush. The float also drops, reopening the inlet valve. (The refill tube, meanwhile, returns water to the toilet bowl. The toilet bowl must be kept full so the trap will function effectively.)

The weight of water in the tank normally holds the discharge-valve stopper in place. But a problem will develop when the stopper wires get hung

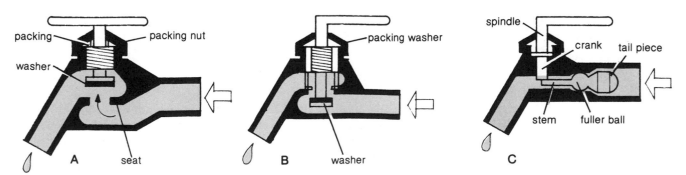

Three basic faucet types. (A) A compression faucet. (B) A faucet suitable for high water pressures. (C) A fuller-type faucet, in which pressure is behind the tail piece.

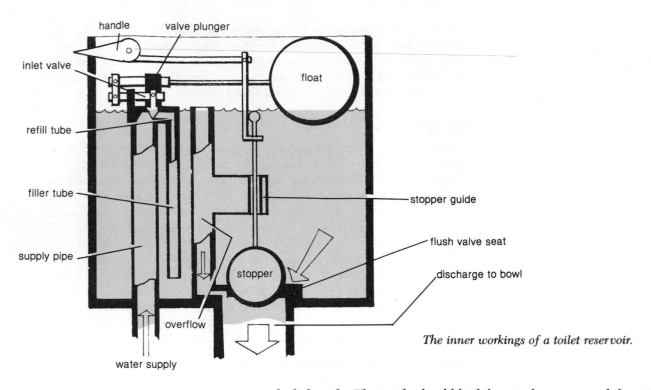

handle   valve plunger

inlet valve

float

refill tube

filler tube

stopper guide

supply pipe

flush valve seat

discharge to bowl

stopper

overflow

water supply

The inner workings of a toilet reservoir.

up in a fouled guide. The guide should be lubricated once in a while with a petroleum jelly like Vaseline. Leaking at the discharge will make the tank's intake valve turn off and on repeatedly. If the rubber discharge stopper is worn, it should be replaced. If a leak in the *intake* develops, it can be repaired much like a faucet. The valve stem is taken out simply by removing a screw or two, releasing the mechanism at the top of the valve housing. And a new washer can be pressed into place.

Leaks in Pipes

Leaks may occur in galvanized steel pipe, when threads are faulty, pipe walls are thin, or fittings go bad. Often this can be corrected just by tightening the fitting with a pipe wrench. In more extreme cases, the section of pipe will have to be replaced, using a union coupling and "pipe dope."

Leaks that show up in copper pipe are usually at a poorly soldered fitting. The entire section of tubing should be drained by opening all faucets and any stop-and-waste valves in the line. (*Any* water in the line will make soldering impossible.) Heat the joint with a blowtorch to break it, clean both the pipe end and the inside of the fitting with steel wool, and resweat the joint. (82)

Obstructions

Stopped-up fixtures can usually be opened easily. Most likely there's an obstruction in the trap or stopper mechanism. In a bathroom lavatory, for example, twist the drain stopper and remove it to clean out hair and other material in the drain. If there's standing water in a basin or toilet bowl, use a plunger—an item that should be standard equipment in any home. Commercial preparations for freeing clogged drains are widely advertised and available everywhere. These are effective but should be used cautiously, since they may contain toxic chemicals that can damage fixtures, your septic system, and *your* body's internal plumbing.

THE HOME WATER SUPPLY

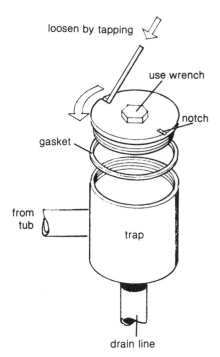

loosen by tapping

use wrench

notch

gasket

from tub

trap

drain line

How to open a bathtub trap.

If none of these measures corrects the stoppage, you'll have to remove and clean the drain trap. Put a bucket under the trap before loosening the packing nuts. This is to catch any water that spills out. Once the clog is removed, check the washers before replacing the trap. Then make sure the nuts are snugged up tight.

A bathtub trap has a cover that must be removed with a wrench. Turn the wrench on the nut at the cover's center. If the nut is stripped (not unusual) or the cover is stuck, you may have to loosen it with a hammer and punch in notches cut into the cap with a cold chisel. Check the fiber gasket before replacing the cap, and replace the gasket if necessary.

A blocked toilet trap *may* require a specialized tool. Still, renting a small "clean-out auger" may be cheaper than calling in a plumber to handle this particular job.

Water Treatment

High quality water-treatment equipment is typically covered by an excellent warranty that reflects the manufacturer's confidence in the product. But it will still require periodic attention. If you own a water softener, your main job will be to keep the brine tank supplied with dry salt, so salt solutions will be automatically made up between regenerations. (61) Electrically operated timers control regeneration cycles in the newest water softeners, and the timer should be set by the installer. These timers have proven virtually trouble-free in recent years, but they should be monitored. An electrical outage can throw the cycle out of whack. Or maybe the setting causes the softener to regenerate too often, or not often enough. To reset the timer, or to regulate the brine concentration, follow the instructions received with your unit. These instructions should also include a trouble-shooting chart. If something goes wrong, consult *it* before calling the plumber.

Filtering Units

Filtration units will demand attention from time to time. An iron filter may be the most troublesome. It will need its prescription of potassium permanganate refilled. This refill might be as infrequent as once a year, or as often as once a week, depending on how badly the water supply is polluted with iron. (60) Handle the potassium permanganate cautiously. *Domestic Water Treatment* describes it as a "powerful oxidizing material. Explosive in contact with sulfuric acid or hydrogen peroxide. Reacts violently with finely divided, easily oxidizable substances. Increases flammability or combustible materials."

Activated carbon filters, once they're saturated, can absorb no more contaminants, tastes, and odors. In some cases the old carbon can be vacuumed out, backwashed clean, or simply dumped and replaced with new medium. More often, however, it's simpler (and probably more economical) to replace the entire unit. (64)

Clarifying filters, used to remove turbidity, will lose their effectiveness when the filter bed becomes overloaded with sediment. Since water turbidity can vary throughout the year, it's hard to know when to schedule regular backwashing. Pressure at the filter discharge should be watched closely. Whenever it falls below an acceptable level, the filter should be backwashed. (63)

Neutralizing filters correct a water's pH, as we know. (65) Acidic water gradually dissolves limestone and marble chips in the filter bed, and the medium must be replenished whenever it's necessary. Furthermore, the filter bed, which may also collect some sediment, should be backwashed—maybe as often as once a week in extreme instances.

A chemical feed pump may need more attention than any other water-treatment device. A strainer is designed to remove waterborne particles before they enter the feeder. If it's doing its job it will become clogged regularly and will need to be cleared. Any chemical feeder contains highly corrosive material. Chlorine is the most obvious example. It will do its best to weaken valves, springs, and synthetic "O rings." These components will need to be inspected, cleaned, and replaced whenever they're damaged. The other vital maintenance step, of course, is to keep the chemical storage tank filled.

Reverse osmosis (RO) units (69) are expensive and all but maintenance-free. But the RO pressure pump is meant to apply as much as 400 psi of force against the membrane. A sudden and drastic increase or decrease in pressure—as indicated by the gauges in the system—suggests either a fouled RO membrane, a defective pump, or weakened seals. So the gauges should be watched closely.

87. FOOT VALVES, CHECK VALVES, AND FLOW-CONTROL VALVES

Specialized valves may be used to control automatically the quantity and the direction of water flow anywhere in the lines. The ideal home system will have a small amount of stored water, held under pressure at all times, for emergencies. (A good backup system might include a standby gasoline-powered electric generator which would permit the pump to operate during an extended power failure.)

A *foot valve* can be installed in a well at the base of a suction line or below a submersible jet pump. Its function is to prevent backflow and to maintain pump prime in a jet-pump or turbine system. Sometimes the foot valve is placed at the end of a *tail pipe*, a water line that extends below the lowest theoretical drawdown of the well. The tail pipe operates like an automatic throttle, assuring that the well can't be overpumped. The foot valve keeps the tail pipe full of water, even when there's no pumping action.

It's best not to skimp on the quality of a foot valve. Use the best one available. It's difficult to replace. It should have good flow characteristics. That is, it should *not* cause a lot of vacuum or head loss, particularly at that low point in the well. Centrifugal or turbine pumps, remember, are meant to pump little or no air. By insuring prime, the foot valve is protecting the pump's seals, rings, and other parts that might otherwise be destroyed by an overheated pump, working "dry."

A check valve, mentioned several times earlier, is used in suction lines and discharge lines from submersible pumps. It's also used in situations

A check valve permits water to flow in only one direction. In this case the valve is closed.

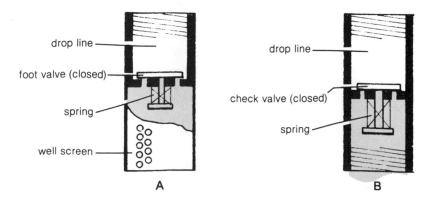

Two types of valves frequently found in wells. (A) A foot valve for maintaining prime in jet-pump systems. (B) A vertical check valve to prevent backflow.

where more than one pump is supplying water to the same delivery line. In this case, possibly harmful pressure generated by one pump is not permitted to reach the other, thanks to the check valve.

Prevents Backflow

Basically, a check valve is an anti-backflow mechanism. Normally check valves are spring-operated, and like foot valves, they should have good flow-through qualities and shouldn't produce a lot of friction in a water line. More sophisticated check valves include stemless guide types, diaphragm types which have no moving parts, and streamlined stemless guide types, famous for generating very little head loss.

Often a submersible pump will be equipped with two check valves. The first is located at the top of the pump; the second near the pressure tank inlet. There should be a check valve between any reciprocating pump and the pressure tank. Its function is to hold water in the hydropneumatic tank and distribution lines, preventing any water from running back into the well line or into the pump.

Flow-control valves have the opposite effect on water-delivery lines. They're used where there's a very limited water supply or when a pumping system is weak. Flow-control valves restrict and regulate, keeping too much water from moving through a line too quickly. In areas where water conservation is becoming a way of life, small flow-control valves are now being installed in branch distribution lines. In a sense, they serve as water-saving fixtures, limiting the gallons-per-minute flow to showers and other appliances. (99)

88. NOISE CONTROL

Humorist James Thurber lay awake worrying about "things that go bump in the night." He may have been hearing the plumbing. Good plumbers reduce water hammer—the thud or strong vibration in distribution pipes—in several ways. First, they build long sweep bends into main lines, so large

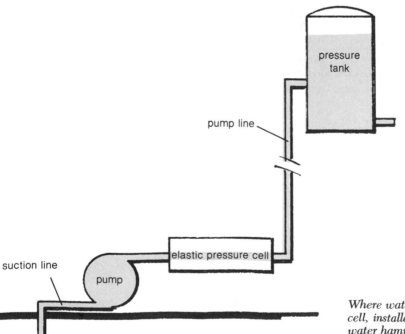

Where water must be pumped uphill, an elastic pressure cell, installed near the pump, can be used to cushion water hammer.

amounts of water don't have to turn sharp corners. Second, they install air chambers, sometimes called risers, near each faucet. (77) Third, they hang hot water lines with hardware that allows for pipe expansion. Last, they may use plastic fittings designed to dampen pipe vibration and reduce noise.

The water hammer Thurber may have been hearing may not have been in the house distribution lines at all. The pressure tank, common to almost any modern setup, alleviates a lot of thud. The sounds may have been in an earlier portion of the water system. Noise can be a particular problem where water must be pumped great distances uphill through a long delivery pipe. When the pump starts and the column of water is suddenly moved, or when a valve is closed and the water's movement is quickly stopped, a pounding sound can result.

In some cases this problem has been solved by using two pressure tanks: one at the level of the pump (if it's above ground) and the second higher uphill at the delivery point (the tank's normal location). But, as the AAVIM reminds us, "This often creates air problems in *both* tanks. The air supply in the lower tank is under high pressure so the air is absorbed by the water readily and delivered to the upper tank. This makes it difficult to keep the lower tank properly charged with air." If a diaphragm tank were used at the lower level, this problem could be reduced.

The best solution may be to locate elastic pressure cells (56) near the pump, and possibly at the upper level near the pressure tank. These pressure cells should provide enough cushioning to absorb any noise.

89. PRESSURE SWITCHES AND FLOW SWITCHES

Electrical controls for small domestic water systems fall into two categories. *Operating controls* dictate when pumping equipment is to work, and when it's to shut down. *Safety controls* might also instruct a pump to stop or start, but their additional purpose is to protect the machinery from damage during a malfunction, or in the event of dangerously low water level in the well. The most common operating controls are *pressure switches* and *float switches* discussed here. Safety controls, including *low-water cut-offs* and *low-flow controls*, are described in the following section.

A pressure switch is in a small gray box mounted on the pump, on the line between the pump and the pressure tank, or on the tank itself. It senses pressure on the delivery side of the pump. Its chief component is a flexible rubber diaphragm. Pressurized water is always in the open connector between the switch and the water line. Water pushes upward against the diaphragm. The diaphragm, in turn, pushes upward against a range spring, compressing it. As the spring compresses, it moves a small lever and camwheel mechanism that trips a toggle switch, breaking the "snap-acting" electrical contacts. This break in contact is what gives the pressure switch its distinctive "click" as it shuts off at the appointed pressure point—usually forty, but sometimes sixty psi.

Almost all pressure switches operate the same way. Remove the plastic cover and you'll see a differential adjusting nut which allows you to change the tension on the lever spring. (The lever spring is smaller than the range spring. The differential adjusting nut is also the smaller of the two nuts.) You can increase or decrease the break pressure—normally factory-set—without changing the pressure point at which the pump starts up. But the *Water Systems Handbook* says,

Caution: Adjustments to pressure switches of any kind should be made by someone familiar with the type of switch employed. It's quite possible on

Pressure switch controls operation of pump.

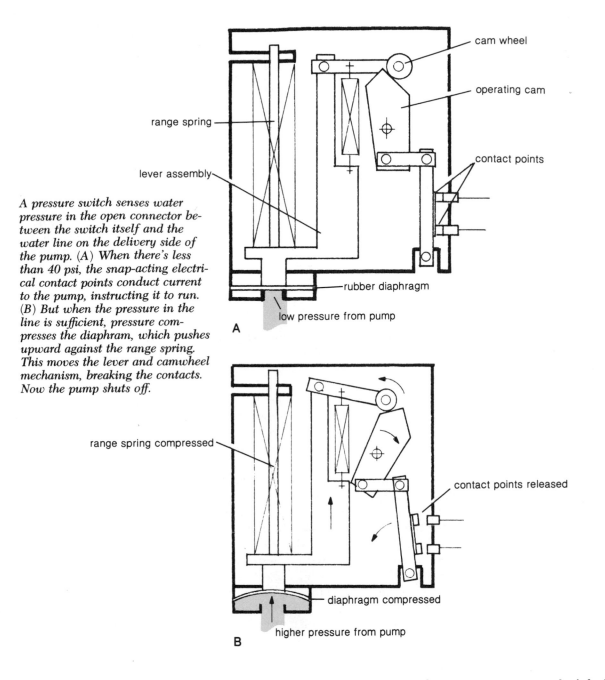

cam wheel

operating cam

contact points

range spring

lever assembly

A pressure switch senses water pressure in the open connector between the switch itself and the water line on the delivery side of the pump. (A) When there's less than 40 psi, the snap-acting electrical contact points conduct current to the pump, instructing it to run. (B) But when the pressure in the line is sufficient, pressure compresses the diaphram, which pushes upward against the range spring. This moves the lever and camwheel mechanism, breaking the contacts. Now the pump shuts off.

rubber diaphragm

low pressure from pump

A

range spring compressed

contact points released

diaphragm compressed

higher pressure from pump

B

any switch now manufactured to obtain a pressure setting that's higher than the capacity of the pump it's controlling. In such cases, the motor may overheat and fail or other pump parts may fail.

A float switch is used to control the water level in a gravity tank or individual reservoir. (49) It looks and works very much like a pressure switch except the switch controlling the circuit to the pump is activated by a float arm rather than a diaphragm. The float itself moves up and down with the water level, just like the float in a toilet tank. When the water level lowers, the float arm trips the switch and the pump is started. When water rises to its prescribed level near the top of the storage tank or reservoir, the electrical contact points in the switch are broken, stopping electrical current to the pump. The pump then stops.

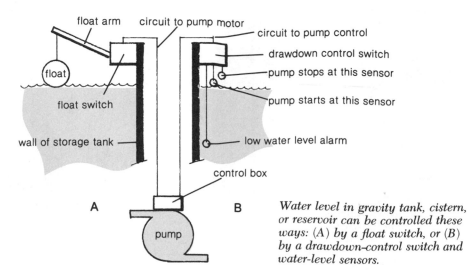

Water level in gravity tank, cistern, or reservoir can be controlled these ways: (A) by a float switch, or (B) by a drawdown-control switch and water-level sensors.

90. LOW-WATER CUTOFFS, LOW-FLOW AND LOW-PRESSURE SWITCHES

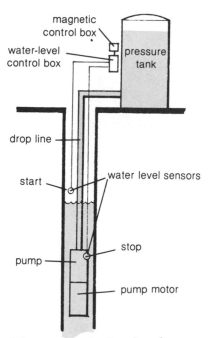

A low-water cut-off or drawdown-control switch can be used in a well with limited yield. It insures that the pump can't start when water reaches a dangerously low level.

A low-water cutoff, or *drawdown-control switch*, as it's often called, is a safety control consisting of a relay box and two (possibly three) electrodes suspended in a well, gravity tank or reservoir. Its purpose is to start the pump when the well casing or tank is filled to the appropriate level, to shut it off again when the water reaches the desired drawdown point, and *most important*, to be sure the pump cannot start when water reaches a dangerously low level. A low-water cutoff is meant to be a safeguard in a well that has very limited yield.

The lowest electrode, or sensor, is usually placed in a well just a few inches above the submersible pump. The upper electrode is suspended somewhat higher, at a distance depending on the well's recovery rate. When the water level reaches the lower electrode, the relay box breaks off the current to the motor, and it stops until the water level has recovered to the height of the upper sensor. This way the pump can never run "dry."

A drawdown control switch is installed to operate in conjunction with a normal pressure or float switch. But this low-water cutoff should be wired to override the pressure switch if need be. In other words, if the lowest drawdown level is reached, the pump will shut down, even if there's insufficient pressure in the tank, according to the pressure switch. The pump motor should not start again until the water level has climbed back to the top sensor.

Low-flow controls sense when there's too little water in a delivery line to the pressure tank. One type consists of a *rotatable* or *bendable vane* installed in the inlet line to the tank. When the flow is reduced to a dangerous level, the vane detects it, tripping a time-delay circuit that shuts off the pump within thirty to ninety seconds. This kind of low-flow control may be reset manually, or it can be set to restart the pump after a predetermined period of recovery time.

A second type of control measures the pressure at the check valve leading to the hydropneumatic tank inlet. When the pressure is inadequate, a time-delay circuit is triggered to stop the pump. These pressure-sensing switches can also be set to stop the pump immediately, without any time delay.

Any of these devices are meant to anticipate low-water levels as well as weakened flow—to be sure the pump never runs out of water. Of course, a water-level sensing device cannot detect a clogged well screen, nor can a

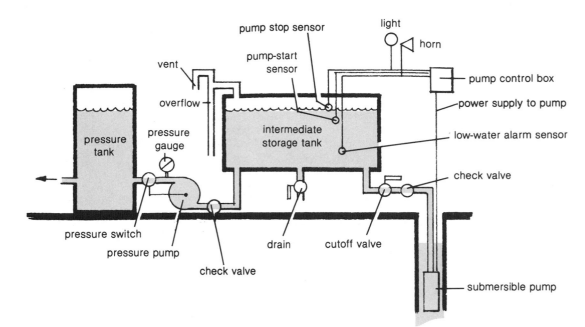

pump stop sensor

pump-start sensor

light

horn

vent

overflow

pump control box

power supply to pump

pressure tank

pressure gauge

intermediate storage tank

low-water alarm sensor

check valve

pressure switch

pressure pump

check valve

drain

cutoff valve

submersible pump

In this elaborate layout, an intermediate storage tank takes up the slack in a system where the well capacity can't possibly meet all of a family's demands. The light and horn signal too low a water level in the tank. Pressure is supplied not by the low-capacity well pump, but by the second pressure pump near the pressure tank.

low-pressure device detect the absence of flow. For peace of mind you might want a second set of these auxiliary protective controls to back up the pressure switch.

91. AIR-VOLUME CONTROLS

Air-volume controls keep the proper balance of air and water in a hydropneumatic tank. Such a control may not be necessary in a pressure tank with a good absorption barrier or diaphragm. (56) Where air and water are isolated from each other, there's little opportunity for air to be absorbed in the liquid and be carried away. New air *might* have to be pumped into this sort of tank once a year or so. If the water level in a plain steel tank gets too high, however, a valve of some kind must open to draw more air into the tank. A pressure tank might also have an air-release mechanism for times when there's too *much* air inside.

Air-volume controls are among the most fascinating minisystems in all of plumbing. They employ floats, jets, springs, diaphragms, and an ingenious little device called a *snifter valve*, which reacts to pressure by opening or closing, letting air in or out of places where it's needed.

Pumps Air, Too

The simplest air-volume regulators are called *shallow-well float-type controls,* which are designed for shallow-well piston pumps. They take advantage of the fact that a reciprocating, positive-displacement pump is able to pump a certain amount of air, along with water. (38) The air-volume control is connected to the pump through an extra loop of tubing. When the water

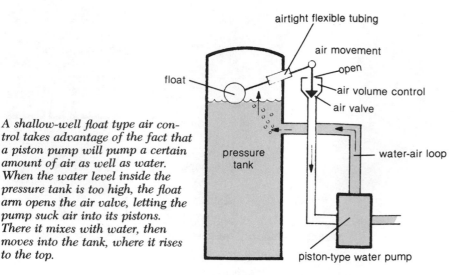

airtight flexible tubing

air movement

open

float

air volume control

air valve

pressure tank

water-air loop

piston-type water pump

A shallow-well float type control takes advantage of the fact that a piston pump will pump a certain amount of air as well as water. When the water level inside the pressure tank is too high, the float arm opens the air valve, letting the pump suck air into its pistons. There it mixes with water, then moves into the tank, where it rises to the top.

inside the tank gets too high, a float-and-arm mechanism opens an air valve in the control unit, and lets the pump suck air into its pistons. Here it mixes with whatever water is already moving through the pump, and is passed along to the tank. Once inside the tank, the air separates from the water, rising to the top of the interior space.

Once enough air has accumulated in the tank, the water level is lowered. The float drops, the air valve in the control is closed, and the pump moves water only. There's one catch in this system: if the water source is at the same level as the pump, or higher than the pump, there won't be enough suction developed to pull air through the pump pistons. To solve the problem, add a valve to the suction line, restrict the water flow with it, and in that way increase suction.

Deep-Well Pumps

Deep-well piston pumps often have an *air-pump air-release control* that moves air into the tank all the time the pump is working. When the water level gets too high, a similar float keeps the air valve closed, and all the air coming into the tank remains there. If there's too much air, the float lowers, and the air valve is opened, letting air escape. To regulate the amount of air leaving the tank, a pressure valve is located in the outer chamber of the control. The pressure valve prevents the air pressure from dropping below about thirty psi.

Centrifugal, jet, and turbine pumps (39 through 41) can pump *some* air without losing their prime, but they become very inefficient when air is introduced. So several ways have been devised to move air into the tank without it ever passing through the pump. The first, a *diaphragm-type air control*, looks like a swollen disc that's attached to the outside of the pressure tank. A line is run from the control back to the pump's suction line. Within the disc is a rubber diaphragm and spring.

When the pump starts, a partial vacuum is created in the connecting line as water moves through the suction line. Suction pulls the diaphragm against the spring—toward the connecting line. This in turn produces a partial vacuum on the tank side of the diaphragm. Since the vacuum must be filled, a snifter valve lets air into the disc-like control for as long as the pump is pumping. Once the pump stops, the diaphragm is no longer pushed against the spring. In fact, the spring pushes it back the other way, the snif-

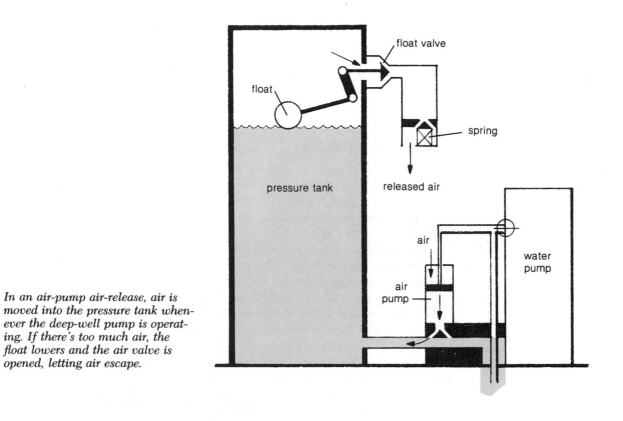

float valve

float

spring

pressure tank

released air

air

water pump

air pump

In an air-pump air-release, air is moved into the pressure tank whenever the deep-well pump is operating. If there's too much air, the float lowers and the air valve is opened, letting air escape.

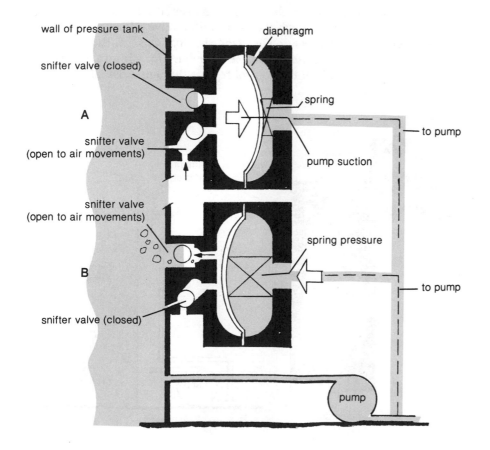

wall of pressure tank

diaphragm

snifter valve (closed)

spring

A

to pump

snifter valve (open to air movements)

pump suction

snifter valve (open to air movements)

spring pressure

B

to pump

snifter valve (closed)

pump

Diaphragm-type air-volume controls are mounted on the side of a pressure tank. (A) The diaphragm is pulled out by pump suction as the pump is running. Air moves into the control through the snifter valve. (B) When the pump stops, the spring forces the diaphragm in toward the tank, sending a burst of air into the pressure tank.

CONTROLLING WATER

ter valve is closed, and a small charge of air bubbles through the opening into the tank.

This control is set at the desired water level within the tank. If water is *below* the level of the control, the snifter valve never opens, and air already in the tank moves into the control. When the pump stops, the same air returns to the tank. In other words, the tank receives *new* air from the diaphragm control only when needed. This type of control, by the way, depends on the pump's turning off and on frequently.

Little Suction Needed

The beauty of another control—a *water-displacement type*—is that very little suction is needed to make it work. It looks like an obese cylinder that's also connected, through a tube, to the pump's suction line. If water is above the control when the pump starts, water from the tank is pulled into this cylindrical air charger. But as it comes out of the tank, it passes through a jet. The tiny jet stream means reduced pressure nearby. To take advantage of this partial vacuum, a snifter valve is placed right above the jet, to let air into the chamber together with water.

After a certain point the air-control cylinder can't hold any more water-and-air mixture, and a float valve seats in the opening to the connector tube. When the pump stops, water pressure in the tank, the suction line, and the connecting line equalizes, forcing the float in the cylinder upward. And the air in the cylinder is forced into the tank. As in the diaphragm-control, when there's already enough air in the tank, no new air is introduced.

Another type of water-displacement control uses suction from a jet placed in the supply line *leaving* the pressure tank. Water flow in the tank's discharge line is drawn through the jet, creating another partial vacuum. This suction draws water from the air-charger unit. As water leaves the cylinder, it's replaced by air moving through the open snifter valve. When water flow in the discharge line stops, pressure equalizes, the float valve in the cylinder is forced open, and water is pushed into the cylinder. *This* pressure closes the snifter and forces the air in the control to pass through a ball check

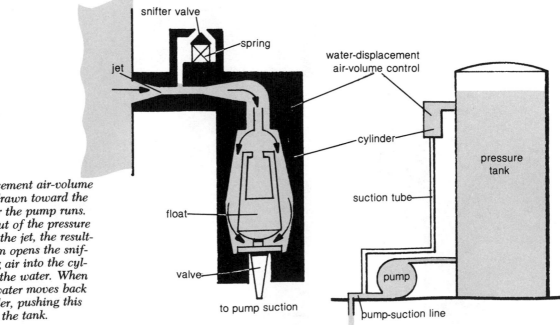

In a water-displacement air-volume control, water is drawn toward the cylinder whenever the pump runs. As water passes out of the pressure tank and through the jet, the resulting partial vacuum opens the snifter valve, drawing air into the cylinder, along with the water. When the pump stops, water moves back up into the cylinder, pushing this new air back into the tank.

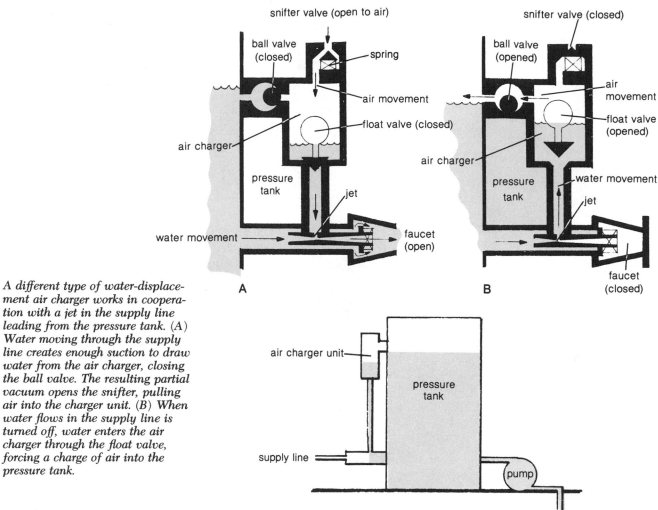

snifter valve (open to air)

ball valve (closed)

spring

air movement

float valve (closed)

air charger

pressure tank

jet

water movement

faucet (open)

A

snifter valve (closed)

ball valve (opened)

air movement

float valve (opened)

air charger

pressure tank

water movement

jet

faucet (closed)

B

air charger unit

pressure tank

supply line

pump

A different type of water-displacement air charger works in cooperation with a jet in the supply line leading from the pressure tank. (A) Water moving through the supply line creates enough suction to draw water from the air charger, closing the ball valve. The resulting partial vacuum opens the snifter, pulling air into the charger unit. (B) When water flows in the supply line is turned off, water enters the air charger through the float valve, forcing a charge of air into the pressure tank.

valve into the tank. If there's already plenty of air in the tank, it's simply passed back and forth between the tank and the cylinder, without any new air entering.

Submersible Pumps

Even submersible pumps have air-volume controls. They're very simple, as well as effective. If a bleeder valve is installed in the well just above the pump on the discharge line, the entire column of water can be drained from the discharge line whenever the pump is not running. It happens when the bleeder valve opens. Water in the line just runs back into the well casing.

If the check valve in the line to the pressure tank also has a snifter valve, you're in business. As water drains out of the line through the bleeder below, air is sucked through the snifter in the check valve above, and the line fills with air. As the pump starts, both the bleeder and snifter close, and the column of air is blown into the tank. If the tank receives *too* much air, the excess escapes through an air-release valve higher on the tank.

Finally, a *venturi* and *air-release* air-volume control can be installed between a pump and pressure tank. This little unit has a pressure-drop adjuster valve, which can be closed just enough to force some of the water in the line to bypass through a venturi. Once more, the venturi is teamed up

water displacement units

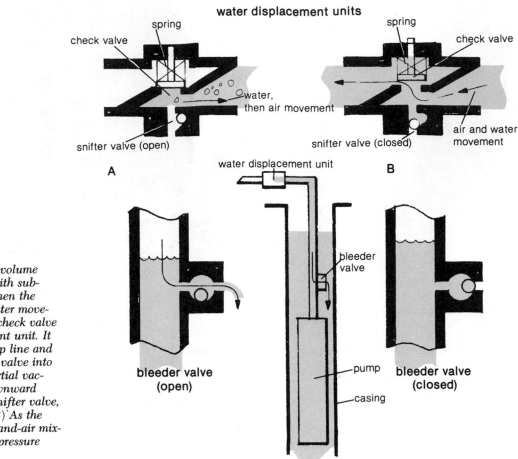

check valve · spring

water, then air movement

snifter valve (open)

A

spring · check valve

air and water movement

snifter valve (closed)

B

water displacement unit

bleeder valve

pump

casing

bleeder valve (open)

bleeder valve (closed)

Water-displacement air-volume controls are also used with submersible pumps. (A) When the pump stops, upward water movement is blocked by the check valve in the water-displacement unit. It runs back down the drop line and out through the bleeder valve into the well casing. The partial vacuum created by the downward water flow, opens the snifter valve, allowing air to enter. (B) As the pump restarts, a water-and-air mixture is pushed into the pressure tank.

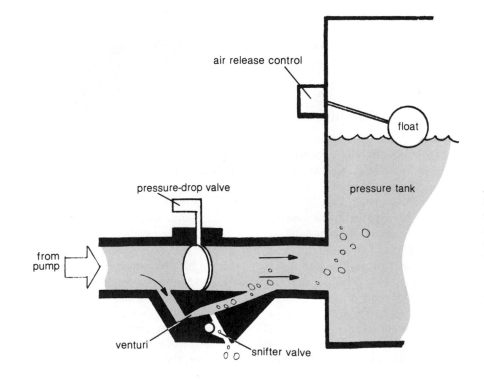

air release control

float

pressure-drop valve

pressure tank

from pump

venturi

snifter valve

A venturi, mounted in the line between pump and pressure tank, might work in conjunction with an air-release control mounted on the side of the pressure tank. The amount of water being diverted through the venturi is controlled by adjusting the pressure-drop valve. A partial vacuum in the venturi pulls air through the snifter valve. The air combines with water entering the pressure tank. Whatever excess air exists in the tank escapes through the air-release control.

THE HOME WATER SUPPLY

with a snifter valve. The jet created as water is squeezed through this small opening and draws air into the line and then into the tank. Again, excess air is released through the air-release control. This type of venturi and air-release is often used with centrifugal and turbine pumps.

92. PRESSURE-RELIEF VALVES AND GAUGES

Pressure-relief valves, which cost less than $10, are cheap insurance for any water system. Pressure gauges vary a great deal in price, but pay for themselves by keeping you informed about what's going on within the system. They can also be helpful trouble-shooters if and when something goes wrong.

Pressure-relief valves should be installed with any shallow-well or deep-well piston pumps. They're spring-loaded and designed to pop should the pressure switch malfunction. It must open, of course, before there's enough pressure to damage the pump. These safety valves may not be necessary with centrifugal or jet pumps, because when pressure in these units builds too high, the pump simply stops—before any damage can be done to either the pump or the hydropneumatic tank.

In building solar water heaters, I've installed several pressure-relief valves at critical points in the lines. I was advised by a plumber friend to use valves that were factory preset and nonadjustable. He thought it best if I was not tempted to monkey with the setting. The AAVIM agrees, saying,

> Note that the relief valve has a *pressure adjusting screw* so it can be adjusted to work at higher or lower pressures. It is important that an inexperienced person not tamper with this adjustment. If adjusted for extra high pressure, it may provide no protection for the pressure tank. A pressure tank explosion can cause considerable damage.

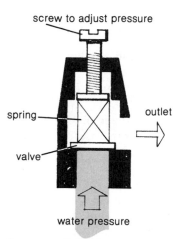

screw to adjust pressure

spring

valve

outlet

water pressure

Pressure-relief valves protect a water system from excess pressure.

Pressure gauges do more than tell you how much pressure is being developed by the pump. They can help locate problems anywhere in the system, and become more valuable as the system becomes more complex, particularly if water-treatment units are installed. If you need to change the setting on a pressure switch, for example, it would be impossible without a gauge. A pressure gauge is also necessary where there's a deep-well jet pump. Enough water, under the right amount of pressure, must be returned to the jet below if the pump is to do its job. (41)

93. LIGHTNING SURGE PROTECTION

Motor overloading and lightning are a pump's two worst enemies. I'm told that during a thunderstorm electrical power lines are almost never hit by lightning directly. But a bolt of lightning nearby may produce an electrical surge in the lines that can ruin the insulation in a pump's motor windings, causing the motor to short out. The *Water Systems Handbook* tells us that utility companies protect their own equipment and lines from lightning surges, but that their 10,000-volt protection is much higher than most home appliances—including water pumps—can stand.

All of this is to say that lightning arresters and grounding are a necessity in almost all rural situations. Grounding connects power lines to moist earth, and is meant to offer a path of least resistance for a sudden abundance of voltage seeking an avenue to the ground. When a surge exceeds the amount of voltage acceptable to the home's electrical system, it's reached what's called the *impulse sparkover voltage*. This is when a lightning arrester takes over. The *Water Systems Handbook* does a better job than I could of describing how these devices work:

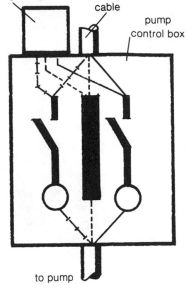

Lightning arrester mounted on pump-control box.

... Two types of arresters are available, the expulsion type and the valve (pellet) type.

An expulsion arrester consists of an air gap and a gas generating material. During normal voltage, the air gap insulates the power lines from the ground. If the line to ground voltage exceeds the arrester impulse sparkover voltage, the air gap "sparks over" and short-circuits the line to the ground. The resulting current through the special material in the arrester produces a gas which "blows out" the arc. An expulsion arrester is designed for outdoor use only.

The valve type arrester consists of many pellets of nonlinear material separated by small air gaps. The material presents a low resistance to high voltages and a high resistance to low voltages. At the impulse sparkover voltage, the air gaps spark over and the nonlinear pellets short-circuit the power line to the ground. When normal voltage returns, the resistance of the pellets automatically increases and the air gap voltages are reduced to the point where current ceases to flow.

With the advent of the submersible pump, it was widely believed that these in-well water lifters would be particularly vulnerable to lightning surges. Although this has proven *not* to be the case, when lightning does damage submersibles, it tends to be extensive, and expensive—to say nothing of the inconvenience. For this reason you might consider lightning arresters in places besides those normally recommended.

Two of the most typical locations for lightning arresters are where service wires connect to the house's service entrance cable, and on the switch box where the wires to the pump motor originate. The advantage of an arrester at the service entrance is that it helps protect the wiring in all of the home's electrical system.

A lightning stroke often follows underground wiring. If it struck somewhere in a cable between the control box and a submersible pump, for instance, the surge could travel in both directions—to the house *and* the pump motor. In this case the arrester on the control box would be of little help to the pump. A safer arrangement might be to install another arrester at the well head, or to encase the underground cable, leading from the house to the well, in a metal conduit.

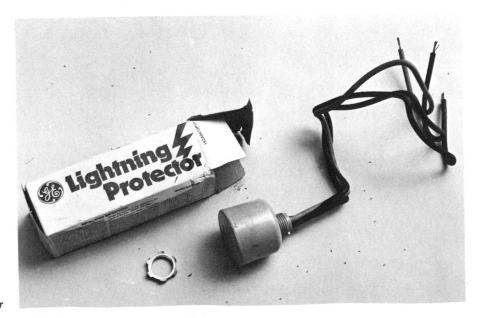

Lightning arrester

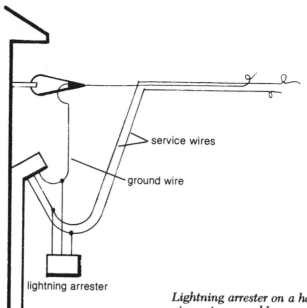

service wires

ground wire

lightning arrester

Lightning arrester on a home service entrance cable.

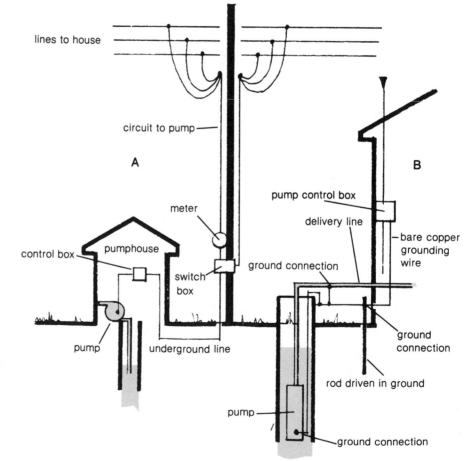

lines to house

circuit to pump

A

B

meter

pump control box

control box

pumphouse

delivery line

bare copper grounding wire

ground connection

switch box

pump

underground line

ground connection

rod driven in ground

pump

ground connection

Two safeguards. (A) A separate pump circuit may be run underground from a metering pole to the pump control box. If there's a fire in the home, the pump should still run. (B) A water system should have ground connections at least at these three points.

CONTROLLING WATER

187

94. OVERLOAD CONTROLS

An overloaded pump motor will, of course, overheat. When it gets too hot, the motor windings burn out. This could happen if the pump's rotor were somehow to lock up, if the pump were short-cycling for too long, or if its normal means of cooling were threatened. If for some reason the water level in a well got below the submersible pump, the motor, dependent on water for cooling, would be in grave danger. Likewise, centrifugal pumps, which are designed to push water against a certain amount of pressure, can be harmed if they pump for too long at full capacity with a free discharge of water.

Circuit breakers, time-delay fuses, and magnetic switches are all designed to provide overload protection. Any motor protector must let the motor continually receive the most current it can accept (it needs all it can get during start-up), yet trip in a no-load situation, or if the motor *fails* to start for whatever reason. It's also an important maintenance procedure to keep air vents in an above-ground pump free of dust or other material that could obstruct the passage of cooling air.

Thermostats are a part of many motors. And *overcurrent protectors* are meant to prevent overloads. Here a heater strip, placed close to a bimetallic strip, heats up and warps whenever there's too much current being delivered to the motor. The warping releases a trigger, breaking the electrical contact points and opening the circuit. The motor stops. When the bimetallic plate cools down enough to restraighten, the motor can be started again with a reset button.

Unfortunately overcurrent protectors don't guard against overheating from lack of cooling. And a thermostat may not act fast enough to save a motor which does not start. So newer motors are equipped with *inherent thermal protection,* meaning that both thermostats and overcurrent protection are on hand.

Submersible pumps also may have some inherent thermal protection, but they rely on external back-up protection too, in the form of fuses, circuit breakers, and low-water (drawdown) protectors. (87 and 90) In addition, *low-flow protectors* break off current when the submersible pump seems to be operating all or most of the time, but is producing less than a predetermined minimum flow.

Your pump dealer is probably the best source of information about pump motor overload controls, and should install whatever devices best suit your particular system. If he can't satisfy your further curiosity, additional information about electrical controls can be obtained by writing the AAVIM (American Association for Vocational Instructional Materials), Engineering Building, Athens, GA 30602. Ask for the publication called "Electric Motors—Selection, Protection, Drives."

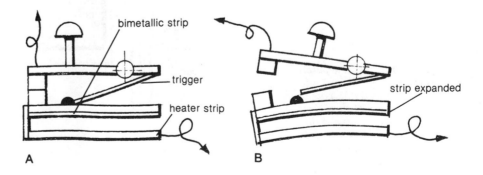

An overcurrent protector works this way: (A) Current passes through the heater strip. The heat expands and warps the bimetallic strip, which breaks the circuit (B). Now the overload control needs to be reset.

9 PROTECTING AND CONSERVING WATER

95. COMMUNITY SYSTEMS

It sounded like rock-n-roll. Visitors walking past the tiny pump house shielded by bushes would ask, "Where's that music coming from?" Somehow the combined thumps of the ancient pump and chlorine feeder were so harmonious they could have been a muffled bass and drum backing up a band. It made you want to dance.

The music, if that's what you'd call it, was actually the heartbeat of a small community water system in Vermont, one that's been in operation, in one form or another, for nearly a century. We took from its erratic plentitude for many summers, along with eighteen other families. The pump in question drew water through a long suction line which sank twenty feet or so below the surface of Lake Champlain.

Lake water was mixed with chlorine in the pump house, then pushed uphill to a ramshackle barn that housed a large wooden cistern. I don't know exactly how big this container was, but I climbed the ladder on its side more than once, and peered into the darkness. It had to be twelve feet across, and if I'd fallen in I would have had to swim. It was that deep.

This cistern sat at the point of highest elevation on the lakeshore peninsula, and it functioned as a gravity tank, pressing water back downward to the nineteen cottages in the co-op. Since the archaic bylaws of the Cedar Beach Association made it illegal for anyone to winterize his cottage and try to live there year round, the water distribution system remained a tangle of galvanized pipes that ran along the surface of the ground. The old pipes were ugly, and until you learned where they were, you'd probably stumble on a valve or fitting one night, walking home in the dark. So it was dangerous, as well as unsightly and costly. But nobody complained much. At least the pipes were easy to get at.

The system would be started up each May, and drained again in October. (Each family was responsible for filling, draining, and looking after the plumbing in its own cottage.) Not rarely, something would go wrong. Pipe joints, nudged and shifted by frost each winter, would develop problems. Or a delivery truck would back over a line, breaking it and putting everybody out of water—sometimes for hours, sometimes overnight, sometimes through a weekend, until replacement parts could be found on Monday.

Everyone Helped

When this happened, association members would be enlisted to man the huge pipe wrenches and help replace the damaged section. I grew to know the system more intimately than I cared to, and my taste buds grew sensitive to the varying degrees of chlorination in our water. About the time it became unbearably strong, somebody would do something about it. I began

189

to get inklings of the myriad problems that arise when many people share a water source and dole it out among themselves. In those years I'd return each autumn to my funky farmhouse and its jerry-rigged water system with a sigh of relief, and a renewed sense of freedom.

South Lake Tahoe, California/Nevada, is a year-round resort city, beside another lake a continent away. Now we live there for six months each year and share water with as many as a quarter of a million others during busy times. I've made it a point to know almost nothing about the municipal water system there, except to realize that water comes from the lake (which remains virtually pure), and that our sewage is pumped, at great expense, out of the Tahoe Basin, to be treated elsewhere. (This particular engineering project has been dubbed a "failure" by many.) I don't know if, or how much, the water is treated.

I do know what comes out of the tap. The water is clear, odor-free, very cold, soft enough to make laundering easy, and absolutely delicious. Put some in an old-fashioned seltzer bottle, inject carbon dioxide from a cartridge, and you make sparkling water that puts both Canada Dry and Perrier to shame. I have yet to be aware of the system's failing, and I hear no complaints.

The political struggle surrounding the water in Lake Tahoe has been a painful and bitter one, and it's destined to worsen in the face of frightening population pressures and drought. But for the moment, the product is a triumphant testament to compromising environmentalists, engineers, developers, and the U.S. Forest Service, all of whom had a hand in putting together this community water system.

But Tahoe is an exception to the rule. Generally our communal waterworks, particularly the gargantuan systems in our largest cities, are rickety, ill-kept, highly vulnerable, and in some cases a menace to health and well being. *U.S. News and World Report* claims that old pipes in New York City leak an average of 100 *million* gallons a day. They say the Boston system, even worse, leaks two gallons for every one it delivers. The contamination potential with so much leakage is horrendous.

Not long ago, vandals managed to wreck two aqueducts in Newark, New Jersey, and according to former *New York Times* reporter Fred Powledge, the breakage "threw the system into chaos." It was later discovered, ironically, that the city's "chief of security," whose job it was to protect the system, actually lived in Florida.

"Bad" Pipes

Televised reports from the West Coast's Bay Area say there are at least 6,000 "bad" pipes in the San Francisco water system. And there's six times the acceptable lead level in that city's drinking water. In neighboring San Jose, California, there's an echo of the Love Canal, albeit a hushed-up one. Chemicals from an industrial plant have allegedly seeped into city wells, polluting the drinking water. This contaminated water is believed to have caused birth defects in children.

"Is the Water Safe to Drink?," a multi-part article which appeared in *Consumer Reports*, suggests that even city water that's been processed in sophisticated treatment facilities still contains serious contaminants.

All too often, they say, water treatment personnel are poorly paid, receive little training, and are shoved into a situation where they're told, "OK, here it is. Turn this valve and make sure everything is pumping." When something goes wrong, or somebody gets sick from the water, these people are to blame, though often they don't have the foggiest idea why.

Recontamination

Municipal water purification as it now exists is a step in the right direction, but the finished product that comes out of the kitchen faucet is discouraging. Recontamination often happens *after* treatment. It comes from one of two sources, according to *Consumer Reports:*

1. Fresh water picks up impurities from the system's copper, lead, galvanized, or plastic pipes. Solder in plumbing joints contributes cadmium. In some cases cement pipes give off carcinogenic asbestos.

2. Further impurities come from poorly maintained or faulty "cross connections" between fresh water and nonpotable sources. Sometimes backflow, which results from too little pressure in water or sewage lines, adulterates purified water with polluted water.

In short, municipal water problems are almost too large to grasp, though probably not insurmountable. Upgrading town and city waterworks, large and small, will present a staggering burden to taxpayers. Those of us who move beyond community systems will continue to have our own sets of problems, but we may count ourselves lucky. With this in mind, it's all the more important to protect and conserve what we have.

96. WATER RIGHTS

When Robby Adams got his bulldozer stuck in my pond site the first time, I wasn't that surprised. I warned him. The 5.28 acres I own in Stowe Hollow is part of the old Peterson Farm, which at one time accounted for much of the land on the north side of the hollow. When Mr. Peterson got too old to farm—in his estimation—he sold off a major portion of the land to a man who then subdivided it. When I bought Lot #13, Charlie Burnham, the surveyor who laid out the subdivision, gave me a map of my land and the land adjacent.

On that map, immediately off my property line to the east, was a small square clearly marked, "Peterson spring." From there a dotted line ran across my parcel marked, "Peterson spring line." The deed includes several "covenants," one of which says,

> "Lots 12, 13, 14, 15 and 2 are subject to certain spring and pipeline rights of record in Book 80 Pages 569–72 of the Stowe Land Records. No building, structure, or part thereof, shall be erected on said lots, the outside of which shall be less than twenty-five (25) feet from said existing pipeline."

The records explained the deal between Peterson and the developer. The land would be purchased for X-amount of dollars, and the developer was to pay the cost of drilling a well near the Peterson farmhouse. In addition, Peterson and his heirs would forever reserve the right to the spring and to the buried line running from it—across five lots, all the way to his barn.

The bulldozer found and severed the polyethylene line, which proved to be right where it was supposed to be. It gushed a ¾-inch stream of spring water and mired down the cat. Aware of the covenant, I went straight to Mr. Peterson, who was rocking on his front porch, as usual.

I allowed as how we'd just cut his spring line, and would repair it as soon as possible. He was civil enough about the whole thing, said the well was working fine, and that he'd not been aware of the break. But he didn't let me off the hook. The spring was his "back-up," the only water source to his barn, and he wanted it. By late that afternoon we'd restored the flow, and he was satisfied.

Weeks later I attended an evening meeting of the Stowe Planning Commission, to lend moral support to a friend who'd been called on the carpet because one of his buildings was purportedly too close to the town road. The case preceding my friend's *also* involved a spring line, but it had been far less peaceful than my own with Mr. Peterson. The dispute involved a local resident (who also had a well) and an out-of-state developer who was trying to gain approval for a condominium cluster on the adjacent parcel of land.

The developer's representative was a smooth talker, armed with very professional color renderings of the proposed complex, as well as a sense for saying what he thought the commission wanted to hear. The only fly in the ointment was one silly spring line, which again was only a back-up. But it was enough to stand in the way of approval, though everything else in the plan seemed to conform to Stowe's requirements. The local officials were buying nothing of the plan—despite the presenter's attempts to gloss over the problem. What they said was "Get your water problem worked out, and we'll listen. Otherwise let's hear the next case." I don't know exactly where it stands at the moment, but I know the complex has not yet been built.

Riparian Rights

In the eastern United States, where water generally abounds, arguments like this are usually settled in accordance with a sensible set of laws based on the idea of live-there-and-you-own-it. Most state water laws in the East conform to the concept of *riparian water rights.* (The adjective, "riparian," is defined as "of, relating to, or on the bank, as of a river.")

Riparian water rights permit the use of water from lakes, streams, and rivers by those who live immediately adjacent to them. They also include the *underflow*—groundwater beneath one's property. The Water Supply Division of the Environmental Protection Agency defines riparian rights as "rights that are acquired together with the title of the land bordering or overlying the water source." In other words, own the land and you own the water on it or in it, so long as you don't conflict with similar rights of owners downstream. In parts of the country east of the 100th meridian, this is the dominant legal doctrine. It only gets sticky in cases where land changes hands, but water rights don't. Then it becomes like a right-of-way question.

Rights in West

In the West (except for the damp Pacific Northwest), the story is altogether different because water is scarce—particularly scarce west of the front range of the Rocky Mountains. The history of the western United States is largely a tale of feuds over water. Directly or indirectly the plot of every cowboy movie involves the question of water rights.

Log of a Cowboy by Andy Adams is the real-life journal of a real-life drover, written well over a century ago. For years the life Adams recorded consisted of driving herds of cattle from the Rio Grande in southern Texas, more than 1,000 miles north to the greener summer grass of Montana. In the fall, when cold set in, they'd drive the herd back to graze in Texas.

At the time, the vast ocean of grassland east of the Rockies was "open range"—to be used freely by anyone passing through. Adams and his cohorts moved their bovine charges lazily and according to the weather, stopping to drink at whatever water sources they happened upon. When they neared a railhead like the one at Dodge City, Kansas (later to become the setting for the mainly-fictional *Gunsmoke* series on radio and TV), a portion of the herd would be cut out, sold, and shipped East to places like Chicago for slaughter.

During the sale, cowboys who had been at home on the range for months were given leave to spend a day or so in town. As we know, their drunk-and-disorderly conduct created problems for law-enforcement officials like the legendary Matt Dillon. But fracases among drovers in the Long Branch Saloon were minor compared to the range wars which were to follow.

As settlers began to homestead the open range, they naturally looked for places where there was water. When they found it, they laid claim to it, and built fences around it. The cattlemen, looking for waterholes to slake the thirst in thousands of steers, resented the new fences and the homesteaders, and tried to overrun both in many cases. That's when *real* trouble began, and the results were often bloody.

The fledgling system of law tried to deal with this sort of conflict (and other disputes arising from miners' uses of water) by establishing a different legal doctrine, with precedent in ancient Moorish law, centered around *prior appropriation*. Basically it said, "First come, first served."

The EPA's modern definition of *appropriative rights* is a bit more vague than that of riparian rights—as is the whole concept of owning water that comes from, or through, land somewhere else. Appropriate rights, they say, are "acquired by following a specific legal procedure," which may be another way of saying that a lawyer can lay a perfectly legal claim to water on behalf of somebody who wants to appropriate it from elsewhere. Whoever is first to divert water from its source to his own property takes all he can prove his need for.

Prescriptive rights are "acquired by diverting and putting to use, for a period of specific stature, water to which other parties may or may not have prior claim. The procedure necessary to obtain prescriptive rights," says the EPA, "must conform with the conditions established by the water rights of the individual states." In some states, then, water can be shuffled around between prescribed areas, but the legalities can get complicated. Fred Powledge in his fine book entitled *Water*, says

> Appropriative rights may be sold and traded and switched up- and downstream. Usually such rights are administered through the offices of the state water engineers (with ultimate settlement of disputes in the state courts), and the quantity of water to be diverted is clearly specified. A claimant who establishes a right to water but who doesn't use it can forfeit his right to it, and so the irony of the western doctrine is that it can encourage waste.

It would be wise not to "borrow" somebody else's water in the West (or elsewhere) without obtaining legal permission first. Failure to do so may result in a serious skirmish with a neighbor, and conceivably with the federal government.

Bigger Battles

Although the basic thrust of this text is to help us all deal with private water problems, it would be profoundly shortsighted to limit a discussion of water rights to those of individual claimants. The July 1981 issue of *Life* had a cover story called, "America the Dry." In it this statement is made: "Water politics in the West is a bitter business. It is a familiar tale of the haves and have-nots, played out in inches of annual rainfall rather than in currency. . . ." On the other hand, Glen Sanders, the man credited with writing much of Colorado's water law, remarks cynically, "(In the West) water runs uphill to money." (103)

The focus of the *Life* article, like so many concerned pieces in the early 80s, is on the death of Mono Lake, the "oldest continuously existing lake in North America." It's about ordinarily peaceful residents of Owens County, California, who have dynamited reservoirs and aqueducts that "steal" their water and spirit it away to cities hundreds of miles away.

It's about the furor surrounding the proposed Peripheral Canal, a forty-three-mile, $5 billion project meant to trap northern California water bound for the ocean in the Sacramento River, and divert it south to thirsty Orange, Los Angeles, and San Diego Counties. Northern Californians are calling it "legal rape," and the fight over the Peripheral Canal could escalate into a twentieth century range war.

Pumping Too Much

It's about land that's *sinking* in Houston, Tucson, parts of New Mexico, and Florida. (One sinkhole in Florida swallowed up a house and six Porsche sports cars, while other holes threaten whole apartment complexes.) It's all because we're pumping water out of the ground—"mining" it or "over-draughting" it—faster than Mother Nature can replenish it. And the subterranean void simply collapses. It's about the 800-mile Ogallala Aquifer that stretches from Nebraska to West Texas. This granddaddy of an underground sea, that's stored water for 10,000 years, is being sucked dry by huge irrigating robots that spray the water over 160 acres at a clip. Most of it evaporates.

The Colorado River, which begins in the Rocky Mountain National Park and flows through the Grand Canyon on its way to the Gulf of California in Mexico, doesn't reach its ultimate destination anymore. It supports more people than the Nile. It's already the most used, tampered-with, and disputed river in the world, taking its water from seven states and contributing to three. It's first dammed before it hardly gets going, less than ten miles from its headwaters. By the time the emasculated river gets to the Gulf of California, it's nothing but a mud flat.

Battles over its flow are fierce, because more water is allocated from the Colorado River than it holds. The 1963 U.S. Supreme Court case of Arizona versus California over Colorado River water, was the longest oral argument heard by that court in the twentieth century. (The majority of justices found in favor of Arizona, denying water to southern California.)

Water watchers Lorus and Margery Milne find the Colorado an internationally significant test case. "Real rivalry for fresh water from a limited supply," they say, "as seen in the American Southwest, portends the future in many parts of the world."

An ever-growing California offers a more specific preview of what's to happen elsewhere. Its water-transfer system is an engineering marvel, to be sure, but it's complex, highly political, and corrupt. (The popular film *Chinatown* is based on water corruption in Southern California.) Already the energy expended just to move water around that state equals all the energy used in Los Angeles.

Powerful Agency

Southern California's Metropolitan Water District (MWD) is just one powerful (and some would say arrogant) government agency in a tangle of federal, state, local, and private claims to water rights. The area between Los Angeles and San Diego, known as the "southcoast region," has been dependent on imported water since the 1920s. In the fertile San Joaquin Valley, there's far more farmland than can be irrigated with existing surface water. So much has been pumped from underground aquifers that the land has sunk thirty feet in some places. The San Joaquin problem raises the question of whether California, where water has been the single most pressing problem ever since the days of the Gold Rush, can support both its cities *and* its agriculture.

Water wars in this country are sure to pit agribusiness against industry, city against city, state against state. The tension, already mounting in the West, is spreading to places like Wisconsin, Virginia, and Delaware, of all places. New Jersey, which may have the most massive water-*quality* problems of any state except Florida, found to its dismay that it has too little public water storage. During the drought of 1980 reservoirs started to run dry, then threatened to overflow later during rainy periods.

Our ninth largest river, the Tennessee, is so overdeveloped and "harnessed" by the Tennessee Valley Authority (TVA) and the Army Corps of Engineers that it can be practically turned on and off like a faucet. Government agencies continue to build dam projects of questionable value throughout the nation, according to Fred Powledge in *Water*. They're apparently immune to the water laws governing the rest of us. And all the building is at taxpayers' expense.

Battles Ahead

Indeed, the U.S. Forest Service, given its druthers, would demand that all water rights used by permittees on public lands be in the name of the U.S. Government. So a battle brews over water rights on gigantic tracts of land the government holds in "our" name.

"Developers might be willing to pay tremendous amounts of money for that water, and we believe the public's right must be protected," said one Forest Service spokesman. "We feel the public interest is only served if the water rights are in the name of the public.

"Right now a lot of questions are being raised. The Justice Department is making a review. If they tell us we don't have the right (to appropriate rights in the name of the government), we'll stop."

Meanwhile the eerie and desolate Mono Lake Basin in Owens County, California, continues to dry up. Four of its five feeder streams, which used to bring water from the Sierra Nevada, are now diverted to Los Angeles. Since 1941, when the diversion began, the lake level has fallen at a rate of two feet per year. The rare and endangered briny shrimp, one of two species that have always existed there, is dying out. And the gulls and other birds that fed off the tiny shrimp are all but gone. Paiute Indian legend has it that when their sacred Mono Lake goes dry, the world will come to an end. . . .

97. WATER LOSS

By the end of the nineteenth century, the flush toilet had been perfected, and it has proven to be a water-loser ever since.

Water loss is no laughing matter. Rural folk, like their city cousins, who statistically tend to be more wasteful of water, are just now becoming aware of how much modern conveniences are—and *will*—cost us in terms of water expenditure. The toilet, to cite just one universal example, uses as much as five gallons of water per flush, to put a few ounces of human excrement out of sight and out of mind. We now know the same job can be accomplished with as little as two quarts.

Once we comprehend the hydrological cycle (6) and the finite nature of the world's water supply, we begin to realize we're all in this together. Our water is everyone's water, we know, but it begins to take on aspects of any other commodity subject to the basic laws of economics. Its cost will be based on supply and demand. To put it bluntly, the age of cheap and plentiful water is gone forever, like the era of inexpensive energy.

Waste and Evaporation

The two biggest factors by far in water loss are waste and evaporation. Our cities are only magnified reflections of our individual systems. In New York, *billions* of gallons are wasted each year as a result of apathy, confusion, incompetence, lack of funding, and simple neglect. Street hydrants are opened by youngsters trying to cool off in the summer heat (and by oldsters wishing to wash their cars), and the hydrants are left running for months. Thieves go into abandoned buildings to steal faucets and other plumbing fixtures for resale, and water pours from the unplugged pipe ends—literally for years. That's to say nothing of the tremendous leakage already mentioned. (95)

Urban areas are draining groundwater far from the cities themselves. And it's an acknowledged fact that the water table in many parts of the country has been lowering for generations. For every 100 gallons taken out of the ground, only about 74 are being naturally restored, according to Charles McGinnis, who recently headed a study on water problems for the National Society of Professional Engineers. What water is still in the ground is rapidly being polluted. (104)

As "rural users" we account for just 1 percent of the national water withdrawals, and our per-capita water use consistently proves to be more efficient than that of our city counterparts. (Westerners use about twice as much water as Easterners on the average, mainly because of the dry western climate. If water used for hydroelectric generation is included, Westerners use three times as much.) Before any country people pat themselves on the

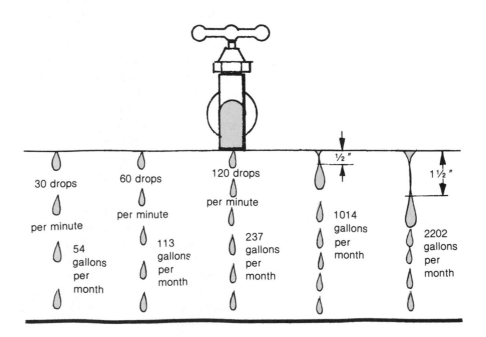

Average water loss from a leaky faucet over a period of one month.

back, however, we should realize that we waste plenty, and allow even more to be lost to the atmosphere.

Within our individual rural systems, needless water loss can be counteracted through vigilant maintenance to detect and stop leaks, efficient utilization and storage of what water we have (100), water-saving devices, and recycling of gray water. (99) Unnecessary energy loss is as ridiculous as water loss. To preserve heat, our hot water tanks can be bundled up in extra insulation. Hot water lines should also be insulated.

Simple conservation (105) can be practiced without any significant change in our lifestyle, as whole populations in California, New Jersey, New York, New Mexico, Texas, Arizona, and suburban Washington, D.C., have proven very comfortably. Says *Water,*

> Conservation . . . is an obvious key component in solving the water crisis and in avoiding future problems. It is an obvious way to provide the equivalent of a vast, previously untapped reservoir of clean, potable water. It is as obvious as elementary school mathematics, halving the demand for water (or anything else) is equal to doubling the supply. Every serious examination of what is happening to water today, and of what threatens to happen to it tomorrow, comes to the conclusion that conservation is of extreme, possibly premier, importance. And yet the subject is studiously ignored by politicians, leaders, builders, planners, agriculture, and industry, and their unwillingness to pursue it is a leading contributor to the crisis.

Of the thirty or so inches of annual rain that falls over the United States on the average, about twenty-one inches are lost through plain old evapotranspiration. In the world as a whole, it's estimated by the United Nations that between 12 and 50 billion metric tons of valuable topsoil are carried away by erosion each year. Land contouring, which slows runoff, helps control erosion as has been universally recognized since the beginning of this century, and it also slows water enough to let it run into the ground and escape evaporation. This, and the selection of indigenous crops and other vegetation which loses less water through transpiration, are other solutions that can be handled on a personal level.

Water Consumption Levels

Per Capita Use (gallons per day)	Family of:					Conservation Rating
	Four	Five	Six	Seven	Eight	
100	400	500	600	700	800	**Very heavy,** no conservation evident
75	300	375	450	525	600	**Heavy use,** including lawn & garden watering
60	240	300	360	420	480	**Normal Use,** with some outside lawn & garden watering
45	180	225	270	315	360	**Moderately Conservative** with little or no grass watering and some selective garden watering
30	120	150	180	210	240	**Very Conservative** household use, no outside watering

In rural America, our irrigation practices are destined to change. (100) To quote again from Powledge's *Water* text,

> Farm irrigation is a big user of water; for 1975 the usage was 140,000,000,-000 gallons a day, or 34 percent of the national total, applied to 54,000,000 acres of farmland. About 56 percent of the irrigation water withdrawn was consumed, and 16 percent of it was lost in conveyance. The U.S. Water Resources Council, a federal body made up of several cabinet heads that is charged by 1965 law with keeping track of the nation's water assets, has used the existing drainage basins to establish twenty-one water regions for the nation, eighteen of them in the coterminous states. The 1975 statistics showed that the nine Western regions used 93 percent of the nation's irrigation water.

I'm aware of no really good estimates about what percentage of irrigation water actually reaches the plants it's meant to feed, but it's undoubtedly low. New techniques, which are relatively inexpensive and can be implemented by even the small landowner, will make the irrigation numbers look better.

98. RESTRICTIONS

If you plan to do all or any part of your own plumbing installation, make sure you're familiar with both local ordinances and state regulations before you lift a pipe wrench. Unfortunately, as water-moving machinery gets more sophisticated and we discover more about the imperfections water can have, as well as how to treat it, codes become more and more complicated. It's difficult even for professionals to keep up with changes.

As the water situation in this nation and throughout the world tightens, codes will become secondary to the serious water *restrictions* sure to be imposed on us. Government, local and national, has been slow to respond to well-documented warnings about the impending water crisis. Once government agencies *are* motivated to move off center on water issues—stimulated by drought, or flood, or catastrophic pollution—the tendency is toward *over-reaction*. Whole community systems may be shut down, and private wells condemned by health departments, as was the case in Gray, Maine. (104) We'll have no choice but to comply.

What's Ahead

Water rationing, a fact of life in some communities now, will become more widespread. First, residents will be restricted to fifty gallons per person per day. Then less and less. If voluntary compliance doesn't work, expect public humiliation to be heaped on those who ignore the new rules. (Televised embarrassment was a political tool used against noncomplying citizens recently—and effectively—by New York City's Mayor Koch.) Further enforcement will include spot checks on water meters. Later, we can anticipate government-installed flow restrictors, followed by heavy fines. There's great social and legal pressure to come regarding our water.

The earliest indicators of restriction are already upon us. Signs in restaurants say, "This restaurant serves drinking water only on request." Next, car washing is not allowed. Then sidewalk flushing is not allowed. Watering ornamental plants is not allowed.

It's a sure bet water rates will climb. And it won't be long before water-conserving devices are specified in local building and plumbing codes. They already are in parts of California. Water metering, resisted for years in many eastern cities, is becoming the rule rather than the exception. (A U.S. Geological Survey reveals families that pay a flat rate for their water use ap-

Consumption of Water

Device	Water Use Comparison		Incremental Costs	
	Standard	Improved	New ($)	Modified ($)
Tank toilet	5–7 gallons per flush	3–5 gallons per flush	0–10	0–6
Shower	up to 12 gallons per minute	3.0 gallons per minute	0–5	1–5
Kitchen & lavatory faucets	up to 5 gallons per minute	1.5 gallons per minute	0–5	1–5
Pressure-reducing valve	80 pounds per square inch	50 pounds per square inch	0–25	25–50
Hot water pipe insulation	Not insulated	Insulated	0.50–1 per foot	0.50–1 per foot
Automatic clothes washer	27–54 gallons per load	16–20 gallons per load	20–30	Not practical
Automatic dishwasher	7.5–16 gallons per load	7.5 gallons per load	0	Not practical

SOURCE: "Water Conservation in California," Bulletin #198, 1976, California Department of Water Resources.

proximately *double* the amount of water used by those whose water is metered.) The meter gives water a positive value, and it can reduce water consumption by as much as 30 percent, as shown in Maryland and Virginia suburbs. We'll see tougher water-use laws in cities and rural areas alike.

In Florida, where state officials finally admit, "Too many people are coming down here to live," well drilling is now controlled by the state legislature. Florida has been divided into five distinct water districts, each with semi-autonomous control of all the water in its region. Citizens in Delaware and New Jersey face similar state controls immediately.

Farther west sits Arizona, another of the nation's fastest-growing states, where water has *always* been a problem. (The newest engineering scheme in Arizona involves pumping water out of the Colorado River at Lake Havasu, then lifting it 1,200 feet over mountains to Phoenix. Ironically, sections of Phoenix have been severely damaged by *flood* waters four times between 1980 and 1982—from the usually nonexistent Salt River.)

Norm Oebker, a population watcher at the University of Arizona in Tucson, predicts, "By the year 2000 we're going to have more people in this state, and eventually there may not be enough water for agriculture." Although water is the most significant ingredient in any future development, Arizona shows no signs of restricting its own marketing efforts to attract more people to their part of the Sun Belt.

99. WATER-SAVING DEVICES AND RECYCLING

The *Wall Street Journal* forecasts that in the 1980s, business will pick up for manufacturers of plumbing hardware, including pumps, water-treatment equipment, water-recycling equipment, waterless toilets, and the chemicals needed for treatment and recycling. (At the same time the *Journal* predicts declines in the overall building industry.) New water-conservation technology will become big business too, as consumers understand the cost-effectiveness of water-saving plumbing fixtures like restrictors and low-flow shower heads. We should all count ourselves among these enlightened consumers.

Cavalier attitudes about water use and waste are out of fashion. Habits are changing, and will change more. Leak detection will be a serious pastime for homeowners. We'll sniff out drips in faucets, toilets, pipes, and hoses. We'll look more closely at water loss in our ponds and pools, and we'll invest more money in covers for them, to reduce evaporation loss.

We'll also run full loads in our washers, keep drinking water in the refrigerator, so the tap needn't run so long to provide cool water, and use garbage disposers less than we do now. Appliance salesmen will interest us in water-saving washers with sixty-minute cycles that use 7½ gallons rather than the ordinary 13 to 16. On a personal level, conflict will develop at times between the conscience-soothing feeling of conserving water and an unsatisfactory dribble from a restricted shower head. We'll face such moral dilemmas with a sense of humor—we hope.

Per capita, the average (and maligned) Californian *used* to use about 140 gallons of water per day. (A camel needs only 10. A European about 40.) Statistically, California *was* at least 40 percent above the national average in water consumption. Citizens in other parts of the West resented all the water used in California. Many still do. (96)

To their credit, those "spoiled" Californians, used to responding to effective public-relations campaigns beamed over the electronic media, quickly became the most innovative water-saving population in the world. California not only has an Office of Water Conservation (OWC), it has a DWR (Department of Water Resources), which publishes *Water Conservation News*. Children in California public schools read *Captain Hydro* comic books during class time. They're provided by the teacher for "water-conservation training." Creative PR for conservation is widespread. TV weathermen promote it. Newspapers cover it in front-page stories. Free water-saving kits are handed out door-to-door in Los Angeles. And they're getting results.

About 85 percent of the water California consumes is used in agriculture. Farmers there use enough to cover the entire state with forty-two inches of water. That's 33 million acre-feet annually. But they're learning about selective breeding of livestock, and are developing "non-thirsty" plants that produce more nutrition per unit of water. (100)

Now CIMIS, the California Irrigation Management System, has set up a $6.5 million computer network in cooperation with the University of California. CIMIS tells consulting farmers, who contact the computer from at-home terminals, when and how much to irrigate their crops. Modern computer technology will also help design more efficient irrigation systems, which are surely part of California's picture in the future.

Water-Saving Devices

Water-saving devices may be the best and least expensive long-term approach to water conservation for the nation as a whole. Although most semi-modern plumbing has been developed *without* an eye to conservation, but to deliver whatever the demand calls for, simple gadgets like the ones described below fit easily into almost any system. First, they save water. Second, they reduce waste flow—and possible pollution as a result.

Water-saving toilets are now required by law in some parts of California. They use 3.5 gallons of water per flush, instead of the standard 5. (It's worth remembering that a good toilet depends more on the *velocity* of water being flushed than on the quantity of the flush.)

200

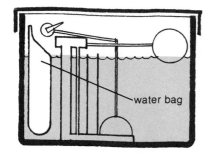

Any device which will display its own volume in water decreases the volume of water in each toilet flush.

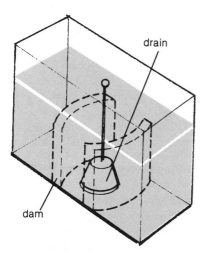

Dams can also be used to hold back water in a toilet tank.

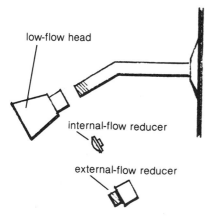

One of these three types of flow reducers can lower water use in almost any shower.

Plastic bottles, placed in a toilet tank, take up space and hold back the amount of water that can be flushed in a conventional toilet. This is an improvement on the old brick-in-the-tank trick. A soaking brick eventually disintegrates, discoloring the water and fouling up the plumbing. Plastic bottles, of course, are nonbiodegradable, but they have to be weighted down to keep them from floating in the toilet tank. Fill them with water or sand.

Toilet inserts accomplish the same thing, by damming off part of the toilet reservoir. Anybody can install one without tools.

Improved ballcocks, which plug the flush opening in the bottom of a toilet tank, are now available everywhere. Because they create a better watertight seal and depend less on the weight of water in the tank to do so, a lower water level can be maintained in the reservoir.

Dual-flush cycle toilets have been around in Europe for years. We'll see more of them here. One flush cycle is for solids; one for liquids. The solid flush uses 2.5 gallons; the liquid flush 1.25 gallons. A long pull on the handle gives you a long flush. To eliminate liquids in the toilet, give a short tug.

Faucet aerators are already common in this country. They expose water to air, save water, provide an even water flow, and prevent wasteful splashing.

Spray taps, also used in Europe, spray small amounts of water into bathroom basins instead of running a single flow.

Flow-control devices are dime-sized orifice-restrictors for showers and faucets. They look almost like ordinary faucet washers. By blocking water movement through the opening, they conserve as much as 60 percent. Typically they permit three gallons of flow per minute, instead of four or more. (Some regular shower heads spray up to ten gpm.)

Pressure-reducing valves may be placed near a home's water-supply inlet. They keep pressure in the interior plumbing at a maximum of fifty to sixty psi, even if the pressure approaching the system is higher. (90)

Water-conserving appliances, touched on earlier, make adjustments for load size. A small wash load needn't use the same amount of water as a large load, as is the case with many washers now.

Thermostatically controlled mixing valves combine hot and cold water near the tap. Because these make it so easy to get water at the right temperature right away, less water is wasted adjusting hot-and-cold mixtures.

Air-assisted toilets and showers, vacuum toilets, gas-burning toilets, mineral-oil recycling toilets, and detergent-flush toilets are possible answers already in the offing. Unfortunately they wear high price tags at the moment.

Expensive Leaks

Leaks in faucets can amount to a loss of twenty gallons a day. A runny toilet can lose 200 gallons a day! A dye tablet, free for the asking at health agencies nearly anywhere in California, can be dropped in a toilet tank to demonstrate, almost immediately, if there's a leak. Over time the dye will detect even the slightest wasteful seep. Food coloring will do the same job. So will turning off the supply line to the toilet tank and watching the water level inside for several hours.

People in metered water systems have a quick and easy way to check for leaks. Make sure everything in the house is turned off, so the system theoretically is using no water. If the meter still shows some water input, water has to be leaking somewhere. In an individual water system, finding leaks becomes a more painful trial-and-error search.

There are a number of other common-sense water saving tips:

- Minimize rinsing dishes before putting them in the dishwasher. Scrape them instead.
- Run only full loads in both the dish and clothes washers.
- Plan ahead. Remove ice trays from the freezer early, so you don't have to run water on them to free the cubes.
- Don't thaw *anything* with running water.
- Double up in a shower or bath.
- Don't flush the toilet *every* time. (Odors in a toilet bowl can be concealed by adding chlorine bleach, vinegar, or liquid detergent.)
- Don't sprinkle lawns and gardens, particularly on hot, sunny, and *windy* days.
- Compost vegetable waste instead of running an in-sink garbage disposer.
- Save cooking water for soups and stews. (Nutritionists have been pushing this for years.)
- Wash cars from a bucket of soapy water. Then rinse quickly with a hose.
- Install "pistolgrip" nozzles on hoses. They shut off water flow when released.
- Insulate hot water pipes, so the hot tap doesn't run so long while you wait for warm water to reach it.
- Catch whatever water must be run before the mixture is hot or cold enough.
- Take a "military shower." Get wet. Turn the water off while you lather up, then turn it back on to rinse.
- Use "gray water" for watering plants, and in toilet tanks.

Gray water, water that's been used for washing but contains no sewage, can be recycled. Experts expect extensive plumbing modifications in the home of the near future. Pipes will run gray water from appliance drains to recycling points throughout the house. Many homeowners discharge gray water from washers into a dry well. From there it may be pumped out for use elsewhere, or simply allowed to percolate back into the subterranean water supply. If it passes through at least ten feet of porous soil before reaching an aquifer, it should be thoroughly filtered in the process.

Recycling will take on other more dramatic forms.

Closed Circuit

Here's the scene: You want to live in an arid place—where land is cheap because water isn't. Even catchment is too unpredictable.

Or: You want to live in a very wet place, where a high water table makes sewage disposal difficult, maybe impossible.

Or: You want to live in a ledgy place, where bedrock near the surface and lack of absorbent soil make a septic tank and leach field prohibitively expensive.

Or: You want to live in a tightly controlled municipality where permits for hookups to water mains and connections to public sewage treatment facilities are hard to come by because the demand is so high.

There may be a way out of any of these problems. The PureCycle Corporation (1668 Valtec Lane, Boulder, CO 80306) has developed what may be the ultimate water-conserving mechanism. It's a closed-circuit system, that, once charged with an initial 1,500 gallons of water, recirculates and recycles that same water indefinitely, without need for added water. It's a single-family sewage treatment plant and mini-hydrological cycle. Water can be used in the normal way, and in normal amounts—except for irrigation outdoors, where evaporation makes the water impossible to recover.

A little squeamish about drinking your own waste water? The PureCycle system has already been approved by health departments in Colorado, Wyoming, Arizona, and New Mexico, and other states are expected to follow suit. The five-stage purification process is constantly monitored by a micro-electronic control, better known as a *microprocessor* or small computer, that's connected to the homeowner's telephone.

In the first stage, household waste water is *digested* in a biological reactor. Here, organic matter is devoured by oxygen-using and nonoxygen-using bacteria. Next is the *ultrafiltration* stage, where suspended particles, as well as most bacteria and viruses, are removed when "black" water passes through an automatically backwashed membrane. The membrane screens out anything larger than nine millionths of a millimeter.

Third is the *adsorption* phase, designed to remove any traces of organic matter that somehow have survived stages one and two. This is done with the help of an activated-carbon filter. Fourth comes *demineralization*, a water softener essentially, where heavy metals, nitrates, and phosphates are removed. Finally, there is *sterilization*. Here, claims PureCycle vice-president Robert Mankes, intense ultraviolet light will kill 100 percent of all known bacteria, including any pathogenic organisms. The resulting liquid is tasteless, similar to distilled water.

Gordon Bellen, a chemist with the National Sanitation Foundation, an independent nonprofit food- and water-testing laboratory in Ann Arbor, Michigan, says he has "more confidence in the PureCycle system than in many municipal systems that are downstream from a lot of industries."

PureCycle has a documented 99.3 percent recovery rate. If a family uses 300 gallons of water a day, that means about 2 gallons will be lost in various ways throughout the recycling process. But beer, soda, water from canned goods, and other liquids poured into the system each day will more than make up for the deficit.

How much does all this cost? The selling price is around $18,000, including installation, but not including delivery, site preparation, a needed outbuilding, and plumbing connections. The pretested system is delivered, as-

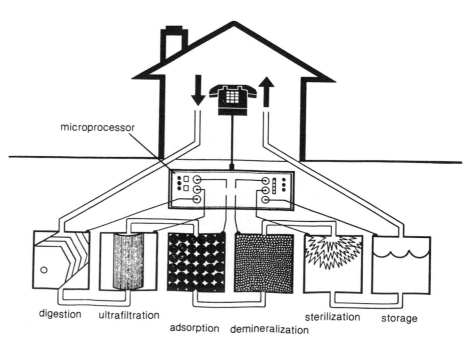

microprocessor

digestion   ultrafiltration   sterilization   storage
                        adsorption   demineralization

The PureCycle installation

sembled fully, and housed in a 600-cubic-foot structure that sits on a concrete slab next to the house. Installation, they say, takes about four hours.

If any sensor in any one of the five processing stations detects a malfunction or a quality-control parameter that's been exceeded, the minicomputer takes corrective measures. If the correction isn't made within a specified time, the computer automatically reports the problem to the nearest service center, via telephone, then shuts the system down. Before technicians in white coats pull up in a white PureCycle van, the family can draw water from a 400- to 500-gallon reserve tank.

Service centers are expected to spring up throughout the western states. They'll provide regularly scheduled maintenance as well as continuous monitoring. The cost of this ongoing service is around $35 a month.

For the time being, it seems one must be in the affluent category to afford a closed-circuit system such as the PureCycle. But like calculators, digital watches, home computers, and electronics of all kinds, the price is likely to come down as the market for recycling devices becomes more competitive.

Water is constantly recycled in nature, and there seems no reason it can't be done inexpensively in our homes. Gray water that's produced in washing machines, showers, and tubs, will contain some unappealing lint and perhaps detergent residues that could be harmful. As we make better use of gray water, we'll find ways of improving its quality. Using a biodegradable detergent, such as Shaklee's Basic H for example, should make waste water safe for the garden, certainly for fire protection, and for use in toilets. We'll also filter it.

Black water, on the other hand, is less suitable for immediate recycling because it contains a much higher concentration of organic matter and biological waste. It needs more complete sewage treatment. Dual water-delivery systems, one for potable water, one for nondrinkable but otherwise useful water, will become common in many new homes. Although more expensive to install, they seem more feasible economically than total recycling. We'll also see dual waste-water systems. One will allow us to collect and reuse gray water while the other sends black water directly to treatment.

100. DROUGHT GARDENING AND IRRIGATION

In 1847, two years before the greedy rush for gold began in California, the Mormons quietly began irrigating Utah's Salt Lake Valley. In a sense, they were the first American irrigators of any significance. And their knowledge about the art of applying water to land has spread throughout the world. They wrestled with the age-old problem of furrow irrigation: just how much grade does an irrigation canal need to keep water flowing—without filling with silt, yet without eroding? Laser land-leveling technology and computers are now being explored by the Mormons, as well as others. The goal is to accurately control irrigation—water flow.

In Utah today, irrigation still depends on streams flowing out of the Wasatch Mountains, now famous for dry powder snow and the ski resorts that naturally followed. The Utah State University Drought Committee monitors the snowpack at high elevations very closely. Too-early spring thaws can be cause for concern. If the deep snows melt too soon or too fast, too much moisture is percolated into the soil and lost. If the snowpack melts too slowly, much of the water is lost to evaporation, and residents of the Salt Lake Valley start to worry about drought.

Learning to Adjust

Agribusiness in all quarters is learning to adjust grain and forage crops to drought conditions. South Dakota has a special Drought Task Force to keep close tabs on the water supply and make planting, irrigating, and grazing recommendations to farmers and gardeners. The task force keeps a steady flow of up-to-date printed material coming out of Extension Service offices.

In dry times, they remind us, livestock must be culled more severely, so there are fewer thirsty mouths to feed. Gardeners would do well to learn about shorter-season crop varieties—fast-maturing plants that will need water for a shorter time. The recommendation is to plant early and irrigate most in the spring, when water is most plentiful. Plant in beds and wide rows where neighboring seedlings can shade each other as well as the ground. Avoid wide walkways between rows.

Mulch as soon as the soil warms up. Organic matter like leaves, hay, and straw will eventually rot and feed the soil. Many commercial growers, as well as home gardeners, use plastic mulch, like black polyethylene, to hold water in the soil.

Staked Plants Exposed

Later on, remember that staked plants get exposed to more air as they're raised off the ground. This means they transpire more, giving off precious moisture to the atmosphere. A bed of organic mulch should keep tomatoes, for instance, from touching the ground (the purpose for staking in the first place), thus insulating them from disease organisms in the soil.

Soil itself, particularly clay, should not be allowed to compact. When it gets too packed down, soil becomes "hardpan," which accepts little water. Instead, add as much organic matter to the earth as you can, so it holds water like a sponge. And think about shading devices and air flow. A windbreak that slows the movement of the air mass across a garden will close the door, part way at least, on evaporation. Soil type has a large effect on how much irrigation water must be used. The higher its concentration of organic matter, the greater its ability to retain moisture.

As important as knowing the soil is awareness of how much water various plants require. Crop varieties that are drought-resistant must also be salt-tolerant. As we allocate less of our water to irrigation, salty residues will not be readily flushed from the soil and will gradually accumulate. *Salinity* is already a problem in places where irrigation is prevalent.

Since 1977, when big drought meant big headlines, a number of fine books have been published on the subject of drought gardening. They explain that the best time to water is at the end of the day, when there's less evaporation. They encourage smaller, more intensive, mulched gardens because they lose less water than more spread out patches. They suggest growing more crops in partial shade, which also keeps the ground from drying out. More help is available from seed companies, who now push seeds for drought-resistant plants. These seeds are featured in all the major catalogs.

Homeowners, particularly those with extensive landscaping, represent a recognizable percentage of our total irrigation needs. We're bound to see public encouragement of flatter slopes in private yards—terracing and contouring in home landscapes, so water runs off less and sinks in more. It's easy to foresee tax credits for farmers and gardeners who invest in irrigating equipment that saves *both* energy and water. That's all well and good. . . .

Water Battles

But a broader look into the crystal ball suggests the biggest legal battles coming up will involve vast quantities of water—*not* petroleum. (107) Pivot-center watering machines that pump out groundwater and spray it on round fields deliver water at a rate of 800 gallons a minute. In some places, such as over the Ogallala Aquifer, this rate of underflow depletion is unacceptable, and more and more farmers will be forced out of business as the supply quite simply disappears. Many farmers in West Texas (at the southern end of the Ogallala Aquifer) have already gone belly-up. (96)

The American Vegetable Grower, an authoritative periodical for the pro-

'Hands On' Guide to Soil Moisture

	Sand	Sandy Loam	Clay Loam	Clay
Moisture Available for Plants		Feel or Look of the Soil		
Close to 0. Little or no moisture available.	Dry, loose, single-grained. Flows through fingers.	Dry, loose, and flows through fingers.	Dry clods that break down into powdery condition.	Hard, baked, cracked surface. Hard clods difficult to break. Sometimes has loose crumbs on surface.
Up to 50% Nearly time to irrigate.	Still appears to be dry. Will not form a ball with pressure.	Still appears to be dry. Will not form a ball.	Somewhat crumbly, but will hold together with pressure.	Somewhat pliable. Will ball under pressure.
50% to 75% Enough available moisture.	Same as above.	Tends to ball under pressure, but seldom will hold together.	Forms a ball, somewhat plastic. Will sometimes stick slightly with pressure.	Forms a ball. Will ribbon out between thumb and forefinger.
75% Plenty of available moisture.	Tends to stick together slightly. Sometimes forms a very weak ball under pressure.	Forms weak ball. Breaks easily. Will not become slick.	Forms a ball and is very pliable.	Easily ribbons out between fingers. Feels slick, like modeling clay.
Soil won't hold any more water.	After squeezing, no water appears, but moisture is left on hand.	Same as for sand.	Same as for sand.	Same as for sand.
Waterlogged soil.	Water appears when soil is bounced in hands.	Water will be released with kneading.	Can squeeze out water.	Puddles, and water forms on surface.

SOURCE: Adapted from "Saving Water in Landscape Irrigation," free from the Public Service Office, University of California, Davis, CA 95616.

fessional farming community, is *very* conservative in its estimate that only 81 percent of all the water consumed in the United States is for agriculture. They admit, however, that at least 53 percent of all our irrigation water comes from groundwater sources.

A more likely assessment is that about 90 percent of our fresh-water supply goes for agricultural use, and most of that directly for irrigation. It's nobody's fault that irrigation is so inefficient. At very best, half of the water used in conventional irrigation reaches the plants it's intended for. The rest is lost to runoff and evaporation. One admittedly crude guess is that about 25 percent of the water from an overhead sprinkler is actually used by the plants themselves. Traditional surface irrigation, through canals and furrows, may be somewhat better—33 percent efficient.

About forty years ago, an Israeli engineer by the name of Symcha Blass noticed that a fig tree next to a leaky water spigot grew much faster than those around it. And a light went on in his head. Blass experimented with ways to bring a consistent supply of water to plants at a steady rate. Today Blass is regarded as the inventor of *drip* or *trickle irrigation*, a technique that, only now, is catching on in this country.

Overhead irrigation, as any experienced gardener knows, spoils plants by encouraging them to grow shallow roots, and thus be weaker and more dependent on surface water. It also waters weeds, which compete for sunlight, space, and nutrients—as well as water.

Direct to Roots

A trickle system works more like a home gardener's soaker hose, but on a much larger scale. It delivers water directly to the plants' roots, which grow deep and strong. Crops use less water and grow more uniformly. Plants are not left wet, so disease is reduced, and fields are mud-free. Fertilizers, herbicides, insecticides, and fungicides can be injected safely and directly into the water-carrying system. And because the flow is targeted only at the crop itself, less fertilizer is lost through leaching.

A trickle irrigation system is laid out in rows. Tubing is laid in the soil two or three inches deep, four to six inches to the side of a row center. Small plastic "emitters" are spaced along the tube every two feet, each in a hole drilled in the polyethylene tube. (Home garden trickle kits are available in many hardware stores.) Each emitter delivers only one to two gallons an *hour*.

Moving less water takes less energy, naturally, so pump and mainline pipe sizing can be reduced. (Trickle systems require only five to fifteen pounds per square inch of pressure, so there's no need for a high-pressure pump *or* beefed-up tubing. In fact, if you're working off ordinary household plumbing carrying twenty to sixty psi, you may need a pressure *reducer*.)

Still, for all its efficiency and ability to conserve water, a trickle irrigator needs regular flushing, inspection, and maintenance to keep the emitter holes from becoming clogged. Algae, sand particles, organic matter, mineral deposits, and dissolved chemicals can quickly put a whole row of emitters out of commission.

Can Be Timed

Filtering and/or chemical treatment will improve the quality of water passing through the system, and should do a lot to cut down on fouling problems. If you want to get fancy, your drip irrigator can be set up with an automatic timer. Large systems even have *tensiometers* to measure soil moisture. These automatically turn water on when it's needed.

Trickle irrigation, touted as *low energy precision application* (LEPA) by the food-growing industry, is not cheap to install. Costs run between $500 and $600 an acre. In some places the price tag is as high as $800. Further, it does *not* operate as frost protection like a fine mist sprinkler. Finally, I'm sorry to report, rodents have a fondness for chewing holes in polyethylene drip-irrigation lines. Either exterminate the rodents or carry on a continuous struggle with them.

Watering Guide

Type of Plant	Frequency		Methods	Comments
	Newly Planted	*Established*		
Evergreen	Weekly, especially into fall and winter months.	Twice a month, year round.	Slow running hose, or soaker hose. Use water lance for greater depth.	Soak ball when planting and continue once a week to fill root hole with water until ball has integrated with surrounding soil. Provide basin (ponding terrace) for future watering and regularly break up hard soil around tree base so water can soak in. Avoid "winter kill" by watering in fall, winter and spring.
TREES				
Shade	Once a week until firmly established.	Twice a month in summer and fall. Late winter or early spring soakings also may be required.		
Evergreen	Once a week.	Twice a month, year round.	Soaker hose around base of several shrubs or slow running hose for single plants.	Lack of sub-surface moisture will kill evergreens any time of year. Other shrubs, though dormant in winter, also require root moisture to stay alive. Deep soaking to roots is required for all types of shrubs.
SHRUBS				
Other (such as burning bush)	Twice a week.	Once a week in growing season, and twice monthly in fall and spring.		
Flower	Three times a week.	Once a week during growing season.	Soaker hose supplemented by sprinkling.	Flowers and vegetables use water rapidly. Soaking to a depth of six to eight inches is recommended in addition to above surface sprinkling when required to prevent leaf wilting.
GARDENS				
Vegetable	Every other day until above ground.	Once a week during growing season.		
Blue Grass & Fescues	Daily until established to keep surface moist.	Water as infrequently as possible, but water heavily during those parts of the season when it becomes necessary.°°	Sprinkler, moved to cover entire area. Soaker hose, used where slope permits water to spread: Underground sprinkler system.	Newly laid sod should not be allowed to dry. Use water plentifully to integrate sod with the soil base. *All grasses need about one inch of water (applied at one time) without runoff.* This is sufficient to moisten the lawn soil to root depth. Some grasses go dormant in August but revive in late summer, if there is sufficient moisture.
GRASSES				
Zoysia & Bermuda	Daily until established.	Seldom need water in the summer.°°		

SOURCE: This chart was prepared by the Washington Suburban Sanitary Commission, for use in the suburban areas of Montgomery and Prince George's Counties, Maryland.

NOTE: Experts generally agree that *watering of plants and lawns should be accomplished during the mid-day hours* (rather than in the evening) *to prevent the spread of fungus diseases.* Mid-day watering also helps your water supplier, since peak essential household requirements (washing, drinking, and cooking) normally have to be met in the morning (6 to 9 A.M.) and evening (5 to 9 P.M.) hours.

101. EMERGENCY WATER

We probably won't be prepared. Emergencies, by definition, are usually unexpected. When one hits, emergency water might be held (and found) in bulk tanks, indoor pools, bathtubs, cisterns, hot-water tanks, toilet reservoirs, in canned or fresh fruit juices, and in fruits and vegetables themselves.

Surface water should be thought of only as a last resort during an emergency. Groundwater will be somewhat safer. Containers, such as plastic-lined garbage cans, for transporting water during a disaster, should be cleaned and disinfected, if possible. Civil Defense, National Guard units, and fire departments may become involved in a major emergency or disaster. Theoretically, these people should have the capacity to haul tanks of potable water to those who need it. (Water stored in fire trucks, however, can't be considered potable. Often corrosion-preventing chemicals have been added to the tanks.)

Emergency water can be disinfected in four different ways:

1. Boil it vigorously for at least five minutes.

2. Add four drops of chlorine bleach to one quart of water. The mixture should stand for at least thirty minutes before the water is used.

3. Add five drops of 2 percent iodine solution (what's usually found in a home medicine cabinet) to a quart of water. It too should stand for at least half an hour before it's consumed.

4. Buy water-purification tablets in most drug and sporting goods stores. They contain *titratable iodine*. Almost any water is bacteriologically suitable once it's treated with these tablets. One tablet is added to a quart container filled with water, before the container is tightly capped.

After three minutes the container should be shaken thoroughly so the screw heads are rinsed with iodine solution. The cap can then be tightened, and the water allowed to disinfect for ten minutes. Directions from one manufacturer of these germicidal tablets read, "If water is very cold or contains rotten leaves or is dirty and discolored, use two tablets. Wait twenty minutes before drinking." At less than seven cents apiece, these should be stocked in everyone's medicine cabinet—tightly capped. If they're exposed to air or moisture, they lose their effectiveness.

Storing Water

Emergency water can also be canned. Fill quart Mason jars, cover with regular jar lids, and process in a pressure cooker for ten minutes at fifteen pounds of pressure. Store these jars in a cool root cellar, or wherever other canned goods have been stored.

The best-selling book, *The Fate of the Earth,* by Jonathan Schell, was excerpted in three issues of *The New Yorker* in 1982. In it the author creates a vivid scenario of what will happen in the event of even a "minor" nuclear war. He says atomic warfare will be so totally and incomprehendably destructive to life on this planet that only a few insects and certain species of grass will remain once it's over. In the process of painting this picture, Schell all but ridicules man's futile plans for survival following a nuclear holocaust.

Nonetheless, the U.S. Department of Agriculture recommends a fourteen-day supply of fresh water for each family member, to be stored in case of a nuclear attack. Allow one gallon a day per person. (A human in a bomb shelter might survive on a half-gallon per day, but one gallon is proposed.) Surface water will of course be contaminated by nuclear fallout. But radioactive particles will be filtered by soil, meaning that most groundwater will be protected during and after a nuclear explosion. Any water in a pressure tank, hot-water heater, and interior plumbing is also safe from fallout.

A high content of nuclear radiation in water is "rare," the Environmental Protection Agency tells us. Yet it does exist in some places, and must be considered an ongoing source of worry, particularly in light of events like the Three-Mile Island accident, and the confusing issue of what to do with nuclear wastes.

In some instances radioactive water comes from natural sources as well as man-made ones. The EPA goes on to say, "The effects of human exposure to radiation or radioactive materials are viewed as harmful, and any unnecessary exposure should be avoided." This may be history's greatest understatement.

WATER'S FUTURE

102. POPULATION AND DROUGHT

We have too many people. Population demands and increased usage visibly diminish the world's supply of fresh water each day. That's hardly late-breaking news. In *Water*, Fred Powledge addresses the shortage:

> ... Competition for usable water seems to be increasing, both nationally and globally. The world rate of population growth is believed to be slowing somewhat, but there are so many people now on the planet that even a slowed rate will result in just a few years in vastly increased demands for food, and therefore for water. Most of the population growth that is expected in the near future will occur in the less developed countries, where adequate food is even now something of a luxury. Coupled with this is the continuing decline in worldwide cropland, a product of increased human development (and need for land on which to put the houses for all the people) and erosion of the soil. One UN document asserts that one-third of the world's arable land will disappear in the next twenty years. Another survey says that continuing deterioration in the land and water environments that produce the things we want and need, together with population growth, has resulted already in a decline in the per-capita production of resources such as cattle, grain, fish, and food.

Closer to home, in our own country it's the age-old problem of unequal water distribution. Seventeen of our western states, totalling roughly 60 percent of our land area, receive a quarter of our rainfall. The eastern states, comprising the other 40 percent of our land, get more water than they need. West of the Great Divide, water quantity is a perpetual question mark. (In California the demand for water is 3.8 times greater than the annual rainfall.) Those in the East have to worry less about where their water will come from, but must chew their nails every bit as much about its *quality*. (104)

Below ground, approximately 25 percent of the groundwater being pumped from our western farmlands is not being replenished. Yet, on the surface, the equivalent of thirty-six acres of prime topsoil is being washed away each day throughout the United States. Demographers and census analysts tell us of the great population migration to the Sun Belt, but point out in the next breath that it could all be halted by something as fundamental as water shortages in the southwestern states.

Growth that continues in that part of the nation will be at the expense of agriculture. So far, water does not seem to be a major factor in industry's decisions to move to the Sun Belt. But long-range forecasters see the trend reversing, as both employers and the labor force march back north.

It's the rural poor, of course, who are least capable of moving at all. And pure water continues to be these people's most pressing need, just as it's always been. Huge and costly construction projects, meant to provide jobs, control flooding, and deliver power and water to rural areas traditionally stricken by drought have been marginally successful at very best. Of the 8,000 or so flood-control dams in the United States, the Army Corps of Engineers now labels one-third of them unsafe.

(From the highway, eight miles from my home, I now look at green grass and shrubs growing in what used to be the bottom of the Waterbury Reservoir, a flood-control project on Vermont's Winooski River, completed by the Army Corps of Engineers and the Civilian Conservation Corps in 1938. Its dam was reconstructed in the 1950s. In summers past this man-made lake was filled with white sails and water skiers. Now, because the dam has serious "seepage problems," according to one government employe, the reservoir stays empty. The seepage has been "under investigation" for the past six years, and the reservoir remains empty. Locals say the dam should never have been built there in the first place, because it sits atop a large spring.

(Meanwhile more artificial lakes, built by the Tennessee Valley Authority and the Army Corps of Engineers, an outfit one *New York Times* writer calls "the federal agency that has done the most to damage the watery environment," are filling. These projects in California, Tennessee, and elsewhere, ruin fast-flowing rivers, kill off endangered wildlife, and flood thousands of valuable acres of farmland.)

Restrict Construction

"Rather than take the water to the people," nongovernment water experts recently told *New Roots* magazine, "(we must) restrict construction in water-poor areas. . . . Let the people go to the water." Apparently only when public outcry reaches a deafening level can such environmental manipulation be stopped. The dams don't work, but the building continues. There's no doubt that drought is going to force new population patterns. And it's no longer just pessimistic soothsayers who say the water crisis in the 1990s will make the energy crisis of the '70s and '80s seem like a child's birthday party.

Yes, we're in the midst of drought. And the situation is likely to get worse before it gets better. The wet-weather cycle we've recorded (and enjoyed) since 1900 may *not* be normal. At least that's what one meteorologist, Edwin Cook of Columbia University, thinks.

We're finding out we have a greater impact on the hydrological cycle than anyone ever thought possible. Southern Florida is a scary case in point. Both coasts of that swampy peninsula-state have been "capped with concrete," and land development in the previously soggy interior known as the Everglades has drained much of the wetlands. The result is a deadly "man-made drought."

Sheets of water which always flowed from the Kissimmee River through Lake Okeechobee—the second largest body of fresh water entirely within the United States—then into the vast flood plains of South Florida, no longer do so. Nobody could have predicted that artificial drainage and human land coverage would disrupt whole weather patterns and rainfall cycles. But we've managed to throw a monkey wrench into the "rain machine."

Everglades Threatened

Now the whole Everglades National Park is threatened, along with all its fish, animal, and plant life. Also endangered is the nearby sugar-cane industry—the largest source of sugar in the nation. Farmland is drying out, and fire is a constant danger.

WINOOSKI RIVER FLOOD CONTROL PROJECT
WATERBURY DAM

CONSTRUCTED 1935-38 ··· MODIFIED 1957-58
UNDER SUPERVISION OF U.S. ARMY, CORPS OF ENGINEERS
IN COOPERATION WITH WATER RESOURCES BOARD, STATE OF VERMONT

THIS DAM IS ONE OF THREE DAMS CONSTRUCTED BY THE CORPS OF ENGINEERS, U.S. ARMY, TO CONTROL THE FLOW OF THE WINOOSKI RIVER AND ITS MAIN TRIBUTARIES SO THAT THERE MIGHT NEVER BE A DISASTER LIKE THAT OF NOVEMBER 1927 WHEN FLOOD WATERS CAUSED DAMAGES OF $13,000,000 AND THE LOSS OF 55 LIVES IN THE WINOOSKI RIVER DRAINAGE BASIN.

THIS DAM, IN ADDITION TO PROVIDING FLOOD CONTROL PROTECTION IS UTILIZED FOR THE GENERATION OF ELECTRIC ENERGY. AN AVERAGE OF 15 MILLION KILOWATT HOURS ARE GENERATED EACH YEAR.

THE DAM IS OF ROLLED EARTH FILL TYPE, CONTAINING 2,200,000 CUBIC YARDS OF SELECTED MATERIALS INCLUDING 490,000 CUBIC YARDS OF CLAY IN THE CENTER PORTION. THE TOP OF THE DAM IS 633 FEET ABOVE SEA LEVEL AND THE DAM IS 2130 FEET LONG WITH A MAXIMUM HEIGHT OF 158 FEET.

AT NORMAL CONSERVATION POOL ELEVATION OF 592 FEET, THE RESERVOIR CONTAINS 36,800 ACRE FEET OF WATER AND HAS A SURFACE AREA OF 845 ACRES.

IF THE WATER SHOULD RISE TO ITS MAXIMUM FLOOD CONTROL ELEVATION OF 629.5 FEET, THE RESERVOIR WOULD CONTAIN 82,100 ACRE FEET OF WATER AND HAVE A SURFACE AREA OF 1,600 ACRES.

A REINFORCED CONCRETE SPILLWAY 153.5 FEET LONG AND THREE TAINTER GATES AT THE EASTERLY END OF THE DAM PROTECT THE EARTH SECTION FROM OVERFLOW.

THE STONE RIP-RAP ON THE FACES OF THE DAM WAS HAND PLACED DURING THE ORIGINAL CONSTRUCTION STARTED IN 1935 AND COMPLETED IN 1938. A TOTAL OF 2,000 MEN OF THE CIVILIAN CONSERVATION CORPS WORKED ON THE PROJECT DURING THIS PERIOD.

THE DAM WAS MODIFIED IN 1957 AND 1958 TO PROVIDE FOR THE SAFETY OF THE STRUCTURE, IF LARGER FLOODS THAN ORIGINALLY ANTICIPATED WERE TO OCCUR.

THE STATE OF VERMONT FURNISHED ALL LANDS AND RIGHTS OF WAY AND OPERATES THE DAM AND RESERVOIR IN CONJUNCTION WITH THE GREEN MOUNTAIN POWER CORP.

It sounded great in 1935, even in 1957

But the dam leaks . . .

And the whole project is gradually turning into a neglected mudhole.

Study any world map and you'll see that most of the world's great deserts sit at almost exactly the same latitude as South Florida. More than a few state and local politicians and experts from the Department of Interior fear that desert conditions are in the cards for Florida—unless the water-robbing development process is reversed. And soon.

We're not completely to blame, but it's hard to know what *is*. Is the eruption of Mt. St. Helens causing sudden shifts in our national weather? Some think so. Some say it's the eleven-year sunspot cycle. Others with an astronomical bent say that when Jupiter, Saturn, and our own moon line up in space to form what's called the "Grand Junction," gravitational pull on Earth is increased and our weather is affected—in much the same way as the moon's pull causes tides.

Whatever the theories to explain it, we seem destined to be abnormally dry for a while. Even the wet Northeast is in for an extended drought, one that will probably be worse than the parched period between 1877 and 1880. The year 1980 foreshadowed things to come. Precipitation in New England was 25 percent below normal. Thirty towns in Massachusetts declared water emergencies. One hundred and fourteen northern New Jersey communities began rationing water at fifty gallons per family per day. Reservoirs for Boston and New York held 84 percent of their normal capacity, and crop losses throughout the country, particularly the Midwest, were heavy.

103. WATER AND DOLLARS

I don't consider myself a rich man, though I know I'm wealthy in water. I squander it sometimes, taking inordinately long showers, letting it run while I'm brushing my teeth and at other times, using the convenient garbage disposal instead of composting vegetable wastes as I know I should. We use a dishwasher and a clothes washer, and try always to do full loads. But we don't always. Like everybody else, I've been naive about water. I've taken it for granted, as I've confessed already.

But not long ago I began to wonder exactly how much all of this luxury was costing. In 1980 I built a new house. Looking back over the bills, I find that the drilled well, the submersible pump, the pressure tank, and all the connections, tubing, and fittings needed to bring water to the house from under my ground cost just over $2,500. The totally separate plumber's bill, including the price of all tubing, hot-water heater, garbage disposer, fittings, and fixtures for a kitchen and two full baths, one outdoor sillcock (I wish I'd put in more), an outlet in the solar greenhouse, and labor, was just under $5,000. The clothes washer was about $380; the dishwasher was less, about $300.

The pond cost over $5,200 by the time it was finished, and the bill for the new water softener (installed) exceeded the estimate and amounted to almost $1,250. (I don't know exactly how much the salt for the brine tank is going to cost yet, but Mr. Roe helped me figure close to $300 a year.) There's additional drainage around the property, and of course the waste system with its septic tank and leach field.

Electricity for the house runs about $480 a year. If the water system uses just 15 percent of that power, it costs about $72 annually, and gas to heat the hot water last year totaled $103. I have almost $18,000 invested in water alone (enough to buy a decent house in 1965). And I spend about $475 a year to keep it going, assuming there are no repairs—though we all know there *will* be.

Wealthy Use More

I read studies that say water usage rises with income, and I wonder where that puts me. Wealthier people, they say, buy more water-using appliances, for example. Lifestyle improvements inevitably involve more water. More lawn. More garden. More landscaping. More carwashing. More water sports. More pets. Swimming pools. So today, as a total group, we take twice as much water from United States ground as we did in 1950.

I first had serious worries about how much trying to reach better-living-through-water was going to cost, in 1980. Like you I worried first about myself, my own family's water and money problems, along with Floridians, New Jerseyites, and other property owners everywhere in the country. Meanwhile Texans (who may have the most enlightened water-planning policies in the world) worried about whether folks in Arkansas were going to let Texas import some of *their* water. Iowans worried about plans to divert Missouri River water to the high plains of Nebraska where it could substitute for groundwater dwindling in the Ogallala Aquifer.

As if they didn't have enough to worry about that year, with drought and crop losses, other Midwesterners began to worry about having to share their water with Southern Californians, who already have their eye on the Great Lakes. *Alaskans* even, are worried about how to fend off the water-seeking tentacles already reaching out from Los Angeles. (106) The very soul of that thirsty octopus, whose heart is set on the cost-inefficient goal of "making the desert bloom, lies tucked between the briny Pacific Ocean and the Mohave Desert." But Southern California is where the *money* is.

In 1980, President Jimmy Carter had cause for water worries on a grander scale. That year *The Global 2000 Report* he'd requested in 1979, came across his desk. Among other things, it said,

> There will apparently be adequate water available on the earth to satisfy *aggregate projected water withdrawals* in the year 2000; the same finding holds for each of the continents. Nevertheless, because of the regional and temporal nature of the water resource, water shortages even before 2000 will probably be more frequent, and more severe than those experienced today. . . .

> Fresh water, once an abundant resource in most parts of the world, will become increasingly scarce in the coming decades for two reasons. First, there will be greater net consumption . . . so that the total supply will decline. Second, pollution and the impacts of hydraulic works will effectively limit the uses of fresh water—and therefore, in effect, the supply. The deterioration of water basin catchments, especially as a result of *deforestation*, will increase the variability of the supply, accelerate erosion, damage water development projects, and degrade water quality. It seems inevitable that the function of streams and rivers as habitat for aquatic life will steadily be sacrificed to the diversion of water for irrigation, for human consumption, and for power production, particularly in the less developed countries. . . . Scarcities and conflicts are becoming more acute, and by the year 2000 economic, if not human survival in many industrial regions may hinge upon water quality, or water supply, or both. (My italics)

So the future of water will be controlled by dollars. Water will, indeed, flow to where the money is.

Just as supply and demand have recently shifted a larger percentage of world power to the Middle Eastern oil nations, water may become *the* controlling economic factor of the future. On an individual level, this means something so available to man for so many thousands of years that he's hardly ever bothered to put a price tag on it, is suddenly right up there with gold, and oil, . . . and power. If you have water, particularly good water, don't underestimate its value. If you don't have it, never underestimate your dependence on others to help you get it.

104. POLLUTION

What do Perham, Minnesota, Aurora, Missouri, Bumpass Love, Tennessee, Renfrow, Oklahoma, Elizabeth, New Jersey, Hopewell, Virginia, Woburn, Massachusetts, and Gray, Maine, have in common? They're Anytown, USA, like your town and mine. But like cities with more famous names—Atlantic City, New Jersey, Louisville, Kentucky, Cincinnati, Ohio, New Orleans, Louisiana, and Niagara Falls, New York—they're also the sites of ghastly tales about water contaminated with the cast-off byproducts of industry.

Niagara Falls is the scene of the infamous Love Canal incident. The sickness and birth defects connected with that episode are early evidence of the slow self-poisoning process going on everywhere. It's happening in heavily populated areas and it's spreading to the backwoods. There's no escape and there are many who feel that the Industrial Revolution, which held so much promise for so long, will be our demise. Those in the know point to poisoned water as our "biggest problem in the 1980s."

In Perham, Minnesota, homeowners drank water from a normal shallow well, twenty feet deep. But it contained "grasshopper poison" (including 21,-000 parts per million of arsenic) that had been buried nearby in the 1930s. The dump was all but forgotten until illness spread. In 1980, Aurora, Missouri, citizens heard that steel drums containing dioxin, a deadly chemical, had been buried in their ground by a company long defunct. They were buried on one of their neighbor's farms, and the drums were leaking dioxin into everyone's water supply. In Bumpass Love, Tennessee, there were so many barrels of hazardous industrial waste in one dump that a flood resurrected some and carried them down the Nolichucky River, poisoning water all along the way.

One couple in Renfrow, Oklahoma, pumped 2,000 gallons of locally spilled *gasoline* from their water well. When they were finished pumping out all that free fuel, their well was still so bad they had to drill another. In 1979 the *New York Times* reported that Woburn, Massachusetts, had been found to have "almost every known major form of hazardous waste pollution" in its water supply, including solvents, heavy metals, chloroform, even radioactive wastes. The "abnormally high rate of cancer" in that community is attributed to the drinking water.

Cancer in New Orleans

New Orleans also has one of the highest cancer rates in the country. The Mississippi River, which flows over that city's doorstep, carries something like 40 percent of all rainfall runoff in the United States. Unfortunately it's also used as a sewer and chemical dump along its entire length. It's no wonder so many people near its mouth in Louisiana are sick. Cincinnati, on the banks of the Ohio River, rates second to New Orleans in drinking water contamination. Over 700 man-made chemicals have been found in public water there.

As agricultural chemicals and insecticides show up consistently in the aquifers of rural Kansas, wells in Philadelphia, New Jersey, Long Island, and Florida continue to be flooded with toxins. As much as five inches of oil have been found floating on the water table in some of these places. In others, lagoons full of toxic wastes slowly leaching into groundwater have suddenly burst into flames. That's what happened in Elizabeth, New Jersey.

Practically all the individual water systems in Gray, Maine, were polluted by a raft of chemical wastes placed on the ground by their manufacturer and *intentionally* burned. What didn't burn, according to one chemical company spokesman, "just sort of disappeared." Later a group of house-wives banded together to face the problem in Gray, and soon mains were built to bring water from a neighboring town. But as one of the women put it, "Losing the well was like losing some of your independence. It's like the well represented some kind of *freedom* for us. It meant we didn't have to depend on other people so much."

Kepone in Water

Six hundred miles down the Atlantic coast is Hopewell, Virginia, the town to introduce Kepone® to the news-watching public. Kepone® is a roach-and-ant poison that causes tremors, sterility, brain damage, liver damage, twitching, and slurred speech in humans. We now know it also causes cancer in laboratory animals. Life Science Products Company, which manufactured chemicals in Hopewell, disposed of its "kepone-laced leftovers" in the James River. The waste promptly killed beneficial bacteria in the digesters of Hopewell's sewage treatment plant. But nobody shut the system down soon enough, and Kepone® escaped into the municipal water system. Eighty workers from the Life Science Products Company now suffer various symptoms of Kepone® poisoning, and many more are anticipated. Life Science's parent chemical company was convicted and fined, then took the fine as a tax deduction.

DDT and other pesticides have been dumped into landfills for years in Austin, Texas. Bulldozers unearthed these poisons as a baseball field was being built, and rain washed them into a nearby pond, killing fish there. Deadly PCBs have been found in fish taken from the "pure" Feather River in the Sierra foothills. "These are the highest levels (of PCBs) ever found in game fish," say California game officials. The pollutants are believed to come from oils in the road surfaces next to the river.

In 1978 a man confessed to pouring 730,000 gallons of chemical wastes right into a Philadelphia storm sewer—one that led to the Delaware River and a water-treatment plant that treats water for half the city. Another waste hauler in Kentucky was found to have stored 20,000 drums of chemical byproducts on one seven-acre site. In 1978, when the Ohio River flooded, a "large number" of these fifty-five-gallon drums were discovered floating in Stump Gap Creek, twenty-five miles from Louisville.

Toxic Wastes

In Atlantic City, at least a dozen illegal waste haulers have dumped toxic wastes at Price's Landfill, just outside of town, but near city wells. Price's Landfill is basically a twenty-two-acre hole, filled with chemicals that have already contaminated many private wells. And they're creeping underground toward the city water.

The pollution horror stories go on and on. We can read them in any local newspaper and see about them on any evening newscast. Industry is usually depicted as the villain, but government at all levels may be equally guilty, simply for not staying on top of such things. (The Hooker Chemical Company, which dumped the chemicals in the Love Canal, sold the area to the city for almost nothing, but warned Niagara Falls' city fathers that the site was probably dangerously polluted. Ignoring the warning of the "time bomb" below, the city built an elementary school there.)

Finger-pointing is rampant on all sides naturally, but there's some validity to the argument that some dumpers and polluters have done their dirty deeds out of ignorance. Who could have known . . . ? Only now are the contents of the dumps surfacing. Only now are the cumulative carcinogenic effects of chemicals in our drinking water showing up.

There's also the idea that in the past ten years we've learned more about detecting and measuring very small amounts of toxic chemicals in our drinking water, and that what we haven't known all along hasn't hurt us to any "measurable degree." One thing's sure: our knowledge about what to *do* with what we find is lagging way behind our ability to find it. Given enough time, many believe, solutions for our worst water pollution problems can be found. Water chemists assure us that even the most contaminated water can be made drinkable. But at what price?

Alan Kneese, the popular authority on water resources, tells us what we all know by now. "Until recently, attention has been focused entirely on our surface water problems, but about half the people in this country drink water from groundwater sources, usually those living in small- or medium-sized communities." Kneese, who sees the whole water picture as clearly as anyone, is optimistic, even as he foresees how everything in the debit and credit columns of our water account will be brought to the bottom line. "We can adapt," he says.

Brighter Side

For the moment we continue to pollute our water with sewage and chemicals. As individuals we each may be as much to blame as anyone else. But there's one problem that's already a generation ahead. Lake Erie is a model of how legislation like the Federal Water Pollution Control Act Amendments of 1972 can triumph. Eutrophication was choking off the oxygen supply in the water so fast that even fish couldn't survive. The lake was labeled "dead." By now, as the result of a massive clean-up effort along its shores, the pollution problem has been turned around, and nature's healing processes are bringing the lake back to life.

105. OLD IDEAS, AND NEW

In the middle of the Negev Desert of Israel sit many three-foot piles of pebbles, placed there . . . who knows when, or by whom? At night these little mounds of stone cool quickly, and shrink the air next to them. In the morning the ground nearby is moist from the accumulated condensation. Small plants and flowers are nourished by these ancient watermakers.

Much water can be gathered from dew—water vapor from the atmosphere. And it can be condensed and collected regardless of the level of relative humidity. Estimates say as much as fifteen inches of water could be collected through condensation each year, even in the desert. That much water would go far in arid places. An abundance of pure water is ready and waiting in the sea of air surrounding us. We need only to find ways to trap it and hold it efficiently.

Desalination

The oceans, though they seem watery enough at first glance, are far from a viable fresh water source. Although techniques for removing salt from sea water have been understood for a long time, *desalination* is still expensive and too energy-inefficient to make large-scale "desal" operations worthwhile.

Desalination takes two forms. The first is *reverse osmosis*, where salts are removed as pressurized water is passed through a membrane. (69) There is, in fact, a $260 million reverse-osmosis plant in Yuma, Arizona, one of the hottest, driest places on earth to be inhabited by man. The plant desalinates, but the nagging question there is whether the initial expense and huge operating costs are justified.

Distillation is the more widely known method for freshening salt water. Saline water is boiled, the vapor is captured, and the condensed droplets are collected for consumption. Most lifeboats are now equipped with solar-powered stills which do just that. I notice the Spiegel catalog advertises a small home water distiller that sits on your kitchen countertop. It's electrical, distills one gallon of tap water in four hours, and—here's the killer—costs $249.

If it's anything like the desalination plant on Stock Island in Key West, Florida, Spiegel's "Distill Clear" uses a lot of energy. The Key West plant transforms 2,300,000 gallons of sea water into drinkable water every twenty-four hours. The salty water is drawn from three wells near the ocean, treated with various chemicals to remove gases and adjust the pH, then heated in a huge silo. The vapor is cooled and condensed in over 400 miles of ⅝-inch tubing, then the resulting water is stored in tanks.

The consensus in Key West is that the water is "*too* pure," therefore it "tastes funny." So now the water is exposed to coral—marl actually—in post-treatment tanks where it's allowed to pick up some taste. Most ironically, the desalination plant's outmoded boiler is fueled by oil, a substance that looked cheap a decade ago. The cost of generating the heat needed to make the plant work is also making the distilled water *very* expensive.

Ice Caps

Trying to melt portions of the polar ice caps for use as fresh water may be as unrealistic, right now anyway, as trying to recover fresh water from the oceans. The idea of towing great chunks of icebergs to latitudes where they can be melted is another possibility under discussion. The logistical problems are staggering, but the concept is no more farfetched than some of the grand engineering schemes being planned in the Soviet Union and elsewhere. (106)

But it may be a mistake, as some statisticians have done, to include frozen water from the Arctic and Antarctic regions as part of the earth's total fresh-water resources. The capital and technology needed to make those frozen supplies usable appear to be out of reach in the near future. For the moment, we should be trying to amass more and better understanding about fresh water sources as they exist and are available to us now.

Energy Source

Maybe the best news is that we're starting to recognize groundwater as a vast, untapped source of geothermal and solar *energy*. Water from wells can be used to heat and cool homes through *groundwater heat pumps*, devices that have generated much excitement in the otherwise unimpressible National Water Well Association.

Groundwater temperatures throughout the world average about 55° F. (The temperature range in the United States runs from a low of around 48° F. to a high of about 70.) A heat pump takes warmth from the groundwater during the winter months, and delivers it to the home via air. In summer, heat is removed from the air, and returned to the water.

Coefficient of performance (COP) is an important part of the vocabulary surrounding heat-pump technology. The COP tells us how much heating energy the pump is giving off, compared to the amount of energy it uses. A natural-gas heater, for example, may have a COP of .7, meaning that for every 100 Btu of energy it consumes, it produces 70 Btu of heat. In other words, it's 70 percent efficient. Coal and oil burners are typically 65 percent efficient, with COPs of .65.

A groundwater heat pump, on the other hand, has an average COP of 3.3, according to the NWWA, and may go as high as 5. It sounds at first like an impossible perpetual motion machine, but the high efficiency is made possible by an all but limitless supply of relatively warm groundwater, and a refrigerant we know as Freon. Groundwater and Freon make indirect contact in a heat exchanger.

As the liquid Freon moves through the heat exchanger coil it takes heat from the water nearby and evaporates. The Freon gas then moves to a compressor where it's made denser and hotter as it's squeezed into a smaller volume. Now the hot refrigerant is passed along to a second heat exchanger, in the house, where it releases its heat to air flowing through household ductwork.

(A groundwater heat pump raises air temperature to about 105° F. as opposed to 140° F. in a standard fossil fuel furnace. Extra-large air ducts and slow-moving fans are needed to keep the heat flow consistent, making retrofitting to older steam or hot-water systems difficult.)

To cool a home in summer, the heating process is reversed. Freon absorbs heat from the in-house air in heat exchanger #2 and evaporates. The gas goes back to the compressor where its temperature is raised again. In heat exchanger #1, it gives this heat to groundwater that's expelled from the system.

The National Water Well Association says,

> Dr. Karl E. Neilson, professor of physics at The Ohio State University since 1947, may have been the first person in the world to install a groundwater source heat pump system in his home. Neilson designed and built his first system to heat and cool his family's 500-square-foot vacation cottage. The unit performed so reliably that Dr. Neilson installed a groundwater source heat pump system to heat and cool the 1,000-square-foot ground floor of his new home in 1955. The system is still heating and cooling the house today.
>
> A well drawing water from a gravel zone overlain by glacial till supplies both Neilson's heat pump and his family's water needs. Water is discharged from the heat pump into a nearby pond.
>
> The system uses two kilowatt hours of electricity, and two gallons of water per minute to produce 20,000 Btu of heat. Its average COP is 2.9, or 290 percent efficient.
>
> Water in Neilson's area is generally of poor quality, so corrosion, scaling, and the proliferation of iron bacteria were potential problems. However, this system has experienced no growth of iron bacteria, and the cupro-nickle heat-exchanger tubing has been discolored only slightly.
>
> In fact, a slight blockage due to scale and replacement of a faulty starter control have been Neilson's only problems. He maintains his system regularly, and cleans dust from the heat exchanger every two to three years. All homeowners should follow these practices for system economy and longevity.

John Ingersoll, in a *Popular Mechanics* article entitled, "How to Tap the Energy Under Your Backyard," is also enthusiastic, but offers some practical reservations about groundwater heat pumps. He claims the only way to justify the cost is to prove a clear need to both heat a home in winter *and* cool it in the summertime.

Two Wells

Part of the expense of a groundwater heat pump may be the cost of drilling a second well. If it's not possible to discharge the water into a pond or irrigation system, a *recharge well* may be needed to accept water that's passed through the heat exchanger. In this case the system may cost $5,000 or more, and take five to six years to pay back. This is considerably longer than the one- to two-year pay-back period claimed by the NWWA. Both agree, however, that savings can amount to $800 or $1,000 a year, once the initial investment has been repaid.

Further, Ingersoll warns that seven states (Arizona, Maine, Minnesota, Missouri, Oklahoma, Virginia, and Wisconsin) forbid recharge wells, though in several instances there appear to be legislative changes coming along soon. Most other states allow recharge wells by permit only. Alaska, Arkansas, Illinois, and Indiana require no permit. And Georgia allows recharge wells for cooling purposes only.

106. DOWN THE ROAD ...

Times have changed.

In April 1945, Harry Truman walked to a speaker's podium in Kansas City and delivered an optimistic message about water. He said, "When Kansas and Colorado have a quarrel over water in the Arkansas River, they don't call out the National Guard in each state and go to war over it. They bring it to the Supreme Court of the United States and abide by the decision. There isn't a reason in the world why we can't do that internationally."

Then it seemed simple. But it's simple no longer—as we've seen. (96)

Internationally, it's believed today that Canada is the only country in the world with a nearly unlimited supply of fresh water. That would seem to place all other nations in the have-not category. At the opposite extreme from Canada is Israel. Swedish experts Malin Falkenmark and Gunnar Lindh, authors of *Water for a Starving World*, say that small country holds the world's record for "most efficient utilization of water." We'll all be taking lessons from the Israelis in that department.

Nationally, the South Florida Water Management District ordered a 25 percent cutback in water use in 1981, and considered a *60 percent* cutback for 1982, partly because of the weird man-made drought developing there. (102) What's so frightening is that South Florida, in many ways, is representative of much of the rest of the developed world.

In the eight Rocky Mountain states the public outlook on water is turning gloomy. According to a 1981 survey taken by the Behavior Research Center, almost 60 percent of the 1,150 adult heads of household polled believe their states will experience *serious* water shortages in the next ten years.

"Concern about water shortages was particularly acute in Colorado, where 20 percent believe their state already faces such a problem," pollster Earl deBerge told the Associated Press. "Similar views are held by 60 percent or more of Nevada and Utahans, and by over half of Arizonans, New Mexicans, and residents of Wyoming," he said. "Only in Idaho and Montana did less than half hold these views on water shortages." We're all becoming more aware. Slowly.

Acid Rain

In 1981 the National Research Council finally voiced what residents of the Northeast and Canadian Prime Minister Pierre Trudeau have been complaining about for years. The council said, "The interaction of increasing amounts of man-made pollution with natural elements is causing widespread damage in rural and wilderness areas far removed from the atmospheric pollution." They were talking about acid rain.

Eleven years after Truman's speech in Kansas City, U.S. House Speaker Sam Rayburn of Texas spoke much less positively, saying, "The greatest domestic problem facing our country is saving our soil and water. Our soil belongs to unborn generations." Rayburn could clearly see the handwriting on the wall.

Our forests, "green umbrellas that hold our water," are also our greatest soil receptacles. As Rayburn spoke, population growth was achieving the final obliteration of forests in the Heilungkiang Province of China. Now, says *New York Times* China correspondent Fox Butterfield, "Some Chinese scientists believe the destruction of the forests may be responsible for a 50 percent drop in the province's rainfall since the early 1950s." The same thing happened to the Aztecs in what is now Mexico, and to the Anasazi Indians in northern New Mexico. Both tribes originally settled in lush forest, but clear-cut them, and were eventually forced to move. At least they had some place to go. Developmental pressures still cause the removal of 40,000 square miles of jungle and forest each year, making the need for good forest management (and preservation) all the more vital.

As forest areas are diminished, the deserts grow. *The Global 2000 Report to the President* (102) defined "desertification" as "a broad, loosely defined term encompassing a variety of ecological changes that render land useless for agriculture or for human habitation. Deserts rarely spread along well-articulated frontiers; rather they pop up in patches where abuse, however unintended, destroys the thin cover of vegetation and fertile soil and leaves only sand and inert earth."

Some futurists, like the Milnes mentioned previously, see man being *forced* to live in deserts of his own making. As we adjust to water poverty, the prognosticators say, more and more of us will be living underground, and will take on characteristics of the kangaroo rat, a strictly nocturnal creature who lives in the earth and survives on minute quantities of water.

Grand Plans

Instead of halting—or at least slowing—the desertification process, we plan grandiose schemes to counteract it in one fell swoop. If they come to pass, they'll make TVA projects, all the work of the Army Corps of Engineers, and the California Peripheral Canal proposal seem like sandbox play. It's been suggested, for instance, that San Francisco Bay be turned into two fresh-water reservoirs, and that Long Island Sound, on our other coast, be plugged at both ends to make it a fresh-water lake.

That's nothing compared to a plan by the North American Water and Power Alliance (NAWPA), a California-based "entity" which would "build a series of reservoirs, dams, canals, and pumping stations that would take water from Alaska and Canada and ship it around the rest of the continent, including Mexico, but mostly to the Southwestern United States, where it would be put to work naturally, making possible more agriculture and population growth" (quoted from Fred Powledge, *Water*).

Even more incredible is a plan in the Soviet Union, where uncooperative weather continues to cause problems with grain production. In what's been called the "grandest engineering project of all time," the northerly flow of at least twelve major rivers would be *reversed*, to redirect agricultural water south. Original plans included a 1,500-mile canal to be built with the help of nuclear blasting.

Time magazine reports in its June 14, 1982 "Environment" section,

> The diversion, which would take fifty years to complete, would exact an enormous toll. In an area larger than Western Europe, tens of thousands of people would be displaced from their homes. Millions of acres of northern land would be flooded, including great tracts of game forest. Towns and villages would disappear, some of them with onion-domed churches dating back to the Middle Ages. No less disturbing, the diversion would drastically alter climate, not only in the Soviet Union, but throughout the Northern Hemisphere, even as far off as the U.S. and Canada.
>
> . . . More disturbing, some scientists have cautioned that if the Arctic Ocean is not replenished by fresh water, it will get saltier, its freezing point will drop, and the icecap will begin to melt, possibly starting a global warming trend. Other scientists fear the opposite may occur: as the flow of warmer fresh water is reduced, the polar ice may expand. In any case, British climatologist Michael Kelly of the University of East Anglia sees an ironic consequence: changes in polar winds and currents might reduce rainfall in the very regions expecting to benefit from the river diversions.

There are two messages that come through loud and clear from Powledge's dire warning, *Water*. The first is that, so far, government everywhere and at all levels, has failed to recognize the water crisis, thus has failed to plan for it, and has failed to protect us from it. There has been a "shocking lack of leadership," in Powledge's words. ". . . We cannot," says the author, "rely on government to protect us from the bad things that can happen, and are happening, with water. Government's response to problems of water quantity has been frightening in its inadequacy, and its dealings with the quality issue have been a symphony of bad judgment."

The second moral to Powledge's often-accusatory and somewhat apocalyptic story, is that it's a mistake to assume science and technology will come up with ways to solve all our water problems, along with everything else, as it seems to have in the past. The credibility of science is slipping, in his judgment. "We must be very leery about placing our blind trust in the big breakthroughs that may never come," he says. "Particularly in water matters, the old ways of doing things, or perhaps of *not* doing them, have become highly suspect. A lot of clichés by which the nation grew, and which were used to excuse some really relentless and destructive exploitation, must now be abandoned."

It's hard to know what to think. Even harder to know what to do. It's hard to know how to leave all this. Knowledge about water just seems to magnify difficulties and make the overall problem all the more complicated.

Wrapping It Up

On a dry August day I wander outside, wondering where I stand, wondering how to wrap it up in a neat package, wondering where all the answers are. After more than a year of close study I should have a handle on the subject of water. But, in the end, the wide-screen view seems too much to grasp (or at least to accept), and I can only turn back to examining what's closest to me—through my own, personal magnifying glass. I can deal with what I can see and touch.

The water table is way down near my house. In spots, the grass is burned and brown—a sign of drought. Yet on the pond dam, the new grass is green. The more it establishes itself, the less I worry about the dam washing out next spring. The bulldozers and backhoes are long gone. The excavator's bill is paid.

The pond surface is way below the spillway. Another sign of drought. And there's nothing I can do about it. Dowsing rods say the main vein of water running underground to the pond is still strong, but it hasn't rained much and evaporation is taking more than its share of toll.

All's well with the plumbing. Once in a while I notice the click of the pressure switch in the backroom, and am assured the submersible pump is doing its job. The water conditioner is still enough of a novelty for me that I wake early every other morning to listen for its backwash. It's there. On time. Last Monday I panicked to see brown stains in the bathroom toilet, thinking the iron in our water was coming back. But Carol took a brush and showed me the bowl was just dirty. So my bits and pieces of technology seem to be working. The water tastes fine, and I'm never thirsty.

The walk shows me the wood-and-metal cover over Mr. Peterson's spring has collapsed, but the spring box is still full of water—now contaminated. I'll have to stop by his house in the morning and tell him about it. I should also pick up a couple of bags of salt for the brine tank. That's what I'll do tomorrow. By now you know what *you* must do.

As for the bigger picture. . . . We'll just have to wait and see. It looks like rough waters ahead. But I think we'll keep our heads afloat. That's where I stand.

APPENDIXES

APPENDIX A

State Agencies That Provide Water-Sampling Services

State	Private labs?	Certi-fied?	Where should home-owner go first?	Name, address, phone number for more information
Alaska	Y	...	Regional laboratory	Southeast Regional Laboratory, Pouch J, Juneau, AK 99811 (907)586-3586
Alabama	Y	...	County health	Division of Public Water Supplies, 560 S. McDonough St., Montgomery, AL 36130 (205)832-3170
Arizona	Y	Y	Private laboratory	Department of Environmental Quality, 2005 North Central Ave., Phoenix, AZ 85004 (602)257-2200
Arkansas	Y	N	County health	State Department of Health, 4815 W. Markham, Little Rock, AR 72201 (501)661-2000
California	Y	Y	District office	District Office of Sanitary Engineering or State Department of Health, Sanitation Engineering Section, 2151 Berkeley Way, Berkeley CA 95814 (415)540-1576
Colorado	Y	Y	County health	Colorado Department of Health, 4210 East 11th, Denver, CO 80220 Attn.: Water Quality Laboratory (303)320-8333
Connecticut	Y	Y	Private laboratory	Connecticut Department of Public Health, Hartford, CT 06115 (203)566-4800
Delaware	Y	Y	County health	Local county health laboratory
Florida	Y	N	County health	Local county health department, or Health and Rehabilitation Services, Division of Health, Tallahassee, FL 32301 (904)488-4854
Georgia	Y	N	State	Department of Human Resources, Environmental Health Section, 47 Trinity Ave., Atlanta, GA 30334 (404)656-5542
Hawaii	One	N	State	Sanitation Branch, Department of Health, 591 Ala Moana Blvd. Honolulu, HI 96813 (808)548-6478
Idaho	Y	...	Central health district	Bureau of Water Quality, 450 West State St., Boise, ID 83720 (208)334-5867
Illinois	Y	Y	State or county health boards	Illinois Department of Public Health Laboratories, 134 N. 9th St., Springfield, IL 62701 (217)782-6562

State	Private labs?	Certi-fied?	Where should home-owner go first?	Name, address, phone number for more information
Indiana	Y	Y	State	Indiana State Board of Health, Water and Sewage Laboratory, 1330 W. Michigan St., Indianapolis, IN 46206 (317) 633-0100
Iowa	Y	Y	State	State Hygienic Laboratory, Oakdale Hall, Iowa City, IA 52242 (319)335-4500
Kansas	Y	N	County or regional health	Office of Laboratories and Research, Kansas Department of Health and Environment, Forbes Building 740, Topeka, KS 66620 (913)296-1620
Kentucky	Y	Y	County health	Department of Natural Resources, Water Laboratory, Frankfort, KY 40601 (502)564-4446 (bacteriological), 564-3772 (chemical)
Louisiana	Y	N	Parish health	Department of Health and Hospitals, Office of Public Health, P.O. Box 60630, New Orleans, LA 70160 (504)568-5101
Maine	Y	Y	State health	Public Health Laboratories, Statehouse, Augusta, ME 04333 (207)289-2727
Maryland	Y	N	County health	County health departments
Massachusetts	Y	Y	Local health	Division of Water Supply, 600 Washington St., Room 320, Boston, MA 02111 (617)727-2692
Michigan	Y	Y	County health	Sanitary Bacteriological and Chemical Laboratories, Bureau of Disease Control and Laboratory Services, Michigan Department of Public Health, Box 30035, Lansing, MI 48909 (517)335-8059
Minnesota	Y	Y	State health	Minnesota Department of Health, Analytical Laboratory, Room 405, 717 Delaware St. SE, Minneapolis, MN 55440 (612)623-5000
Mississippi	Y	Y	County health	County health departments
Missouri	Y	N	District health	Bureau of Community Sanitation, 320 East McCarty, Jefferson City, MO 65101 (314)634-6418
Montana	Y	Y	State	Water Quality Bureau, Cogswell Building, Capitol Station, Helena, MT 59601 (406)444-2406
Nebraska	Y	N	County agent	County Cooperative Extension Service
Nevada	Y	Y	State	Consumer Health Protection Services, Room 103, Kinkead Building, Capitol Complex, Carson City, NV 89710 (702)884-4750
New Hampshire	Y	N	State	Water Supply and Pollution Control Laboratories, Hazen Dr., Concord, NH 03301 (603)271-3504
New Jersey	Y	Y	Private laboratories	Bureau of Potable Water, Division of Water Resources, 401 East St., 3rd floor, Trenton, NJ 08625 (609)292-2121
New Mexico	Y	Y	EIA (regional)	Environmental Improvement Agency, Central Office, 1190 St. Francis Drive Santa Fe, NM 87503 (505)827-2844
New York	Y	Y	County health	Division of Laboratories and Research, Empire State Plaza, Albany, NY 12237 (518)474-3968
North Carolina	Y	Y	County health	County health departments
North Dakota	Y	N	District health	Health and Public Consolidated Laboratories, Judicial Wing, State Office, 2nd floor, Bismarck, ND 58501 (701)224-2370
Ohio	Y	Y	Municipal health or county health	Ohio EPA, Box 1049, 1800 Watermark Drive, Columbus, OH 43216 (614)644-3020
Oklahoma	Y	Y	County health	County health departments or (405)271-5220 (Bacteriological) and (405)271-5240 (Chemical)

State	Private labs?	Certi-fied?	Where should home-owner go first?	Name, address, phone number for more information
Oregon	Y	Y	County environmental health	Water Resources Department, 3850 Portland Road, Salem, OR 97310 (503)378-3739
Pennsylvania	Y	Y	Community Environmental Control Department of Environmental Research	Bureau of Community Environmental Control, Harrisburg, PA 17120 (717)787-9037
Rhode Island	Y	Y	State health	State of Rhode Island Health, Water Supply Deparment, State Office, Providence, RI 02903 (401)277-6867
South Carolina	Y	Y	County/district health	EQC Water Laboratory, South Carolina Department of Health and Environmental Control, 2600 Bull St., Columbia, SC 29201 (803)758-5496
South Dakota	N	N	County health	Department of Environmental and Natural Resources, 523 East Capitol, Foss Building, Pierre, SD 57501 (605)773-3151
Tennessee	Y	Y	County health	Division of Local Health Services, Department of Public Health, Attn.: James Ault, Nashville, TN 37219 (615)741-2275
Texas	Y	N	Regional health	Division of Water Hygiene, Texas Department of Health, 1100 W. 49th St., Austin, TX 78759 (512)458-7533
Utah	Y	Y	Local health district	Local health district offices
Vermont	...	...	Local health department	Vermont State Department of Health, 60 Main Street, Burlington, VT 05401 (802)863-7200
Virginia	Y	N	County health	County Health Departments or Division Consolidated Laboratories, Bureau of Microbiology, 1 North 14th St. Richmond, VA 23230 (804)786-1115
Washington	Y	N	Private laboratories or county health	Northwest Drinking Water, 217 Pine St., Suite 20, Seattle, WA 98101 (206)464-7670
West Virginia	Y	...	County health	Bacteriological: State Hygienic Laboratory, 167 11th Ave., S. Charleston, WV 25363 (304)348-3530 Chemical: Environmental Health Services Laboratory, Attn.: James Rosencrance, 151 11th Ave., S. Charleston, WV 25363 (304)348-0197
Wisconsin	Y	Y	State health	State Laboratory of Hygiene, 465 Henry Mall, Madison, WI 53706 (608)262-1293
Wyoming	Y	Y	State health	Bateriological: Public Health Laboratory Services, Wyoming Department of Health and Social Services, Hathaway Building, Cheyenne, WY 82002 (307)777-7431 Chemical: Wyoming Department of Agriculture, Courthouse Laramie, WY 82071 (307)766-3381

SOURCE: Domestic Water Treatment, Lehr et al, 1979. Reprinted by permission of McGraw-Hill Book Co.

When You Know		You Can Find		If You Multiply By
Length				
Inches	(in)	Millimeters	(mm)	25.4
Inches	(in)	Centimeters	(cm)	2.539 3
Feet	(ft)	Meters	(m)	0.304 8
Yards	(yd)	Meters	(m)	0.914 4
Miles (statute)	(mi)	Kilometers	(km)	1.609 344
Millimeters	(mm)	Inches	(in)	0.039 370 1
Meters	(m)	Feet	(ft)	3.280 840
Centimeters	(cm)	Inches	(in)	0.393 7
Meters	(m)	Yards	(yd)	1.093 61
Kilometers	(km)	Miles (statute)	(mi)	0.621 371 2
Area				
Square Inches	(in^2)	Square Centimeters	(cm^2)	6.451 6
Square Feet	(ft^2)	Square Meters	(m^2)	0.092 903 04
Square Yards	(yd^2)	Square Meters	(m^2)	0.836 127
Square Miles	(mi^2)	Square Kilometers	(km^2)	2.589 9
Acres		Hectares	(ha)	0.404 685 6
Square Centimeters	(cm^2)	Square Inches	(in^2)	0.155 000 3
Square Meters	(m^2)	Square Feet	(ft^2)	10.763 91
Square Meters	(m^2)	Square Yards	(yd^2)	1.195 99
Square Kilometers	(km^2)	Square Miles	(mi^2)	0.386 1
Hectares	(ha)	Acres		2.471 054
Liquid Volume				
Ounces	(oz)	Milliliters	(ml)	29.574
Pints	(pt)	Liters	(l)	0.473 2
Quarts	(qt)	Liters	(l)	0.946 3
Gallons	(gal)	Liters	(l)	3.785 412
Lb/Foot^3	(lb/ft^3)	Kilogram/Meter^3	(kg/m^3)	16.018 46
Lb/Gal	(lb/gal)	Kilogram/Meter^3	(kg/m^3)	119.826 4
Milliliters	(ml)	Ounces	(oz)	0.033 818
Liters	(l)	Pints	(pt)	2.113 271 3
Liters	(l)	Quarts	(qt)	1.056 747 3
Liters	(l)	Gallons	(gal)	0.264 172 0
Kilogram/Meter^3	(kg/m^3)	Lb/Foot^3	(lb/ft^3)	0.062 427 97
Kilogram/Meter^3	(kg/m^3)	Lb/Gal	(lb/gal)	0.008 345 4
Mass				
Ounces	(oz)	Grams	(g)	28.349 52
Pounds	(lb)	Kilograms	(kg)	0.453 592 4
Grams	(g)	Ounces	(oz)	0.035 275 97
Kilograms	(kg)	Pounds	(lb)	2.204 622
Force				
Foot Pound Force	(ft-lbf)	Joule	(J)	1.355 818
Newtons	(N)	Kilogram Force	(kgf)	0.101 971 6
Joule	(J)	Foot Pound Force	(ft-lbf)	0.737 562 1
Kilogram Force	(kgf)	Newtons	(N)	9.806 650
Pressure				
Lb/Inch^2	(lb/in^2)	Kilograms/Meter^2	(kg/m^2)	703.069 7
Lb/Inch^2	(lb/in^2)	Kilopascal	(kPa)	6.894 7
Lb/Inch^2	(lb/in^2)	Meters of Water	(m)	0.704 089
Inches of Mercury	(inHg)	Kilograms/Meter	(kg/m^2)	345.3
Kilograms/Meter^2	(kg/m^2)	Lb/inch^2	(lb/in^2)	0.001 422 3
Kilopascal	(kPa)	Lb/inch^2	(lb/in^2)	0.145 038 9
Meters of Water	(m)	Lb/inch^2	(lb/in^2)	1.420 274
Kilograms/Meter^2	(kg/m^2)	Inches of Mercury	(inHg)	0.002 896

Metric Conversions (continued)

When You Know		You Can Find		If You Multiply By
1 Atmosphere	14.7 lb/in^2	Kilograms/Centimeter^2	(kg/cm^2)	1.033
1 Atmosphere	14.7 lb/in^2	Kilograms/Meter^2	(kg/m^2)	10 335.0
1 Atmosphere	14.7 lb/in^2	Kilopascal	(kPa)	101.35
1 Atmosphere	14.7 lb/in^2	76.0 Centimeters Mercury	(cmHg)	5.17
1 Atmosphere	29.92 inHg	76.0 Centimeters Mercury	(cmHg)	2.54
Pascal	(Pa)	Newton/Meter^2	(N/m^2)	1.0
Pascal	(Pa)	Kilogram Per Meter^2	(kg/m^2)	0.101 971 6

Power

Horsepower	(hp)	Kilowatt	(kW)	0.745 699 9
Horsepower	(hp)	Watt	(W)	745.699 99
Kilowatt	(kW)	Horsepower	(hp)	1.341 022
Watt	(W)	Horsepower	(hp)	0.001 341 022

Temperature

Degrees Fahrenheit	(° F)	Degrees Celsius	(° C)	(° F-32) 0.555 555
Degrees Celsius	(° C)	Degrees Fahrenheit	(° F)	(1.8 × ° C) + 32

Velocity & Flow

Feet Per Second	(fps)	Meter Per Second	(m/s)	0.304 8
Mile Per Hour	(mph)	Kilometer Per Hour	(km/h)	1.609 344
Gallons Per Minute	(gpm)	Liter Per Minute	(l/min)	3.785 412
Gallons Per Minute	(gpm)	Cubic Meter Per Minute	(m^3/min)	0.003 785 412
Meter Per Second	(m/s)	Feet Per Second	(fps)	3.280 840
Kilometer Per Hour	(km/h)	Mile Per Hour	(mph)	0.621 371 2
Liter Per Minute	(l/m)	Gallons Per Minute	(gpm)	0.264 172
Cubic Meter Per Minute	(m^3/min)	Gallons Per Minute	(gpm)	264.172 0

NOTE: Electrical Terms: Amperes, Watts, Kilowatts, Volts, and Ohms are the same in Metric.

Metric System
SI Unit Prefixes

Amount	Multiples and Submultiples	Prefixes	Symbols	Means
1 000 000 000 000	10^{12}	tera	T	One trillion times
1 000 000 000	10^9	giga	G	One billion times
1 000 000	10^6	mega	M°	One million times
1 000	10^3	kilo	k°	One thousand times
100	10^2	hecto	h	One hundred times
10	10	deka (deca)	da	Ten times
Base Unit 1	10^0			
0.1	10^{-1}	deci	d	One tenth of
0.01	10^{-2}	centi	c°	One hundredth of
0.001	10^{-3}	milli	m°	One thousandth of
0.000 001	10^{-6}	micro	μ°	One millionth of
0.000 000 001	10^{-9}	nano	n	One billionth of
0.000 000 000 001	10^{-12}	pico	p	One trillionth of
0.000 000 000 000 001	10^{-15}	femto	f	One quadrillionth of
0.000 000 000 000 000 001	10^{-18}	atto	a	One quintillionth of

° Most commonly used

BIBLIOGRAPHY

American Association for Vocational Instructional Materials. *Planning for an Individual Water System.* Athens, Georgia, 1973.

American Vegetable Grower. "Making the Switch to Drip." April 1981.

American Vegetable Grower. "New Horizons on Water Management." April 1981.

Boyle, Robert H., and Mechem, Rose Mary. "Anatomy of a Man-Made Drought." *Sports Illustrated,* 1982.

Bucks, D., Nakayama, F., and Gilbert, R. "Is Your Trickle Fickle?" *American Vegetable Grower,* April 1981.

Canby, Thomas Y. "Our Most Precious Resource: Water." *National Geographic,* August 1980.

Cole, Maude E. "Water Appreciation." *Farmstead,* 1981.

Cook, Jack. "Building a Pond." *Country Journal,* June 1981.

DeCrosta, Tony. "Beat the Drought." *Organic Gardening,* May 1981.

Forbes. "Water: Nary a Drop Ever Lost, So What's the Problem?" September 29, 1980.

Gatty, Bob. "Who Says Go on H2O?" *Ski Business,* February 1982.

Golden, Frederic. "Making Rivers Run Backward." *Time,* June 14, 1982.

Helfman, Elizabeth S. *Water for the World.* New York, 1967.

Howells, Harvey. *Dowsing for Everyone.* Brattleboro, Vt.: Stephen Greene Press, 1979.

Hunt, Cynthia, and Garrels, Robert M. *Water: The Web of Life.* New York, 1972.

Ingersoll, John H. "How to Tap the Energy Under Your Backyard." *Popular Mechanics,* September 1980.

Keough, Carol. "Lead on Tap." *Organic Gardening,* May 1981.

LaFavore, Michael. "A Drop of Rain Insurance." *Organic Gardening,* May 1981.

Lehr, Jay H., Ph.D., Gass, Tyler E., Pettyjohn, Wayne A., Ph.D., and DeMarre, Jack. *Domestic Water Treatment.* New York, 1980.

Leopold, Luna P. *Water: A Primer.* Berkeley: W.H. Freeman, 1974.

Life. "America the Dry." July 1981.

Lyon, David. "Drought Worries Flood Northeast." *New Roots,* April 1981.

Milne, Lorus and Margery. *Water and Life.* New York: Atheneum, 1964.

Mitchell, E.W. "Weather, Water and Trickle Irrigation." *Farm Supplier,* April 1981.

National Water Well Association. *Ground Water Heat Pumps.* Worthington, Ohio.

Newsweek. "The Browning of America." February 23, 1981.

Powledge, Fred. *Water.* New York: FS&G, 1982.

Pullen, John J. "The Magic of Springs." *Country Journal,* August 1980.

Pullen, John J. "The Well-Made Well." *Country Journal,* August 1980.

Rogers, Harold T. "Who Will Win the Water War?" *American Vegetable Grower,* May 1981.

Sears, Roebuck and Company. *Do-It-Yourself Plumbing Handbook.* Chicago.

Sheets, Kenneth R. "Water: Will We Have Enough to Go Around?" *U.S. News and World Report,* June 29, 1981.

U.S. Environmental Protection Agency. *Manual of Individual Water Supply Systems.* Washington, D.C., 1973.

U.S. News and World Report. "Just How Safe Is Our Drinking Water?" January 19, 1981.

Water Systems Council. *Water Systems Handbook.* Chicago, 1977.

Westbye, Irene. "Waste Water Tastes Fine . . . If You Recycle It First." *Alternative Sources of Energy,* Number 53.

Wright, Forrest B., Ph.D. *Rural Water Supply and Sanitation.* New York: Krieger, 1977.

Young, D.J. *Build a Pond for Food and Fun.* Charlotte, Vt.: Garden Way Publishing, 1978.

INDEX